WHY THE CENTER CAN'T HOLD

Why the Center Can't Hold

A Diagnosis of Puritanized America by Tom O'Neill

punctum books (P) america & earth

WHY THE CENTER CAN'T HOLD:
A DIAGNOSIS OF PURATINIZED AMERICA
© 2016 Tom O'Neill

First published in 2016 by
punctum books
America & Earth
http://punctumbooks.com

punctum books is an independent, open-access publisher dedicated to radically creative modes of intellectual inquiry and writing across a whimsical parahumanities assemblage. We solicit and pimp quixotic, sagely mad engagements with textual thought-bodies. We provide shelters for intellectual vagabonds.

ISBN-13: 978-0692725474
ISBN-10: 0692725474

Facing-page drawing: Heather Masciandaro.
Book and cover design: Chris Piuma.

Before you start to read this book,

take this moment to think about making a donation to **punctum books**, an independent non-profit press,

@ http://punctumbooks.com/about/

If you're reading the e-book, you can click on the image below to go directly to our donations site. Any amount, no matter the size, is appreciated and will help us to keep our ship of fools afloat. Contributions from dedicated readers will also help us to keep our commons open and to cultivate new work that can't find a welcoming port elsewhere. Our adventure is not possible without your support.
Vive la open-access.

Fig. 1. Hieronymus Bosch, *Ship of Fools* (1490–1500)

Table of Contents

This book is dedicated in gratitude to some of its generous sources:

to Barton Bernstein of Stanford, for eye-opening lectures and for deft guidance to graduate-students like me;

to Joseph P. Sottile of NewsVandal, for relentless reproach when I slacken my attention to current events;

and to my daughter Natasha, for listening thoughtfully to my interminable monologs.

Turning and turning in the widening gyre
The falcon cannot hear the falconer;
Things fall apart; the centre cannot hold;
Mere anarchy is loosed upon the world...

—William Butler Yeats,
"The Second Coming"

Preface

This essay is an exercise in reflection—worse yet, the reflection involves theology. There's not much of new data in it. It revisits themes some may think have been worked to exhaustion. And even in taking up these themes, the writer will be disclosed as sometimes an amateur. That is, there are others whose mastery of individual facts clearly exceeds his. My interest however is not mainly in adding to our information about America, but in taking the weight of quite familiar information.

My concern is that we have not done this. While we have admitted to bumps along the road to progress and to some inconsistencies in our practice of principles, I believe we as a people have never acknowledged some underlying contradictions in the way we conceive our task and ourselves.

So I crave indulgence of the reader. I attempt a revisiting of the American story, and I can imagine time and again the individual reader will say, "Wait—he's got it all wrong; this isn't what I've learned at all!" At such points I ask the reader to hesitate and consider that it may not be sheer ignorance of the familiar story that guides me; rather I'm attempting to tell the story in a way that may shed light on why so many aspects of our current American experience are disappointing to us and seem to have lost their efficacy as guides to the future.

Signs of Accelerating Incoherence

We confront with wholesome skepticism those who say the sky is falling. People have been saying it since the invention of speech — and the sky is still there. Sound enough. Yet the danger of this skepticism can be that even when something is going awry systematically, we may tend to greet each indication as a mere oddity. True, one should not treat the first sneeze as a predictor of pneumonia. But when sneeze follows sneeze, and the throat clogs, and the lungs register congestion, one must at some point acknowledge the onset of illness. That moment of doing so is a positive one; without it one isn't likely to take corrective action.

Today evidence of something going wrong shows up in many places. Consider education for instance. Granted, education is always problematic. Knowledge maketh a bloody entrance. And the effort to set aside immediate concerns for the sake of cultivating more general understandings has always been subject to thoughtful objection. A decision to postpone immediate improvements (say, re-tiling the kitchen floor) to seek a broader understanding of life is open to the charge of impracticality. Add to that that our nation, from the time of its first settlement by Europeans, has been always the site of urgency at some frontier. Our sense of the urgency of things has contributed toward a specifically American form of anti-intellectualism. "He who hesitates is lost." "Let's get this show on the road." There probably aren't many cultures in the world where "egghead" and "intellectual elite" are such effective put-downs as they are here.

All that notwithstanding, something new and worse has been happening lately to education in America. I will speak of "accelerating disinvestment," and this disinvestment I argue is both a matter of morale and a matter of money (often in fact beginning as a matter of morale and becoming a matter of money). I speak of this as a sign of incoherence; the disinvestment runs contrary both to what we've said traditionally and what we say currently in our common discourse about education. So I begin by attending to education as a place that calls for reflection.

After that, I address the profit motive as it currently establishes itself to be the arbiter in America of all other valuation and enterprise. I suggest that here too we have matter for reflection, arguing that our exclusive focus on profit is incompatible with many things we claim to believe in and care about.

Thirdly, I examine our reliance on force as our guarantee of national security. I suggest our quest for a form of absolute security, sought through intimidation, cannot co-exist with our ambition to become a beacon of light to the human race.

At the end of this section I argue there's a kind of coherence amid the incoherencies being identified. Just before that though, I turn to Nature, and suggest there's an ominous contrast between our sense of America as the Promised Land and our actual treatment of the land we inhabit.

1 | Our Accelerating Disinvestment in Education

Our galloping disinvestment in education doesn't need to be proved. By reason of family members and friends—if not from personal experience—everyone's aware of it. On the surface of things it's so obviously counterproductive it seems inexplicable. It's as if a hungry farmer were to say in desperate times: "We'll eat all the seed-corn this year, but as soon as we are again blest with bountiful harvests, we'll start again to put seed aside for planting."

Regarding education, Franklin, Madison, and—in his way—Jefferson were clear that, for government-by-the-people to work, the public would have to be well informed and able to think realistically about needs and prospects. Jefferson tells us "a people who would be both free and ignorant longs for something that can never be." This is why free speech and a free press, along with freedom of religion, were singled out for protection in our first amendment to our Constitution.

Candidates for government office understand this so well that each of them campaigns to become the Education Mayor or the Education Governor or the Education President. Yet what we observe often these days is that the candidates are no sooner in office than they discover, alas, that now is not the opportune time—in our pressing circumstances, education must await more prosperous days.

Here, let me approach the subject matter in a twofold way: both by providing anecdotes that provide a plausible account of what's happening, and by intervening with reflection as to underlying causes for these happenings. While the objection may be lodged that you can't sketch history from anecdotes, let me counter that

if the anecdotes are typical and are set forth honestly, you can—
and we do.

While anecdotes are subject to charges of being inaccurately
presented, slanted, subjectively interpreted, unrepresentative, I
claim that my anecdotes are accurate and exemplary. Whether
this is the case is for the reader to judge.

It's not surprising that the state put Socrates to death. States
don't like criticism. Our own early colonists, particularly those
of Massachusetts Bay Colony, practically defined themselves by
being critical and dissatisfied with the British state; but in the
same breath by which they resisted British control, they regarded
themselves as beyond the reach of criticism and as divinely
assigned to control others.

In the 1630s the stresses and ironies of this situation come to
light in Massachusetts in this first decade of the colony's history.
We look to relations between the Governor, John Winthrop, and
the gifted pastor, Roger Williams. Winthrop acknowledged that
Williams was sincere and charismatic, but found him a terrible
nuisance. Winthrop thought Williams took the position of the
Puritan dissenting church a step too far. For Williams argued
that if the Anglican Church had not the authority to dictate the
beliefs of the Puritan dissenting community, so neither had it—
nor had indeed the British state—the authority to license the
existence of that dissenting church. The dissenting church was
a community of faith which, beyond gratitude for opportunity
to set up shop in the New World, owed nothing either to the
established Church of England or to the British civil authority
which had done the establishing. Further, according to Williams, in the matter of land grants—contrary to the position of
the Puritan civil authority in Massachusetts—Indians as human
beings had rights of possession which were more than equal to
any rights of the white newcomers. How did the colony deal with
this critical thinker? Much as John Winthrop, the chief authority in the Puritan community, wanted his colony to be a jewel of
enlightened thinking and a beacon of light to mankind, he found
this too much, and he acquiesced in the banishment of Williams. Winthrop and his colony believed neither in free speech
nor the rights of individual conscience. Is it a too great a jump
to say one can discover here an early disinclination to promote
education?

This wasn't a solitary instance, in the founding days, of a Puritan attempt to curb freedom of thought and speech in America. Anne Hutchinson too had her way of drawing conclusions from the Puritan protest against Anglicanism. Puritans rightly, she taught, had no use for pope or bishops. But if these man-made offices encompassed no special license to teach the faith, what special claim on such teaching had the appointed male ministers of the Massachusetts colony? Did not the gospel tell us the Holy Spirit was the true teacher of the faith? And was not the Spirit free to blow where it would? One can imagine how the rigorous and humorless Winthrop regarded such a proposition. He saw it as mutiny, and endorsed Hutchinson's banishment as he had Williams's. Later when he heard of Anne's death at the hands of Indians, he felt God's honor and his own had been vindicated.[1]

So while America was brought forth in a protest against England, it would be unhistorical to say this protest was a protest on behalf of tolerance or critical thinking. It was protest on behalf of intolerance, seeking radical limitations on critical thinking and educational development.

All too soon, there were other, glaring indications that America was not conceived in a burst of dedication to enlightened attitudes, freedom of speech, and the advance of critical thinking. When Africans were brought to the shores of "the new world," they brought with them the skills and stamina of people raised in agricultural communities. These traits made them valuable. At the same time, it was expedient that their social bonds be subservient to the uses of those who claimed to be the owners of their labor. In being wrenched from communities in which they had operated familiarly and efficiently, the kidnapped Africans lost too their names, their tribal affiliations, their religions, and their

---

1. Richard Hofstadter, in his treatment of American anti-intellectualism, uncharacteristically fumbles here. While he can correctly cite Anne as an enthusiast and therefore as unimpressed by book learning and college degrees, he would be entitled to see Winthrop and the Puritan divines as stellar examples of intellectualism only if he's right in overlooking their misogyny, their prickly narrow-mindedness in their banishment of Anne, and their emotionally-destabilizing adherence to predestination which nurtured bigotry toward anyone notably different from themselves.

languages. While they were taught the language of those who denied their freedom, the teaching was economical.

Let the enslaved learn the gospel—as it might reconcile them to their state. (And the notion they were creating Christians provided a soothing balm to the consciences of those who claimed to own them.) More urgently, no doubt, let these Africans hear and understand the voices of those who sought profit from their labor. Beyond that, not much. Aside from education for specific tasks, let the fetters of the mind bind ever tighter. Since reading was empowering and since writing enabled partnerships and organization for the pursuit of freedom, the teaching of literacy was forbidden. When misguided whites disregarded the restriction on teaching literacy, one got the likes of Nat Turner and murderous slave insurrections—and who needed that? Such was the near universal perspective within the majority culture. Jefferson, so eloquent and diligent on the importance of education, was even more diligent—by reason of its power—in denying education to those under his control.

The colonial mindset was not promising for the future of education in America. This mindset of the white majority toward denying education to blacks—a mindset often coupled with indifference toward the education of children of poor whites—remained in place right into the start of the twentieth century; and it continues to be alive and kicking, and in fact growing, in blighted parts of America today.

In the middle of the twentieth century, when the Warren Court declared that separated schools are inherently unequal, the deep insight behind the ruling was that education is not some privilege to be earned, but a necessity—like mother's milk—which society must accord the individual if he or she is to grow up wholesomely. For this reason, the situation of an ethnic minority or economic minority is vulnerable and poignant. Unless members of the majority culture open the doors of their schools to the members of a minority, the members of that minority cannot learn the levers and mechanisms, the understandings and style, the agreed-upon wisdom and traditions and linguistic usages by which the mainstream functions. It's not that minorities need to adopt all these; but lacking an understanding of such things, if they do not simply despair, their members seem condemned to become either tools in the hands of others, or resisters or wreckers or mere waste products of an order which would reduce them to tools.[2]

Unanimous though the 1954 *Brown v. Board of Education of Topeka* decision was, from the day it was announced to the present moment there has been widespread resistance to its central idea. White "flight to light" has been a continuing strategy among those whites who find the ruling distasteful. Those who don't want their children rubbing elbows with children who belong to ethnic or class minorities simply move away and found new communities in suburbs where minorities find it difficult or impossible to follow. The cost of this to society as a whole has been steep. The draining from center to periphery of finances and civic stewardship has decreed urban decay at the core of some one-time thriving American cities. At the urban core of these cities, standards of beauty, health, prosperity have dwindled, or in some cases disappeared entirely; and crime has increased. Nor do we find in such places adequate responses to increase governmental involvement and spending on education as a venture to ameliorate things.

Rather the fleeing population have preferred to take their generosity toward education with them, and spend their educational dollars on the places they come to rather than on the places they leave. It seems they'd sooner pay $50,000 or more a year to incarcerate an abandoned human product of urban blight than pay ten or fifteen percent of that amount per student to leave a semblance of good schools behind. As *Brown v. Board* said, the heart of the problem continues to be that separated schools are inherently unequal. If children of minorities are not to be stunted, it's not enough that their schools have some of the amenities of suburban schools; rather they need to be in schools where they can interact with the children of those who run things. (Again, this doesn't mean minorities must replace their culture with white culture, but it does mean they can't afford to be ignorant of the inner workings—the levers and pulleys—of white culture.)

---

2. It is not really as paradoxical as it may seem that some who are closed out seem to find their richest sense of freedom in activities likely to kill them during their youth.

In 1978 in the case of *Regents of the University of California v. Bakke*, the Supreme Court said in effect that UC Davis could not engage in a crash program to increase the number of minority doctors in California unless it was willing simultaneously to open the same program on a competitive basis to applicants from the majority culture; anything less the Court said would violate equal treatment as provided for in the Fourteenth Amendment. The gist of the decision amounted to a declaration that to provide special programs for the down-and-out was a matter of depriving the more well-to-do of the equal protection of the laws. It's as if one were to say a mother would be acting unfairly if she gave an aspirin to a child of hers who was sick unless, at the same time, she offered aspirin to each of her other children. Or if she had an acutely shy son, it's as if to say she couldn't go to his room and read to him unless she invited her other children into his room as well. That they did not share his need was irrelevant. Or it's as if to say that if there were a scarcity of some health-improving remedy like a vacation in the mountains, she could not make it available it to a sick daughter unless she allowed her vigorous and healthy children to compete with the daughter for its possession. That is a very awkward sense of "equal treatment," and no decent mother has ever subscribed to it.

Carefully as it was penned by the gentlemanly Louis Powell, the decision in the Bakke case was insensitive to the urgent need to make medical information and guidance available to the deprived and afflicted amid the minorities of California. UC Davis medical school had wanted—by an effort to recruit from the ranks of minority communities people with skills to bring mainstream medical practice back to their communities—to alleviate one of the major adverse consequences of segregated living. If you can accept the analogy, in effect, Davis was trying to create a corps of medical missionaries, not for Africa or South America, but for Compton and parts of Oakland, Fresno, San Jose, East Palo Alto, and the like. Would it have worked? Powell and company decreed it would be un-Constitutional to try to find out.

Justice Thurgood Marshall, who had been the lead attorney for the plaintiff in *Brown v. Board*, was so unconvinced by the decision that terminated this minority-recruitment experiment that, in addition to joining the dissent of three other justices, he wrote a dissent of his own. In essence, the majority who decided the case had missed the very nature of education. Rather than being some bauble or perk which society puts out there for its best and brightest to compete over, education is something a society owes to each and all its members, and the more deprived any of its members are, the more compelling is society's obligation. His dissent included a withering rebuke to the Court in the form of a history lesson on the ways the law—especially the Fourteenth Amendment—had been used and was being used to deprive blacks of the benefits the law was designed to provide. The fact, in this case, that we were dealing with descendants whose ancestors—with full support of the legal system of the time—had been brought here against their will, could not, Marshall insisted, diminish society's obligation, but could only add to it. Such was at the center of Marshall's dissent.

The elegant language in which the court's majority could "find no compelling reason" that would justify "imposing a burden" of exclusion on whites born into comparative privilege showed the court's majority were indeed color blind. They lacked insight into facts on the ground in the lives of a great many suffering Americans. Priding themselves on being color-blind, the gentlemanly Powell and company refused, on grounds of high moral principle, to regard either the color of deprived Americans or the painful burdens a color-conscious society imposed on it.

The situation of color-prejudice is still with us. And it works to dilute the liberating effects *Brown v. Board* might have been expected to provide. Eventually, our exercise of stinginess toward minorities and toward the white poor has come to provide a precedent for moves toward pricing members of the white middle class out of opportunities for needed education as well. Karma isn't just some whimsical notion. What has been going around is now coming around.

Bad enough. Yet a tradition of blindness to the needs of our minorities and poor, abetted by increasing austerity toward our middle class, isn't the only thing retarding and downgrading educational opportunity at present.

Here are some anecdotes—some glimpses of bits and pieces—I offer for consideration. Each is trivial in itself; and you may want to dismiss me as one who "tells tales out of school" and is simply airing personal grievances over current educational practice. But I suggest the implication of these stories isn't trivial at all. I vouch for the veracity of what follows; the first names I give are real. It's up to the reader to judge whether I'm honest and whether the examples have relevance.

Picture an episode just before Christmas, on Guam, U.S.A., at a Christian school. Father James—a young Anglican priest teaching in this American school—has given the third-grade class a kind of elaboration of his sense of Christmas. He's said that amid the swirl of Christmas presents—amid all the buying and selling that sets up this swirl—the real thing to concentrate on is the gift God has given us in Jesus. To say such a thing was pretty radical. Father James was taking on the lifestyle in which his listeners were being raised. But as he told me in his account, he took a further step. Warming to his subject, he said we should not get lost in the myth of the generosity of Santa Claus, but should celebrate instead the generosity of God—Who created us and showers us with love.

Imagine the recklessness of such a message. And he is speaking in a Christian school, which—being private—depends upon the benefactions of the students' parents for its existence! Father James, as I recall his story, did not reach his dinner table that evening before he heard from the headmaster. The owner of a local bank had called the headmaster, complaining that the rash and insensitive James had ruined the Christmas not only of his eight-year-old daughter, but of himself as well. James had arrogantly used the indiscreet phrase "the myth of Santa Claus," and so in his effort to explain Christmas, he had ruined it altogether. The headmaster communicated news of this outrage to James, and assigned him to write during the holidays a satisfactory apology to the irate father. James did as he was told. He did not show me the apology; but he left the school at the end of the spring term.

Here's another true story. In a middle school in Northern California, picture a Muslim woman hired to teach social studies. I can't remember her name now, but I liked talking with her. She told me she'd formerly been a paid consultant to some agency of the United Nations, and I believed her; for she impressed me as untypically well informed about current events. Well, one day in her social-studies class she was talking about the praying habits of Muslims. She told her students that a devout Muslim is always aware where Mecca is in relation to his or her immediate circumstances. When they asked why, she said it had to do with prayer, and demonstrated by kneeling on the floor and bowing toward Mecca as if getting ready to pray. At least one interested student said "Let me try that!" and, not being forbidden to do so, knelt and bowed. The school had never, so far as I know, had a Muslim teacher before; and in the next term, it was back to normal. The principal told me: "I had to let her go." Evidently a parent, or several parents, had complained she was trying to convert her class to Islam.

Then there's Eric's story. Eric was a colleague of mine in the philosophy section of the humanities department at a community college with mostly middle-class students in Northern California. I often talked with him. He loved philosophy, and his face would take on color when he discussed it. At the start of one term I noticed there was no more Eric. Later I ran into him at a college in Oakland where I also taught.

The story Eric told me—as best I can recall—is this. He was giving writing assignments at that first college, and he was grading the papers meticulously. He gave a C to a paper of a female student, and when she complained, he refused to change the grade, but told her he would work with her on future papers if she wished. Knowing Eric, I believe this; it fit with his sincerity and enthusiasm. He tells me the girl then went to the dean and told her that Eric had wanted to become intimate with her, and that when she'd refused, he'd punished her by giving her a C on her paper. Eric had no tenure—like myself, he was an instance of that great bargain in college education, an adjunct instructor. When the dean summoned Eric, she told him she did not know if the girl's story was true, but that considering how unsavory the charge was, she could not rehire him after the end of that term.

Let me tell you my own story about an experience at the school in Oakland where I heard this story from Eric. I was not terminated from that school, but was amazed when I ran into a dean problem of my own. It, too, was over the grading of a student paper. As I recall the circumstances, a disgruntled student, a black male, had complained to the dean that my grade on his paper was too low. The dean, a black woman—having failed to persuade me to change the grade—sought the high ground with me by asking: "Have you considered the possibility that reading and writing may not be his preferred modalities of learning?" I'm pretty sure the last five words are verbatim or very close to verbatim because the jargon all but knocked me down. I hadn't seen it coming. It seemed to abandon—in the case at least of this student—the long struggle for black literacy. Absolutely I knew my student's "chosen modality of learning" was not reading or writing; that's why I was there. Beyond that, the dean knew as well as I that the accreditation of the college was under review by the state. The state university to which we sent the bulk of our graduates was complaining that, while our students were wonderfully articulate orally, they often lacked key skills in reading and writing. It's significant I think that this same dean was eventually promoted to academic vice president of our college.

Wrangles between teacher and administrator over grades are actually commonplace, and I shouldn't have been surprised at mine. A friend of mine, one of the most entertaining storytellers I've met, was Larry. Larry had taught math at a high school in Northern California for eighteen years. When I asked him why he'd retired two years short of a full pension, he told me that one day his principal called him in to discuss "the trouble" he was having with his students. Larry said he wasn't aware of any trouble. The principal countered there was clearly trouble since students who were getting A's and B's in their social studies and English classes were often getting C's in Larry's math classes. Larry defended himself saying he kept close records of his students' work; when a student's answers were right ninety percent of the time or more, the student got an A; when they were right eighty percent of the time but less than ninety, the student got a B; and so on. The principal said: "Ah! Now I see the problem. I want you to know, Larry, that any answer a student has worked on is a good answer for that student. Once you understand that, Larry, let's hope your grades will come into harmony with the grades of our other teachers."

Larry told me he went back to his classroom and thought "I'd better get out of here before I lose my mind." At the place where I met him and heard this story, he was a very popular tutor of students in math and other subjects; he had not lost his mind, but he had gotten out of there.

I could add more of these stories from creditable, firsthand accounts, but what's my point? When we talk about what's happening in education, we do so usually in terms of "good students" and "bad students," "good teachers" and "bad teachers." We seldom bring administrators into the picture. What though is the attitude toward education of the administrators in the stories I've told?

Is there a common thread running through how these administrators understand their role? There seems to be. Not to paint them as more designing than they are, I think the commonality is that each conceives their role as a role in public relations. They don't so much support and provide education as apologize for it. They apologize for any pain involved, and they attempt to remove pain. In this I think they're more representative of administrators today than members of the general public — those who "don't see the sausage being made" — would like to think. While the administrators I cite lack explicit malicious intent, the effect they have is corrosive and demoralizing.

Let's think over the stories. In each case but mine, a teacher left an institution. (And in my case, when I had to reduce my workload to two classes a semester in order to start collecting my pension, the Oakland college having the generously flexible dean was — perhaps to my shame — among those I let go.)

The fault of Father James was that he wanted to give his students his version of the truth about Christmas. The headmaster might have reminded the irate banker that, when he placed his eight-year-old in a Christian school, he took on the risk that the Christian teachers there might try to tell his daughter the truth about Christianity as they understood it. To say that however would have been confrontational, and the headmaster preferred to leave James responsible to placate the father on his own. James was lost to the institution. One might say — as the headmaster probably had calculated — "neat ending to an unfortunate incident." Whether or not that's how the headmaster saw things, the school lost a sincere and brilliant teacher, and there was also a message to the faculty who remained: never rile a parent — for no one will have your back if you do.

Let's take the case of the teacher who was so rash as to demonstrate the practice of Muslims at prayer. That her contract was not renewed manifests a craven sell-out by the principal involved.

As I've mentioned, it's unlikely the school had ever hired a Muslim to teach there before. Certainly the students weren't over-exposed to Islam. When the principal told me he'd "had to let her go," he was implying she'd crossed a line—the implication being she was out to make converts.

Yet he and whoever had pushed him to take that position knew in their saner moments that wasn't the case. Suppose the teacher had been a Catholic and had, in the course of a lesson on Catholic practice, demonstrated the sign of the cross. Suppose some non-Catholic student or students had imitated the gesture to get the feel of it. Would that have led to a decision not to continue that teacher as an instructor in social studies? I think we know it wouldn't. What seems to have been at work was not a general principle but a mere yielding to prejudice against Muslims and Islam. Educational opportunity was sacrificed for the sake of smooth public relations. It's a costly omission that our k-through-twelve public schools offer so little instruction in the world's religions. While religious views continue to be major forces in current affairs, America's grown-up diplomats and policy-makers often seem woefully indifferent and ignorant regarding the texture of religious beliefs of those they deal with. Their education has done little to inform them. One fears in fact it has tended to confirm them in bigotry.

Let's talk about Eric. The termination of Eric is a clear instance of denial of due process. Even if Eric had demanded access to a grievance procedure, he'd still have had a tough time keeping his job. There was no contract regarding future employment. One can say he had a right in equity to expect continued employment; but equity rights aren't easy to enforce. The dean who terminated him was aware of this. Not unlike the headmaster in the Christian school who left James to twist in the wind, she terminated Eric because that seemed the easiest way to keep the peace. She placated the complainer by telling her the school would no longer employ the teacher whom the student said had given offense. Not only did the institution lose Eric as a result, but if other teachers under her supervision tended to be exacting in the way they graded papers, her act notified them this was a form of self-indulgence she wouldn't defend. I'd listened to this very dean claim her department maintained the highest standards. More accurate—and this wasn't lost on teachers or students—would have been to say her department proclaimed high standards only up to the moment when someone challenged them.[3]

I mention my own confrontation over grading at a college in Oakland to underline how readily some administrators will undermine academic standards. A teacher who tries to hold students to high standards is routinely regarded by some administrators as inviting trouble. Surely the dean in Oakland knew from her own experience the importance of literacy. She was very articulate. My hunch, based on the position she held, is that she was as sharp when writing as she was when speaking. I bet this competence had opened doors for her. Yet she was willing to humor students rather than go to the mat with them over their need for skills like hers. I think it would be no exaggeration to say she'd have been comfortable with a day-care-for-adults program so long as she could call it college. And she fit right in.

Students aren't deceived. At that school in Oakland, it seemed black males in particular had a problem with attendance. In their life on the street, their experience had density; they lived with a vivid sense of their existence. There things had consequences. Dangerous and destructive as their lifestyle regularly was, it sustained their interest and focused their attention. At an all-too-real cost to longevity, they lived dramatically. My theory is that when they came to our place, seeking better opportunities than the street offered, the kind of college they found frequently registered as an anticlimax. They may have begun to wonder if they were they still living in the real world. On the street, failure to pay a dealer for drugs provided on consignment could cost one's life. At the college, failure to meet a deadline, or complete an assignment, or show up for a final often seemed to cost nothing. For some, only the demands of coaches seemed to carry authority. (In hopes of a career in sports, they may have seen the coaches as their only authentic teachers.)

---

3. I owe it to this institution—which I haven't named—to add that when, to the relief of teachers like me, this accommodating dean retired, she was replaced by a dean who said he was concerned that teachers weren't as exacting as they should be in the grading of student essays. Morale improved among students as well as among teachers by reason of his concern. He was greatly missed when he retired.

When we discussed, as we did in my classes (one can see why the dean didn't like me) why their education growing up in Oakland had been so limited, a standard response was that it hadn't been by accident. Analytical and articulate, some young males would claim their relative incapacity to empower themselves through education was regarded by society at large as a benefit. It meant (and I'm quoting here) there'd be inmates for our prisons, recruits for our wars abroad, and cheap labor here at home. While I'd chime in endorsing much that I heard, it was black males who would initiate such statements. Shades of Malcolm! I thought it shameful that a college which provided these articulate young men with demanding athletic programs wasn't willing to pair these programs with equally demanding academic programs.

Looking back on the case of Larry who, as I said, had taught high-school math for eighteen years, in this instance the concern of the principal wasn't about humoring minority students. Minority students were a distinct minority at Larry's high school. The principal's concern was that Larry's conscientious grading and conscientious effort to raise the level of math skills was keeping his, the principal's, school from achieving the reputation of a place where nearly all the students were, as at Lake Woebegone, performing above average. Whether the students actually learned math wasn't among the principal's priorities. Larry, on the other hand, not only had a gift like Mark Twain's for telling outlandish stories, but had—like Twain—a disturbing streak of honesty. He felt compelled to tell students when their answers were wrong.

Let's grant there's room for discussion here. In the early years of school—first, second, third grades—there's a case for humoring one's pupils more than correcting them. More often than not, schools assign these grade-levels to women. The hope is that the really considerable insecurity and vulnerability that nearly all young children experience (and that some young children experience constantly) will be assuaged by a non-judgmental maternal presence. To me this seems quite proper. When a teacher instructs her first-graders to draw a tree, there should be no "wrong trees" held up for criticism at the end of the exercise. When an infant is learning to walk, there's lots of celebration but it would be unimaginable to rebuke or ridicule any awkwardness. While kindness should always be in season, it would not however be a kindness to young people to treat them forever as infantile.

Good coaches know this. I'm surprised that administrators so often don't.

I do not think Larry was in any way unpopular with his students. Chances are they understood his concern and respected him for it. (After he left the high school and took up tutoring, it wasn't unusual for former students of his to come to his new workplace to chat with him.) His crime had been that he did not subscribe to the version of political correctness his principal found convenient. This political correctness holds that no one should ever be made uncomfortable in a classroom. If political correctness like this sounds like a tolerant approach, we should learn to recognize it as a camouflage for indifference. It tolls the death knell of education. If every opinion a student has is "right for him," if every answer a student gives is "a good answer," there's no need for institutions of learning. Much as he'd be surprised to hear it, the program of Larry's principal for raising grades without reference to achievement was roughly as friendly to education as Attila the Hun was to the Roman Empire. Recognizing the madness, Larry did well to leave.

Because it's permeated our educational system, let's delay a bit on political correctness. To do so is worthwhile if it's worthwhile to reflect on what's eviscerating our educational system and thereby making it easier to raise arguments against funding it.

Political correctness has roots in thoughts about equality and the role of tolerance in society—both of which it misunderstands. To say "humans are all created equal" is to say something wonderful. To say "we should be tolerant of another's opinions" is also a wonderful thing to say. To say "since we're all equal, no one has any opinion better than anyone else's" is a terrible thing to say. In effect, to say that is to deny the existence of expertise and thereby cancel the warrant for schools. If one person's opinion is as good as another's, why go to a person with a medical education for an opinion on your health? Why not just ask your postman, or a cashier at the supermarket?

We don't really believe this equality-of-opinion business. Yet in the classroom, teachers are expected to pretend they do. Particularly in public schools, teachers shy clear of manifesting convictions or championing any particular viewpoint. When, by contrast, Aristotle taught ethics in Athens, the whole of what he taught was one huge opinion—namely his—of what was ethical. Today when a person teaches ethics in our public schools, it's notably less likely the person will share personal thoughts, much less deliberately center the curriculum on personal convictions. Rather the typical teacher sets up a kind of cafeteria of ideas. "This is what Aristotle taught; this is what Kant taught; this is what Nietzsche taught." He or she may end with: "And who am I to say which was right or wrong?" Or worse yet: "Should we not say that each was right in his own way?" It's hard to imagine anything more insipid. (Having had for my first nine years of education highly intelligent nuns of strong convictions who endlessly encouraged me and their other students to argue with them, I can't help but feel sorry for young students who have to endure the bland dreariness of much that passes today for public education.)

One time the head of a social-studies department in a public high school bragged to me: "My students haven't the foggiest idea what I think about anything." I suppose I was supposed to say: "How wonderful!" I didn't. I held my tongue. But I thought: "How terrible. Here you are, supposedly encouraging students to practice critical thinking, but you resolutely refuse to model it yourself. How do you expect students to get the hang of it?" (My mother didn't do that with her four children. Neither did any other teachers I've ever had who I thought were worth their salt.)

When I once asked the principal of a middle school: "What's your stand on teaching controversial issues?" he said: "Teachers are free to teach any they want. They just have to be careful not to take a side."

The case for this neutrality is that it does not "crowd" the student. It does not confront any student in his or her comfort zone, or attempt to pull any students out of one. It avoids the danger of brainwashing. However it neuters — de-vitalizes — the teacher and reduces her or him to someone fighting with both hands in their pockets. Sacrificed in the neutral approach is spontaneity and authenticity. There's a world of difference between students and teacher actually arguing in the classroom (something I was very used to with the nuns who taught me), and a teacher conducting with students a discussion about argumentation. More than two millennia after being written, Plato's dialogs continue to command attention because they depict Socrates and the young men gathered about him arguing with each other—not just talk-ing about arguments. (If someone doubts this about how Plato's Socrates behaved, and says, "No! Socrates never took a position!" let them refresh themselves by looking to book 1 of the *Republic* where Socrates takes charge of the premises of Thasymachos and turns them against him to the point where the cool and sophis-ticated Thasymachos runs furiously from the room.) To borrow a bit from Mark Twain, the difference between engaging students in real argument and discussing with them merely the nature of argument is the difference between a lightning bolt and a firefly.

To change the metaphor, the second approach—the politically correct one of laissez-faire—aborts the educational process. It over defends against the danger of brainwashing and underesti-mates or ignores entirely the power of Hegelian dialectic. Hegel tells us the social structure of thinking goes something like this: (1) someone says John is a good man (thesis); (2) this summons some other party to claim John is not really a good man after all (antithesis); (3) a third person is thereby prompted to say that John is a complicated man who demands further study (synthesis). The rebound effect (step 2) is at the same time both spontaneous and predictable. Step 3 is the transition to a general discussion. For the process to start however, someone has to say John is a good man. If the teacher won't venture a thesis (preferably one the teacher believes), and simply begins: "Let us discuss John," the process is stillborn. One gets a replay of Ben Stein's classroom scene in *Ferris Bueller's Day Off*. What makes the scene hilari-ous is that the proceedings are so totally vapid and yet so totally familiar.

One of the reasons the study of religions is systematically avoided k-through-twelve is that religion is a hotbed of contro-versial issues. Out there on the street, there's been so much con-tention over religion—often lethal—that schools where atten-dance is compulsory (i.e., k-through-twelve schools) feel obliged to tiptoe around religion—as if the First Amendment forbade discussion of it. When in college a student elects to take a course in World Religions, a benefit from this delay is that almost all the course's content is fresh territory and new horizons.

That doesn't of course mean the study will be without pain. Recently a Jewish student of mine spoke at length to a World Religions class of her grief that some of her ancestors had been murdered in gas chambers by the Nazis. A non-Jewish student of German descent approached me after class and told me she had been deeply disturbed by the student's talk. I replied I thought her choices came to about three. She could become a Holocaust denier; but that didn't seem to promise much relief. Or she could seek comfort by saying to herself that the extermination effort was something the Nazis had done in spite of the resistance of most Germans; but that seemed a difficult case to make. Or she could as an adult accept that terrible misdeeds had been permitted and perhaps carried out by people who were precious to her. Would this third option leave her in pain? Yes. (Admirably it is this third course that the German government endorses today.)

Education shouldn't dodge these moments; they're partly what it's there for.

Before leaving the theme of political correctness, perhaps there's a further point. Political correctness is usually associated with avoidance of stereotypes. In its extreme form, political correctness is ready to commit to the generalization that any generalization about people is a mistake. The intent is to cut off stereotyping at the root by decreeing generalization regarding human affairs out of bounds. One can see the connection with what I've said political correctness promotes: namely that if generalizations can impinge on people's comfort zone, why not ban them from the classroom?

The problem is that generalization is how human understanding and science proceed. If you exclude generalization about people from the classroom, there isn't much left to say about them. This reduction seems to be going on. "Italians like spaghetti" is a perfectly legitimate statement if one is reviewing a menu for an Italian restaurant from which it's been omitted. But try saying it in a classroom. You'll be lucky if the ceiling doesn't fall on you. "How dare you stereotype Italians like that!" "What's wrong with you?" "What kind of American are you?" Such outrage bodes a loss to the classroom—a part of the evisceration of content that's been going on.

When Reagan ran for governor of California, he promised to clean up the mess at Berkeley. Perhaps he did. Certainly during the eight years he was governor and then the eight years he was president, things became quieter at UC Berkeley and in colleges and universities across the land. The voice of Mario Savio, the charismatic promoter of Berkeley's free-speech movement, became a dim echo from the past, drowned out by the voice of the yuppy. Still later, when students' eyes were sprayed with pepper spray at UC Davis, the school official who did the spraying was awarded $38,000 for the psychological stress he'd felt from responses to his act.

The Chancellor at Davis kept her job on the ground that she'd given the official no permission to do what he did. She was sorry she had failed to exercise the supervisory role she was generously paid to perform, but things happen. So it was really no big deal. Evidently the spraying had been a good-faith effort to get the students to stop protesting, to stop criticizing the way our country is being run, and to get back to their books. One could regard it as a timely warning: use your eyes to learn your assigned lessons, or risk having them sprayed. The real target was critical thinking.

The chancellor had acted—or rather refrained from action— with the same disdain for the motives of students as had Ronald Reagan as governor. That Ronald Reagan remains immensely popular in memory indicates, among other things, the extent to which we've been accomplices in the decline of our educational system. The great agribusinesses of California (the businesses Carey McWilliams has called "factories in the field") have always been scrupulously conscientious about paying as little as they can to the seasonal workers who bring in our harvests (these "lazy Mexicans"—whose labor feeds us Californians, a good part of the rest of the nation, and huge parts of the world at large). That among those workers are many who are in California illegally has made it easier to hold down wages to something about level with the costs of subsistence—of staying alive. Often the owners have only grudgingly provided toilets and drinking water; they certainly have not been proactive toward medical care, day care for children, or education for children.

So when Governor Reagan wanted to reduce funding for education as a form of reprisal for student unrest, he already had on his side a large block of Californians who were sympathetic to lowering taxes and increasing profits by economizing on education. (These Californians likely overlapped with Californians who approved his reduction of funds for the mentally ill. When Reagan "liberated" the mentally ill by closing institutions that housed and fed them, and sent them pouring out into the streets of California's cities to become the new homeless, many voters happily anticipated tax cuts and were grateful for his statesmanship.) Later there was a similar nationwide constituency in his favor when Reagan ran for president. He promised to do what he could to get rid of the Department of Education. Since "government is not the solution, but the problem," he was promising to do what he could to help education by distancing the federal government from its support. As he'd liberated the students of California, so now he was for liberating students all across the nation.[4]

Constraints that began to be felt in education when Reagan was Governor and later when he was president can't be construed as resulting from mere absentmindedness. The constraints weren't limited to restrictions on spending. From the days of the House Committee on Un-American Activities, there had been an acute concern of powerful members of Congress to make sure the movie industry was telling The American Story. When Reagan was president of the Screen Actors Guild, he shared this concern and supported the House Committee's agenda. As governor of California (and later as president of the United States), Reagan believed that our schools, even more than our movies, should exemplify and teach The American Story. Out of this concern, Reagan worked to have Clark Kerr removed as President of the University of California.   Eighteen days after Reagan took office, Kerr was fired The American Story is that America is the land of the free and the home of the brave, with liberty and justice for all; and that we are the last best hope for mankind; and that all our adventures abroad—the war in Vietnam included—have been inspired by our desire that others abroad may come to share the same democratic institutions that we Americans cherish here at home. Clark Kerr had allowed a cacophony of voices to challenge that story.

Reagan himself was very good at telling The American Story. Indeed, a key factor in his election to the presidency in 1980 is that he was far better at it than Carter was. Carter was not good at telling The American Story. Before the election, Carter had been saying that something was going awry in our souls, whereas Reagan in his campaign promised Morning in America.

---

4. The extent to which he had liberated his and Jane Wyman's adopted son Michael can be read in Michael Reagan's book *On the Outside Looking In* (New York: Kensington, 1988).

Though it's not much attended to, there's an impact of all this on our school curricula. There's a connection between all this and Student Learning Outcomes (or SLO's, as their friends like to call them). Reagan did not invent Student Learning Outcomes. If any one person should be given more credit than others for these marvelous entities, it would be Harvard's late behaviorist B.F. Skinner.

Skinner did not believe there exist such things as autonomous human beings. We must, he said, transcend the mythic notions of freedom and dignity.[5] Because all things are totally under the iron law of cause and effect, human beings are totally under the iron law of cause and effect. At any given moment, the apparent choices you and I make are really just the inevitable outcomes of our genetic inheritance and the totality of circumstances in which we act and the contingencies that have formed us to be the individuals we are. Mother Teresa is not to be praised, and Charles Manson is not to be blamed. Neither of them has ever had any alternative but to act as they did. Mother Teresa had simply Mother Teresa'd. What else could she do than perform the acts of the person she had become? Charles Manson had simply Charles Manson'd. What else could he do than perform the acts of the person he had become?

If for some reason you prefer a person who ministers to the dying homeless of Calcutta to a person who sends disciples into the Hollywood hills to murder rich people, know, says Skinner, it's a sign of misapprehension to seek an increase in the number of the first (the ministers) and a decrease in the number of the second (the murderers) by some ladling out of praise and blame. While praise and blame may have some limited influence, they are rooted in ignorance. When you praise Mother Teresa, you imply she could have done differently. When you blame Charles Manson, you imply he could have done differently. In both cases, you imply that an agent acted freely. You may have to do so, says Skinner, because you don't know any better. But the actual way to bring about the increase of the Mother-Teresa-type and the decrease of the Charles-Manson-type is to increase the operant conditioning that produces the first, and to decrease the operant conditioning

---

5. See B.F. Skinner, *Beyond Freedom and Dignity* (New York: Bantam, 1972), especially chapter 9.

that produces the second. Praise and blame tend to confuse the issue; they tend to distract the praiser-and-blamer from where true leverage resides. There were happenings by which Mother Teresa happened, and there were happenings by which Charles Manson happened. Identify and control those happenings, and you can engineer a world in which there are only Mother Teresas and no Charles Mansons.

For all the fairy-tale character of this approach, there's a modicum of truth in it. Aristotle at one point says "the way one raises a child isn't just one factor that bears upon his prospects for happiness; rather it makes all the difference." The statement seems to override Aristotle's conviction that each of us is responsible for the adult we become, but he says it anyway. At that moment, Aristotle seems to be making Skinner's point. Skinner's denial that we make free choices also seems to get some confirmation from the way heroes quite regularly deflect praise. A man goes into a burning plane at great risk to himself and comes out bearing in his arms a stranger's child. Afterward, he's asked why he acted as he did. The man's face goes blank. He cannot process the question. When he composes himself, he replies, perhaps with notable irritation, "I did it because I heard a child crying in the plane." He doesn't seem at all to acknowledge a moment of decision. Likewise, at the other end of the spectrum, a serial killer is asked why he killed all those people. Again, the first reaction may be a blank face. When the questioner refuses to let the question go, eventually the killer may reply: "I don't know. It seemed like the thing to do."

One salutary consequence of the Skinnerian approach is that it might make our criminal justice system abandon executions and some other punitive aspects. While it seems altogether necessary to keep Manson under lock and key, if a normal citizen is asked how guilty Manson is, an honest answer probably has to be: "I don't know; I cannot imagine the inner state of Charles Manson."

For all that, there's something missing in Skinner's behaviorism. As Sartre taught, the experience of freedom is as palpable as the experience of trees and rocks; the fact one's experience of freedom isn't directly observable by a second party is no reason to deny it. By and large, Americans agree with Sartre regarding the trivial decisions of their everyday lives. What's strange then is that a nation which professes in all its public announcements to value freedom has, nonetheless, taken to heart an educational approach whose central premise is that there is no freedom. The resolution to the paradox comes when one realizes that what is sought in our schools is not so much education as control. "By the third week, 65% of the students will be able to associate 45% of the states with the names of their state capitals." As Skinner seems to suggest, many who support education (including many who administer it) seem to think: "If only we could teach our students to behave as well-trained pigeons, all would be well."

For all that, the SLO approach frequently can be appropriate. In a weight-training class, it may certainly happen that "by the fourth week, 90% of the weight-lifters will be able to press comfortably at least 10% more weight than they were able to press at the start of classes." The trouble comes when one gets into areas where quality seems more at stake than quantity, where affect and sensibility seem more at stake than information, where consciousness seems more involved than muscle. Try the plausibility of this: "By the fifth session in the study of Shakespeare's *Hamlet*, 40% or more of the students will have come to appreciate the ambivalence and ambiguity that typically accompany human decision-making, and 25% or more will also, by reason of their exposure to Shakespeare's diction, have increased by 30% or more their sense of the creative opportunities which are provided by the English language." The defenders of SLO's will immediately holler: "C'mon, you're not being fair; you've deliberately chosen to write an SLO where the intended outcome is not easily subject to confirmation by an observer." Exactly.

The trouble with SLO's is that they tend to rule out just such behavior as that cited in the SLO above. The operational rule seems to be: "Since that sort of behavior is not directly observable, it cannot be a legitimate goal of education." According to some of the true believers, it's not even a behavior. The consequence is that an immense chunk of human experience gets discarded from the educational project. A lobotomy occurs. My nagging hunch is it occurs in order to clear the way for agendas of control. If I may invent a seagoing metaphor, SLO's have been employed to drive people from the deck and so make it harder for anyone to rock the boat.

Teachers will not rock the boat if their lesson plans are devised within the context of approved SLO's. Students, it is hoped, will not rock the boat if the lessons they receive systematically exclude all lessons on boat-rocking.

And indeed students seem generally docile. As students emerge from a class these days, they do not typically cluster into excited groups to discuss at greater length the content just presented in a class. Typically, they do not rush to the library to research further the issues the class may have raised. They reach instead for the latest incarnation of their cell phone so they can re-inhabit their favorite place in cyberspace.[6] They live em-bubbled lives. I've watched them walk right into one another and make no apology, but simply grunt, move a bit to one side or the other, and continue down the road of their disengagement from immediate surroundings.

Skinner devised a Skinner box for his daughter so he could increase his control of the inputs which would determine who she became as an adult. As an adult, she's laughingly said he meant well and she's forgiven him. Today, we do not have Skinner boxes; rather we have schools scattered across America that aspire to become such. (Since, as I've indicated, these schools are outside the student-bubble-space, student feelings toward them are mildly aversive.)

The cost of our present condition is high. Aristotle, the Jewish prophets, and Aquinas had said that we have rights—freedoms—by reason of natural law. The Enlightenment in the eighteenth century echoed this. A corollary of this teaching is that any civil law conceived in violation of our natural rights is, in fact, a mere pretense of law—one that cannot rightfully command the obedience of the citizenry. Jefferson's committee put this doctrine at the center of the Declaration of Independence. Yet it is unlikely you will find this revolutionary doctrine provided for in the SLO's of today. Skinner denies that freedom exists. Human dignity is a myth, and the concept of rights is therefore, for him, an empty one. To follow up on an earlier suggestion, the outcome often envisioned by our SLO's seems to be

---

6. Is this why students tend not to worry about climate change—that they are living in an alternate space-time continuum where the climate seems always improving?

well ordered day-care centers, presided over by avuncular types who enjoy Reagan-like gifts for telling The American Story.

When we talk of someone "going postal," we're suggesting it's not exactly that someone went berserk at a post office, but that work of the type done at a post office was conducive to the berserk behavior.

When one turns to think about similar events in our schools, one must tread softly. Children have been murdered. Terrible wounds remain open. One must not casually and callously use cruel tragedies to score points. Yet—in an understandable, indeed inevitable, effort to draw a lesson from it all—we often turn in these tragedies to an examination of gun laws. That seems natural enough. It's less often, however, that we turn to an examination of schools. A sense of fair play seems to forbid such a turn. On many occasions, school personnel have put their lives on the line, and some have died heroically, to mitigate or interrupt such tragedies.

Nonetheless, there's material here that invites inquiry. Around 2014, I heard a talk show host say there had been over 175 outbreaks of lethal violence in our schools since Columbine in 1999. I don't know just where that count came from, but certainly the actual number, whatever it is, is high.

Why at the schools? "Well," comes an answer, "that's where lots of vulnerable people are." This may call forth a counter statement: "But there are lots of vulnerable people all over the place." That in turn can elicit the reply: "People in those other places have been targeted too."

Still, why so many schools? There are enough instances to make a pattern, and patterns invite speculation.

At our schools, most of our students find niches in a circle of friends. They find enclaves that support their emotional and intellectual lives sufficiently so that they are reasonably comfortable, and do not go off the deep end. As noted above, they are further nurtured and buffered by the extension of their enclave into cyberspace. Facebook and twitterings provide this. While their parents may both be working, and are, for older teen students, more often divorced than not, and while family life may not be the support system it once was, most students find sufficient compensation in make-do family arrangements and other immediate social relationships, supplemented by social media, to get along.

The problem is when it comes to loners and misfits. Some of these are very bright people. In fact this may be why others often don't see trouble coming. And it's here that what I'm driving at can get very controversial. It is my hunch that the intensely introspective, the sensitive and easily wounded, might perhaps be able to get by if the curriculum were rich enough to feed their curiosity and nurture their lonely souls. But the curriculum is all too sure they have no souls.

Too often the curriculum has internalized Skinnerian thinking that there's "no autonomous person," and in ignoring the freedom and dignity of the persons it's supposed to nourish, not only does the curriculum not provide for freedom and creativity but in its actual performance too often works toward stifling these things. "In the fourth month of instruction, the student will be able to perform the following six operations, and perform them up to at least the third level of competence, as the levels are set forth in the schedule below." SLO's often sound like phrasing from *Brave New World* or *1984*.[7]

While I don't want to come across as more sure of what I suggest than I am, it is my hunch that some of the violence we're experiencing in our schools these days can be laid at the door of SLO's and the Skinnerian behaviorism in which they are anchored. In an ironic way, Skinner is right: it's a predictable behavior of human beings that when their freedom is disregarded, they become unruly and unpredictable. Operant conditioning works. Even whales revolt.

---

7.   An analogy with recent events in Afghanistan comes to mind. Not long ago in Afghanistan, at an American base where American soldiers were supposedly training Afghan soldiers in how to make their people good Afghans, the American soldiers were experiencing so many violent attacks from their Afghan trainees that they had to build a high wall through the base to protect themselves from their nominative students. Violent attacks of Afghan "allies" continue as I write. On the evening news one can hear the bafflement of an American officer: "Why aren't these people more grateful for all the things we're doing for them?" The obvious answer is "these people" don't see us as acting on their behalf.

Lest this section itself slip out of all bounds, let's make an end. We could go on. We could delay at length on the breathtaking indifference of American businesses to the insufficiencies of American education. ("We bring in brains from abroad!" Alternatively: "We send our business overseas—where the people are better educated, and cost less.") We could also discuss the obscene salaries many educational administrators command while they shed crocodile tears over the financial burdens of the students.[8]

Let's close by returning to the kinds of questioning addressed by my former students in Oakland: "Is the dilution of content and the currently accelerating cost for education the result of a conspiracy?" The answer depends on how one defines a conspiracy. If "conspiracy" implies "something carried on in secret," the disinvestment in education isn't a conspiracy. The attack on education is carried on in broad daylight. If though, all that's required for there to be a conspiracy is what the etymology of the term demands—namely, "an action or plan of action carried on by a number of people who share a common spirit"—then beyond all reasonable doubt there's a conspiracy today against American education.

---

8. As I will elaborate on later, I once heard a well paid economics professor say: "It is not only desirable but a moral duty that an employer pay a worker no more that the lowest wage at which he can persuade the worker to work." Taking my moral duty to heart, it was hard for me not to raise my hand and inquire whether we did not then owe it to ourselves to convene a committee to see whether the professor himself could be persuaded to work for less than the generous salary he was receiving.

2 | The Growing Ascendance of the Rich

Regarding the Puritans

"You didn't land on Plymouth Rock; Plymouth Rock landed on you," Malcolm X used to say in his sermons to black males. It was a way of guiding them toward a revision of The American Story—a story they must always have found incredible. An admirable thing about Malcolm's statement is that it doesn't take the Fourth of July, 1776, as the birth date of America. To run with his metaphor a bit, let's note the rock's first target wasn't the black Americans who came eventually to feel its crushing weight; the first target was the Native Americans of New England. Let's note too, the rock's first truly asteroid-like impact wasn't on those Indians who helped the Pilgrims through their first winter at the start of the 1620s; rather it was on Pequot Indians to the west of them in 1637.

We often speak of Washington as the Father of Our Country. He was in a number of ways our homegrown exemplar of the Enlightenment, and in a number of ways he acted with disinterested wisdom in our behalf. Still, America wasn't conceived in the closing years of the Enlightenment; it was conceived a hundred and fifty years earlier in the time of our Puritan ancestors. If one looks back for a Father of Our Country in the days of our conception, it wasn't Captain John Smith or John Rolfe; the most plausible candidate is the John Winthrop spoken of in the first chapter, for it's his DNA we find flowing in our veins today—and, as already suggested, if we take freedom of thought and tolerance as earmarks of the Enlightenment, Winthrop was neither the Enlightenment's forerunner nor its child.

By reason of our highly principled separation of church and state, while we may know something of Winthrop as Governor of Massachusetts, most of us have successfully evaded any inquiry into his religion. His religion was, as his label as a Puritan suggests, a subset of Protestantism—one which found most Protestantism insufficiently pure. Perhaps a secondary reason why our teachers have had so little to tell us about his motivations is that Puritanism is a notoriously difficult mentality to objectify—not the least because we have all inherited it.

When we arrived at Massachusetts Bay in 1630, we may have wished to establish a new Eden. We quickly found ourselves scrambling however for a place in the sun. There were impediments. They presented themselves as "wilderness." More existentially, they came to be personified as "Indians" or "savages." In order to tame the wilderness, we had to tame, subdue, or exterminate the savages.

Beyond that, we brought with us special sources of internal tension. It wasn't just that some of us who affirmed we were God's people found amongst us others—Roger Williams, Anne Hutchinson, Quakers—who, though thinking differently from us, claimed inconveniently to be God's people as well. For beyond that, each of us was confronted by a highly personal problem of such a nature it couldn't be resolved this side of the grave. No problem could be more urgent and no problem more impossible to solve. It presented itself in the question: Am I who count myself among God's people truly one of them? Am I actually among the Elect?

No decision of mine, no baptismal ritual, no imitation of Jesus nor approval of me by the Christian community could put the question to rest. As Luther had protested, indulgences in the form of contributions to the church were the shabbiest of scams—as if some fellow mortals could sell us the grace of God. Likewise, for that matter, it was blasphemous to say any other work I might perform could merit that grace of redemption which was altogether in God's hands to bestow or withhold. What human has a right to think he or she can force the hand of God? How incredibly lacking we must be in a true awareness of our state if we think we can oblige God to let us share in the eternal bliss that is God's life.

In this matter, Calvin was particularly clear. If as said we knew the decision about our salvation did not reside with us, he said we knew precisely where it did reside. It resided in the eternal and inscrutable decree of God. From all eternity, as Paul's Epistle to the Romans teaches, God has elected a few of us to the life of grace and salvation; the remaining majority, by an equally irrevocable decree, He has destined to burn in hell forever. Nor should we ask why. To ask "why?" is to presume. It's to respond to God with blasphemy. For in asking, we presume we can call God to account. We'd have missed the infinite qualitative difference between our mere selves and God. We'd have assumed God must abide by our trivial human contrivances for justice. Rather the truth is, in this most important matter of life, we have resources neither on earth nor in heaven. Such had Calvin made clear.

Awesome! Breathtaking! Where does it leave us?

It leaves us hoping we are among the Elect, but with no way of finding out. In this Puritan predicament, if we are willing, we can glimpse the remarkably intense motivational context for the whole founding and development of Massachusetts Bay Colony—the colony that laid down the paradigm for the Puritan nation that continues into the present. If the economic and political development has proved spectacular—unparalleled in human history—a part of the explanation is in the drivenness of us who have carried it out.

Max Weber writes, "The Father in heaven of the New Testament, so human and understanding, who rejoices over the repentance of a sinner as a woman over the lost piece of silver she has found, is gone."[1]

It's noteworthy that Weber cites a passage where Jesus compares God to a woman who has found a lost treasure. This passage, and the passages like it, has disappeared from the consciousness of the devout Puritan. One way to speak of Calvin's accomplishment is that he has quite de-feminized the tender God of Jesus. Recognizing what Calvin has done, Weber speaks

---

1. Max Weber, *The Protestant Ethic and the Spirit of Capitalism* (New York: Charles Scribner's Sons, 1958), 103. See Weber's deliberate and scholarly exposition of Calvinism, 98–128.

of "the extreme inhumanity" of the predestined state our ancestors felt they and everyone else had been born into.[2]

That a majority of us found it unbearable brings us to the
paradox at the center of Puritan development. Terrible as was
the prospect of damnation, and helpless as one was to change
the decree of damnation if one was part of the human majority
doomed to it, it occurred to countless of us Puritans that one
could perhaps shelter oneself against the paralyzing fear of such
doom if one could find signs one lived, here and now, in God's
friendship. This thought inspires the unending search for "the
signs of election."

In the book of Deuteronomy, there is a long list of the blessings
Israel will enjoy if it is obedient to God. "The Lord thy God will
set thee on high above all the nations of the earth. Blessed shalt
thou be in the city, and blessed shalt thou be in the field. Blessed
shall be the fruit of thy body, and the fruit of thy ground, and
the fruit of thy cattle, the increase of thy kine, and the flocks of
thy sheep." The list continues for another ten verses. Then there
is an even longer list of curses that will fall on Israel if it is not
obedient. "Cursed shalt thou be in the city, and cursed in the
field. Cursed shall be thy basket and thy store. Cursed shall be
the fruit of thy body, and the fruit of thy land, the increase of thy
kine, and the flocks of thy sheep. Cursed shalt thou be when thou
comest in, and cursed shalt thou be when thou goest out." The list
continues for another forty-eight verses.[3]

Among us Puritans, if one was to take these verses to heart,
one must put them through the purifying filter of predestination.
In truth, man's obedience or disobedience could not be the determining factor in one's eternal lot. God was in charge of everything, and certainly this meant God and God alone made the
decision as to our salvation as vessels of election, or our damnation as vessels of wrath. But could not one use these blessings and
curses as so many indications of which way God had decided in
one's individual case? Could not purity of conduct, and the harmony and prosperity flowing from such, be a sign that God had
eternally befriended one? In general, could not the success of an
enterprise in which one immersed oneself be a sign here and now

---

2. Weber, *Protestant Ethic*, 104.
3. Deut. 28:1–68.

of God's commitment to one's wellbeing? And so commenced our great game of using prosperity as a scoreboard on which were registered eternal victory for the few and eternal failure for all the others.

Living for a mission could provide a kind of reassurance twice over. Let's suppose one had as the governing goal of all one's enterprise the establishment of God's kingdom in the new world. Was not such a human already clearly in alignment with God? Further, if that mission was successful, was it not clear that God was both approving toward the mission and accepting of the person engaged in it?

From the beginning, the Puritans conceive their activity as a mission; and this category "mission" provides a powerful theme for explaining and integrating the moments of our subsequent history. It was our mission to become a city on a hill. As we turned the savage wilderness into God's country, it was our mission to set up a form of government that would constitute the last best hope of humankind. Accomplishing that by our Constitution, we took on in the Monroe Doctrine the mission of being the exemplar and protector and arbiter of good order throughout the entire Western hemisphere. At home it was our manifest destiny to achieve the winning of the West by extending our borders to the Pacific Ocean. After that, it was our God-given duty to bring the Philippines under our Christian control, and then, by holding open the doors of China, to take our rightful place on the planet as the first among equals in the politics and commerce of the world.

Looking back to our Puritan forefathers for the beginnings of all this, notice how "mission" is taken as the implicit principle governing Puritan relations with Indians in the following description by Segal and Stinebeck:

> The Puritan struggle against sin was, in part, a struggle against Satan as personified by the Indian. It was a life-and-death struggle and the Lord directed the Puritan forces in New England. Therefore, what the Puritan did, he did because God urged him to do it. Since the Puritan's relations with the Indians were dominated by his importance as a messenger of God, his gain in a transaction with an Indian was a commensurate victory for God over

> Satan. While New Plymouth authorities declared "there
> was no dealing with Indians above board," these [under-
> the-board] dealings were justified because they were car-
> ried out according to the dictates of God. In the very same
> manner, the Jews had fought the Canaanites for posses-
> sion of the Promised Land.[4]

In this comment by Segal and Stinebeck, there's opportunity
to reflect on the tensions in our ancestors' project. The Puritan
mission was a war against sin. Yet Calvin had insisted it was by
God's eternal decree that sin existed. Before the creation of the
world, Calvin reasoned, God had willed that there be sin. The
logic of his position ran like this: since nothing on earth had an
existence in spite of God, if something did exist, it was because
God willed it. (Many Muslim theologians say the same today.)
The inconvenience however of this splendidly logical doctrine
was that it seemed to drain sin of its essential character, its character of being *contrary* to God. Rather when one sinned, one was
performing God's will. Further, if it is by God's irresistible will
that His creature sins, it was difficult to find a meaningful way
to hold the creature responsible. One is responsible for what one
chooses; regarding sin, according to Calvin, the creature had no
choice—as indeed (in a way anticipating Skinner), he had no
freedom.

This rather stark theological paradox invites us to reflect on
another anomaly. Bear with me while I try to elaborate it. Here
were we Christians in New England seeking to found a new
Eden in which Christ would reign as the restorer of harmony,
as the atonement [at-one-ment] with the Father, as the Messiah
who would reign as Prince of Peace. To establish this was our
Puritan mission. And the open land was our opportunity. Yet, as
said, there was an impediment. The land wasn't quite open after

---

4. Charles M. Segal and David C. Stineback, eds., *Puritans, Indians &*
Manifest Destiny (New York: G.P. Putnam's Sons, 1977), 49. That this work
edited by Segal and Stinebeck has been marketed by its publisher as "juvenile non-fiction" baffles explanation. While I've known bright juveniles, I
doubt I've ever known one who would, without abundant tutelage, be able
to comprehend the message of this book.

all. Once again Satan had intruded himself in what was supposed to be God's garden. And the minions of Satan were the Indians. Quickly therefore the mission we took upon ourselves in 1630 in service to the Prince of Peace became in 1637 a matter of killing Indians. The mission, so brought down to earth and fleshed out, could not easily discover in the four gospels a textual endorsement for the murder of Indian women and children, and—since the provoking of adult Indian males was a conscious strategy of the Puritans—the deaths even of adult Indian males were a problem. But while the gospels provided little help here, fortunately the Bible provided Puritans a whole book of Joshua exemplifying a single-minded readiness on God's part to annihilate Canaanites; and from here we drew biblical justification and warrant. For we were the chosen people of the new order Jesus had come into the world to establish.[5]

There still remained, to be sure, a problem in seeking a warrant in the book of Joshua. Supposing the Israelites had had a divine warrant to kill Canaanites, who was to say that meant we Puritans—freshly chosen people though we be—had such a warrant regarding Indians?

As we try to step outside our Puritan heritage and look to problematic aspects of the Puritan viewpoint, one can wonder how well our ancestral non-Jewish, Anglo-Saxon American forefathers understood the book of Joshua. Having taken Joshua literally, the Roman Catholic Church had quite confused itself by condemning Galileo for saying that night and day are caused by the earth's rotation rather than a daily journey of the sun; the Vatican decreed that if the sun miraculously stood still at the battle of Jericho, that proved the sun at ordinary times was revolving around the earth. Ordinary speech however—including biblical speech—is routinely indifferent to matters of science. We continue to say, without a second thought: "The sun rises in the east and sets in the west." As for accounts of genocidal annihilations that make up most of the book of Joshua, modern archeology

---

5. Characterization of sword as instrument of peace wasn't, of course, an invention peculiar to Puritans and ancient Israelites. Catholics had repeatedly invoked it as they promoted the Crusades. "God wills it!" Catholic jihadists had cried as they scurried eastward pillaging across Europe and hurled themselves into the Holy Land to slay Infidels.

has been unable to find physical evidence of such destruction. To cite the *Jewish Study Bible*: "intense archeological investigation of virtually all the places mentioned in Joshua that can be identified with current sites reveals no pattern of destruction that can be correlated, in either chronology or location, with the period of early Israel."[6] The scholarly consensus today seems to be that what actually took place in Joshua's time—although it may well have involved friction and conflict—was not annihilation but settlement in unoccupied places in the central highlands, leading to gradual accommodation to and merging with native Canaanites. If so, the book of Joshua was far less an historical narrative (in the sense we currently conceive "history") than poetic celebration of God's power (He can make the sun stand still) and of God's generosity to the Israelites—a celebration constructed from numerous folk traditions and set down long after the time of the putative events, having as its motivating purpose the maintenance and promotion of Jewish morale (including, if one reads it carefully, a kind of "commercial" for observing the rite of male circumcision).

When Protestants split decisively from the authority of Pope and Rome, they reached out for something to provide the sturdiness and unity which previously a centralized Catholic teaching authority had provided. Quite in line with the evolving Reformation as it emerged from Renaissance humanism, they sought this in a return to sources, specifically a return to the Bible. A hurdle of understanding of which they seemed only peripherally aware was that they were not Jews. It is undeniably true that Jews yield nothing to Protestants in their reverence for that part of the Bible Christians call the Old Testament. Contrary however to the practice of many Protestants—including, certainly, the practice of Puritans—Jews in general have maintained a sense of their Bible as a compilation from many sources, a compilation including a variety of genres: of histories it is true, but also of poems, fables and other fictional stories, anthologies of sayings, prophetic warnings, and the book of Job. After all, it was Jews who had put it together. They've maintained a sense that the theological convictions and perspectives flowing through this

---

6. Adele Berlin and Marc Zvi Brettler, eds., *The Jewish Study Bible* (New York: Oxford University Press, 2003), 463.

great array of writings were diverse. The book of Job with its non-stop debate between Job and his friends is a microcosm of Jewish intellectual life. This kind of pitting of biblical verse against verse and theme against theme is what has kept the rabbis in business for the last two thousand years. They see the Bible as an inspired invitation for a great argument about God and His creatures. Short of a messianic culmination of human history, these rabbinic scholars do not anticipate an end to this argument. (The statistically improbable prominence of so many Jewish intellectuals and professional men and women—many of them declared secularists—in so many fields of human endeavor can, I think, plausibly be traced in part to the Jewish tradition of originality and creativity in biblical argument; to be raised in such a tradition is to live one's life amid questions regarding the context of everything.)

Protestants, looking to the Bible as the secure and sole anchor of their faith, seem to have required a less complicated, less open-ended, approach. For some, not only is each word in the Bible directly chosen by God, but each word is to be taken literally. This helps explain how Protestants (along with, to be fair, literal-minded Catholics and literal-minded Jews) can find marching orders in the Bible where others may find symbolic statements, allegories, and matter for reflection on the human predicament.

By reason of their strong tendency toward literalism, the notion of being among the Elect easily becomes associated among our Puritan forefathers with the notion of achieving possession of a Promised Land. A doctrine of Divine Real Estate seems altogether plausible to them. "Pure Christians like ourselves," they reasoned, enjoy land by reason of divine promise. John Cotton, an eloquent Puritan preacher, exhorts Winthrop and company before they leave for America to have no scruple about encroaching on the lands of others. For in the case of people like them, God's chosen, the appointment of land is by specific divine decree—as it was for the Israelites. God apportions land to them by "some more special appointment, because God tells them it by His own mouth; He does not so with other people." Cotton concludes his argument saying "others take the land by His providence, but God's people take the land by promise."[7]

---

7. Segal and Stinebeck, *Puritans, Indians & Manifest Destiny*, 54.

It's easy to see what a powerful idea this idea of a special dispensation can be. If we're looking for it, we need no other source for American exceptionalism. This specific exceptionalism is not one that speaks simply of us Americans being exceptionally blessed. That may be part of it; but centrally, it is a belief and claim that we are exempt from law. We do not need to abide by the laws with which we would encumber others. We who place laws on others are, ourselves, outside those laws. As noted, a pilgrim leader had said "There is no dealing with Indians above board." In the immediate situation of the Puritan settlers this meant Christians could hold the Indians to the letter of the treaties forged with them while the Christians themselves remained unbound. Indians could be punished, stripped of their lands, exterminated even, for violations. On the other hand, Indians could not hold "God's people" to any standard at all. Puritans anticipated the statement of a recent American president: "I will never apologize for the American people." The tradition endures. International law is less something that we are bound by than it is something of which we are in charge.

Some have found it strange that we who sometimes say we came to the new world to establish a rule of "laws, not men," should have so routinely set to one side nearly all our treaties with Indians. The basis for this behavior lies here. It lies in our sense that when we aggrandize ourselves, we win a victory for God. To borrow from the wordplay in *Hamlet*'s graveyard scene, it is a sense that both lies deep and deeply lies. It constitutes a pre-emptive triumph by us over Enlightenment thinking about human equality by establishing for us a Puritan division of humankind into the Elect and the Damned. (Our great spokesman for the Enlightenment, after he accepted "all men are created equal" into his declaration against the British, preferred for daily use a Puritan practice; to actually treat all humans as equal was quite alien to Jefferson's lifestyle and mindset.)

What though has all this to do with the growing ascendency of wealth in America?

The template of thinking which we inherit from Puritan forefathers includes a kind of moral somersault. Getting ahead, acquiring wealth, "winning": this kind of thing demonstrates that one is beloved by God. From this it follows that one should devote oneself without restraint to acquisition—but from an altogether otherworldly motivation. (Beyond all wink of sarcasm, there really is a genuine ideological core to the American pursuit of wealth. The most virtuous among us, we think, are those most utterly in thrall to this pursuit. This is an important chunk of what Weber was teaching, and explains why Benjamin Franklin's aphorisms figure importantly in Weber's analysis. It helps explain why, so long as government is seen as facilitating the unrestricted pursuit of wealth, we tend to have no objection to it; it's only when government attempts to place restraints on that pursuit that we seem to remember to complain of it as Big Government.)

I call this Puritan mindset a "somersault" because it's a kind of leap of faith over a familiar objection presented by so many time-honored sages—by Aristotle, the Buddha, and Jesus, among others. The objection states that one condemns oneself to slavery if one pursues wealth as life's organizing goal. Aristotle had argued that to undertake such pursuit is a strategic error, since it takes something whose essential nature is to be instrumental (wealth) and attempts to make it the goal. Such a pursuit, he says, never "arrives;" you can never get enough of what isn't what you really want and need. The Buddha and Jesus posed similar objections. Jesus asks, "What does it profit a man if he gains the whole world, and suffers the loss of his soul?" The Buddha tells us it is open-ended desire that makes human life miserable. The Puritan somersault over such traditional objections consists in regarding achieved wealth as a sign of divine favor. This perspective lifts all restraints, since for the Puritan, there's no such thing as being too confident that God is on one's side. Since one lives always under the shadow of doubt, further acquisitions are always welcome. Indeed they are necessary with an urgency like that with which the addict regards cocaine. (Today, one can note a neurosis of this sort at work in our Puritan selves as we seek "absolute national security." Security of that degree is an ever-retreating horizon; it's unreachable. Each time that we find new means to intimidate our enemies, we find we have both new reasons to fear them and have more enemies to intimidate; daily we intensify the enmity of others toward us and recruit newcomers to their ranks.)

What saves the Puritan orientation from descending immediately into pure economic narcissism, greed, and chaos is partly that the first generation of our Puritan ancestors was, as noted, preoccupied by a sense of being called to a mission. A century and a half before we were "a nation," the seeds of American nationalism were germinating.

A kind of closed loop in the dynamics of faith was operational in this Puritan nationalism: "Our godly mission shows we are God's people; and the fact we are God's people shows our mission is godly." With this as the operating conviction, commitment can be unqualified and, in fact, selfless. The begging of a question here doesn't necessarily indicate invalidity. An elderly couple, for instance, may explain the longevity of their marriage: "Our mutual love has been sustained by the goodness each finds in the other; and the goodness each finds in the other has been fostered by our mutual love." It's quite possible this is true even if it doesn't much help an outsider to grasp the inner dynamic. When Heidegger lapsed into a worship of German destiny and embraced Nazism, it wasn't exactly a surrender to selfishness or some mere lapse of logic he was involved in, but a lapse into uncritical sentimentality and nationalism. Because this lapse was not a lapse into selfishness, Heidegger could never quite find a way to repent of it after the war, or to apologize. Nationalism can anesthetize one to humane ethics, as it does today. We Americans resist socialism — or at least the label of it — as big-government tyranny; but look at all the holidays every year on which we celebrate and ratify our national militancy.

The Puritans' commitment to mission can be regarded as a kind of closed loop, and while some closed loops may be virtuous, there is in these neat and rigid systems the possibility of things going wildly awry. Chesterton remarked: "A madman is someone who has lost everything but his reason." The true-believing that goes on in the Puritan loop may have a simplicity and internal consistency so compelling that it pays no attention to counter-evidence. It was this hunch that led Max Weber to posit something obsessive at the center of the Protestant work ethic. Even Lutherans sometimes charged that the unending search for "signs of election" by Calvinist Puritans had led to a betrayal of the Reformation's great insight into the nature of grace. Were not the Puritans busily scurrying about, some Lutherans asked, in a frenzy to earn grace after all? These Lutherans charged that the Puritans had bootlegged the heresy of salvation-by-works into the Reformation by a back door. They charged that in the actual psychology of Calvinist Puritans, works had become everything.

This gospel of justification-certified-by-acquisition had, as noted, trouble with the Jesus of the gospels. There we find Jesus speaking dramatically of the difficulties of the Rich Man. For all their belief in literal interpretation, the pastors of the first generation of Puritan settlers had in hand a mechanism by which to somersault over this text. Jesus, they said, was speaking of the dangers of wealth sought in a spirit of self-indulgence. Wealth resulting from single-minded efforts to establish God's kingdom here on earth was quite a different matter. Such wealth needed no justification; such wealth was in fact here and now the principal sign granted to us that we are justified.

A negative implication for one who holds this view is that the poor are not justified. This too was believed. The immense epidemics that drastically reduced the numbers of Indians in the early years of Puritan migration were a confirmation to Puritans that Indians were not justified—had never been intended by God for heaven. The miraculous success of us Puritans in a pre-dawn attack on the Pequots as we burnt them alive in their tents demonstrated that we were God's friends and they were not. Clearly these burnt offerings were pleasing to God. Regarding widows and orphans, in the face of everything Jesus and earlier Jewish prophets had to say on their behalf, the sufferings and misfortunes of Pequot widows and orphans provided a thoughtful Puritan with opportunity to question the virtue of these victims of our power. Did not Deuteronomy offer us a reason to question the godliness of those who suffer? Were not then these civilian misfortunes signs? And if God manifested by their sufferings that He had no part with them, why then ought we to befriend them in any way? We hunted and slew nearly all the surviving Pequots we could find. (Later the miserable conditions in which God allowed Jefferson to keep his kidnapped blacks were a reassuring sign to Jefferson that Providence intended them for exploitation.)

So, to sum up yet again: a paradoxical ethos was established. The trademark of godliness was to be sought and captured in an open-ended pursuit of worldly success. That is to say, certified godliness (a deep sense of reliable and comforting personal justification) was a confirmation and guarantee of election to grace that only a successful acquisition of wealth could deliver.

If one says, "Well, sure; that's the way people have always thought," Weber would direct one back to the phrase "open-ended pursuit" and call attention to the weight a relentless theological context added. Weber speaks of the systematic rationalization of work dictated by the Protestant ethic. The humane context had dropped out. One can argue—as contemporary critics of capitalism do—that an unrestricted and unwholesome simplification had taken place. One can argue that things had gotten unwholesomely schematized, and that a great many important human concerns had been abandoned in the process. One can argue also that the true sign of the times was in the murder of Indians, and that we had disastrously misinterpreted it.

America's story, whether good or bad, can be told as one about acquisition. In its romanticized version, we tell this story as a story about our hunger for land and the preciousness we felt for the land we hungered for. We do this in our rich literature of the West. We have our cowboy stories and our little houses on the prairie. Not only in our novels but in our movies this theme has been nearly inexhaustible. One of our all-time favorite stage shows is a musical dramatization of how Oklahoma was opened to homesteading. The first performances of this musical boosted our morale during the Second World War. In all seasons since, there have been multiple performances across America. A few years before that musical play, in the depths of the Depression, we found ourselves gripped by a novel about how troubles in that same Oklahoma had led some to migrate to California in relentless determination to find new opportunity. In the course of the novel, the Joad family comes to personify the indomitable spirit of the American people. To this day, the story resonates with us and its ending can bring tears.

One can say then, our theme has been land, and the plot of our story has been the winning of the West.

But there's a way to de-romanticize the story and say it was about the acquisition of property—and to say that property mattered because it has been a way of keeping score. Considering how we've actually treated the property we've acquired, this version of the story is the more plausible version. People who love the land do not treat it as we have. They do not do to the land the things we are doing as I write.

Also this version can better accommodate the way individual groups have been treated as the story's unfolded. The Oklahoma that was opened to homesteading had been designated earlier as a last refuge for Indians whom our federal government had driven westward from east of the Mississippi. Now, with the "opening" of Oklahoma, the children of those Indians were put under fresh constraints and suffered new losses of land that we'd guaranteed was theirs in "perpetuity." Later, when in the wake of rapacious farming techniques, Oklahoma ceased to nurture the children of these homesteaders, and many were forced to migrate, the California to which numbers of them came had been wrested at gunpoint from Mexico less than a century before. Beyond, then, the wide-eyed wonder at the beauty of nature, and beyond the adventure of turning the wilderness into God's country, was something else. Across the map of what had become the United States a kind of banner had been carried westward which read: "Claims of the sons of Puritans prevail over all counter-claims." The dictum required no legal theory to back it up. It was manifest.

Introducing Adam Smith

Before we try to calculate Adam Smith's influence on our developing Puritan nation, let's look at Smith himself in the latter part of the eighteenth century. The temper of Adam Smith's writing is sweet. His professional career opened with lectures on rhetoric which he delivered in Edinburgh in his mid-twenties. They must have been very good. For what one finds later in *The Wealth of Nations* is a wonderfully considerate pedagogy. While the goal of his writing was theory and prescription, his technique was gently to share with his reader the sources of his convictions. Conscientious about these convictions, he wishes to make available to the reader the experiences and considerations by which he's come to them. Aristotle's advice in his own work on rhetoric can perhaps be summed up: Do not get in the way of the truth you want to disclose. Whether it was from Aristotle, or Francis Bacon, or by his own intuitive sense, this seems to have been Smith's rule. One can open almost any page of *The Wealth of Nations* and understand details there of an argument in progress—even if one is quite unversed in the grand theoretic generalization toward which Smith is working.

The temper of Smith's writing is also benign. While still in his twenties, he passed from being a lecturer on rhetoric to being a lecturer on morality. As such, he was particularly interested to discover the sources and nature of moral sentiments. One can imagine his students were fortunate in the instruction they received. For time and again later in his pages on *The Wealth of Nations,* the reader can find a compassionate, gently Chaucer-like, regard for human affairs. His teacher Francis Hutcheson had taught him to think habitually in terms of what would provide the greatest happiness for the greatest number. Smith argues for generous wages for workers—on grounds similar to those W. Edwards Deming uses in the twentieth century (i.e., good morale of the worker tends to promote high quality in goods and services being provided). Smith celebrates the division of labor not only for its efficiency, but because he sees it as permitting an individual (or a country) to discover what his or her (or their) natural proclivities are and to concentrate on developing those to a point of expertise. The individual and society would benefit mutually—or at least that is what he intended. (Even today, the real work being done in America—I mean the work that sustains us still as a society, not the pseudo-work of financial manipulation—is being done by ordinary people who have achieved precisely the kinds of technical expertise Smith envisioned. So while Smith discourses famously on pin-making, perhaps he'd had insufficient occasion to observe the extreme inhumanity to which the division of labor—as eventually materialized in the assembly-line—could be pushed. I'm willing to grant him that he couldn't foresee the degree to which a worker could be reduced to a cog in the industrial process.)

Smith opposed slavery. Two concerns listed above—maintenance of morale and development of expertise—indicate why. He says the savings one envisions from the work of a captive laborer are illusory; the quantity produced by such a worker will be meager, and the quality poor. (This was not because the captive was incompetent, but because the captive was smart—something an exploiter of captive labor like Jefferson found it inconvenient to admit.)

Smith's argument against the exploitation of colonies—a routine occurrence in the reigning mercantilism—was similar. If colonists are exploited, they will know they are being exploited. They will resent this and will not be willing to pay even those taxes necessary for their upkeep and defense. Smith thought England should let the American colonies go; but he thought also England was not wise enough to know this. Out of pride—not from good economics—England, he thought, would hold on till there was war. His great work, published in 1776, was prophetic—confirmed on this point in the year it appeared.

Not only, in Smith's opinion, was England over-regulating the American colonies; he thought it was over-regulating the people of England. The center then of Smith's program was laissez-faire—but in a far more humanely contextualized sense than the term is defended today. Let the people, acting freely in exchanges with one another, decide the prices of things. Let the workers, freely negotiating with the managers, arrive at wages they're willing to work for. (Unions, Smith says, are a natural exercise of freedom, and laws prohibiting them are instances of governmental excess.) Let the marketplace determine what goods and services will be provided, and in what quantity, and of what quality, and at what price. Let there be no tariffs, protective or otherwise, on goods crossing borders (except perhaps in the infancy of a newly founded industry). If there must be colonies, let them be treated as equals in matters of trade; and let them participate in their own governance.

All this seemed a wonderful prescription for freeing up the energies of the human race at the time of writing. The emphasis was not on the benefits of capitalism but on the democratization of economics. Parties privileged in the traditional mercantilist system had, of course, reason to resist it. A majority of government officials could be expected to resent it. The tendency of Smith's program was to reduce their influence, their numbers, and their compensations. One finds here anticipations of Thoreau's preference for a government that governs least. It was this tendency that made Smith's message popular. (Tellingly, in his effort to divide labor into "productive labor" and "unproductive labor," Smith was inclined to cite court officials, ecclesiastics, and military personnel as instances of the latter. One can assume these parties were not amused.)

Given this brief summary, let's see what affinities there might be between Smith's prescriptions and the earlier, pre-Enlightenment, thinking of our Puritan forefathers. We may have to meander a bit as we go.

Our Puritan forefathers were nurtured, as we've seen, in a Calvinism that led each believer into a state of stark loneliness. One could not, as perhaps in medieval Europe, belong to the "one true Church" and thereby think oneself saved. Rather our Puritan ancestors situated each person alone before God. One's eternal destiny remained inscrutable. The only thing to reach out to—the telling, comforting sign—was success here and now.

Smith, though clearly an agent and citizen of the Enlightenment, was raised in a place with a history steeped in Calvinism. In attempts to gage the effect of this on Smith, it can be helpful to note his lifelong friendship with David Hume, a fellow Scot. Hume, raised in the same dour environs, toyed all his life with what's sometimes called the Egocentric Predicament. The controlling question for the Egocentric Predicament is: how do I know I'm not the only being there is? Hume's answer: I don't. Noteworthy about that question is how it lands Hume—and any disciple of his—in an isolation that parallels the isolation and quandary arising from the Puritan question: how can I assure myself I'm among the Elect?

While their writings make clear that both Hume and Smith managed to slough off most constraints of the Calvinist mindset, one can wonder whether either was ever entirely free of the heightened individualism that Calvinism stimulated. In Hume's case, I'd say this individualism surfaces in the unrelieved subjectivism for which he makes claims in his most deliberate passages. As indicated, a fair phrasing of the predicament he argues for is that so far as any individual can know, the entire universe is simply a projection of his or her personal subjectivity.

Hume's friend Smith is much more grounded in the extramental world, and his case is more complicated. Historians tell us that, in his and Hume's time, "old light" Calvinism was on the wane in Scotland. Also, we're told by Smith's biographers that his mother was a very devout Christian, and that she—a widow almost from the time of Smith's birth—was the mainstay of her bachelor son's life. It's interesting then to ask what religious content Smith may have drawn from his relationship to her and to the times.

The question isn't easy to answer. "Old Light" Calvinism is often associated with "covenanters." Among its major aspects, the theological emphasis of covenanters can alleviate the horror of predestination by channeling it into activity on behalf of God. This indeed is what Perry Miller believes happened early in American Puritanism. While God is utterly free, God has freely bound Himself to work within covenantal relations with His Elect; belief in this becomes in turn a strong motivation for His Elect to work hard. A waning of that theological emphasis as the Enlightenment gained ground among the professors and other writers and intellectuals of Scotland could plausibly mean that the doctrine of predestination retreated yet further—moving toward a vanishing point. If this was happening in the Scottish Christianity of Smith's day, that was a substantial alteration. Smith's Calvinism, supposing some traces of Calvinism remained with him, would then have been quite different from that of our first Puritan forefathers. I take this to have been the case.

It is not a stretch to hypothesize that both Smith's mother and Smith himself maintained some confidence in a divine providence, but without any accompanying thought that God had predetermined all outcomes in the world God created. Such seems in fact the informal theological backdrop that provides context for Smith's reflections on moral sentiments and for the consequences of these reflections in his economic theory. There are routine references to "nature," to "the plan of nature," to the "divine plan," and to "providence" in Smith's writing on moral sentiments. Providence, he says, has installed in us the capacity to empathize; yet the use we make of that capacity occurs in the arena of our freedom.

What makes it difficult to be definitive here is that Smith seems not, at least when writing as an economist, to insist on some precise theological context. This lets some interpreters say his references in his moral writings to a divine plan are just window dressing, a mere concession Smith makes to the residual religious thinking of his time. Since however Smith was neither a sloppy writer nor a timid one, the simpler interpretation is that he believed in some version of divine providence but felt he had enough on his plate not to argue about it. He felt no impulse to reignite religious wars of the previous century. When the

Scottish Enlightenment arrived, its spirit was to allow its participants a fresh start. One neither had to square oneself with all the old traditions, nor identify oneself in terms of the old labels. What I take to be implied in the way Smith phrases things is:

1) there is a divine plan written into nature—which would mean the atheists were wrong; but
2) there is no predestination—which would mean the original Calvinists were wrong.

This would leave Smith somewhere along the line stretching from a deist to a person of devout temper (like perhaps Darwin's wife in the next century) who believes there is an ongoing and daily divine providence.

Allowing the murkiness here, it seems one can find still a holdover from attitudes of original Calvinist individualism at the center of Smith's thinking. Smith's is, to be sure, a transformed individualism. Unlike the individualism of original Calvinism, it celebrates freedom; but it's still an individualism, and this individualism supplies the motivational theory basic to *The Wealth of Nations*. Just as Hume couldn't see any way out of his egocentric predicament, so Smith couldn't see any other scaffolding on which to construct a desirable economics than upon an inescapable and indispensable self-interest of the human individual.

Make no mistake. He intended to construct; and he didn't see the limit of his labors to be merely in constructing a theory. He intended a revolutionary document. While many an economist has claimed to do nothing more than describe how things are, Smith (like Marx in later days) knew that—beyond providing a diagnosis—he was prescribing. As noted earlier, he intended a prescription to counter mercantilism. No mere spectator, he'd chosen sides and wanted to recruit the reader to the side he'd chosen; for he thought mercantilism attempted, counterproductively, to promote national success at the expense of individual freedom and happiness.

One can imagine, then, the exhilaration Smith felt when he was first visited by the "invisible hand"—by which I mean when this marvelously convenient metaphorical conception dawned on him. (The metaphor makes its first appearance in his writing on morals when he is discussing empathy.) To appreciate what this meant to him, it's necessary to see him as more complicated than either his friends or foes of later times have often allowed him to be. Anticipating utilitarians to come and echoing Aquinas and the scholastics' concept of "the common good" from the medieval past, Smith passionately sought to promote the greatest happiness for the greatest number. Just as we'd lose sight of the Puritans and be substituting some fabrication of our own devising were we to deny the genuineness of their obsession to get right with God, so we'd lose sight of Smith were we to deny the passion of his humanism—the sincere humanitarianism out of which he acted. He was anything but a cold-hearted and disinterested party.

As noted, like the American revolutionaries who were his contemporaries, Smith saw British mercantilism as exploitation and *The Wealth of Nations* of 1776 was written to provide an alternative. An argument can be made that his book has been as influential on American life as the Declaration of Independence of that same year. While Smith's phrases haven't been memorized in the rote manner some of Jefferson and company's phrases have, one can argue that Smith's program, albeit in a garbled version, has been more deeply internalized than our July 4th document has.

The key statement of the Declaration is that all men are created equal. The canonical statement in *The Wealth of Nations*, occurring in book 4, chapter 2, paragraph 9 is as follows:

> He [every individual], indeed, neither intends to promote the public interest, nor knows how much he is promoting it. By preferring the support of domestic to that of foreign industry, he intends only his own security; and by directing that industry in such manner as its produce may be of the greatest value, he intends only his own gain, and he is in this, as in many other cases, led by an invisible hand to promote an end which was no part of his intention. Nor is it always worse for the society that it was no part of it. By pursuing his own interest he frequently promotes that of the society more effectually than when he really intends to promote it. I have never known much good done by those who affected to trade for the public good.

Some exegesis of this central statement is required. Some have claimed that the passage should never have been conceded the key position it's usually accorded as a source for understanding what Smith is about. They point out that the passage is part of a case for demonstrating how a nation's wealth is built from the labor of individuals within its national confines, and that the passage's field of reference should be restricted to making that point. But this will not do. Smith clearly intends a wide reference; he inserts "as in many other cases" to underscore his intention. He reinforces that in the next sentence: "Nor is it always the worse for the society..."—suggesting what he says at this point is offered as enunciation of an underlying principle of wide application.

The last sentence I included here ("I have never known...") is as close to sarcasm as one is likely to find in Smith. It may not be as gratuitous as it seems. Even though Smith speaks of merchants in the sentence that immediately follows (which I have not included above), it could be Smith intends a carom-shot with his sarcasm—a way to take a passing swipe at the bureaucratic mercantilists of the government. In Smith's view, while they pretended to be governing trade for the public good, what they were really doing was getting in the way of honest exchange (and probably getting rich in the process). Still I regard this sentence as unfortunate. It's arguable that his witty dismissal of "those who affected to trade for the public good" was a mistake on Smith's part—opening a door to much misinterpretation in times to come. He can too easily be interpreted as saying "anyone who engages in business from humane and idealistic motives is simply getting in the way." A conscientious disciple of Francis Hutcheson would not say this. Smith did not say this. He had good reason not to.

Most noteworthy, but mostly unnoted, is that the whole argument is an argument on behalf of the public good. Smith is making a case for a better way than mercantilism to promote the public good—the *common* good, if one will allow an affinity in Smith for Aristotle and Aquinas. He's saying if each participant will merely be conscientious about his or her particular task so as to provide goods or services that will command the approval of buyers, everything will be fine; the marketplace is self-organizing, and "the public good" will be secured without the interference of government officials. But note the regularly unnoted underlying implication of making this argument. The underlying implication is that, whatever the personal economic enterprise of the reader, the reader-as-citizen is interested in promoting the public good. As a shoemaker, one should concentrate on making good shoes; but the same person as a citizen is regarded as able to stand back and concern himself or herself with seeing to it that the way shoes are provided is conducive to the wellbeing of society. The shoemaker as citizen, Smith assumes, is quite concerned about the public good after all. Otherwise, Smith's argument would have no traction—would not be addressing the shoemaker and other potential readers on anything they cared about. If people did not care about the public good, there were no potential readers for *The Wealth of Nations*. The book was intended as a manual for those who cared about the public good.

Grasped in the fullness of this context, Smith's argument is astoundingly paradoxical: the public good will be most effectually achieved if people forget about it!

As one can infer, though, from the foregoing considerations, the argument cannot really be that stark. The famous passage on the "invisible hand" is hyperbolic. Joseph Schumpeter faults Smith for this. He says that had Smith schematized things less sharply, and had he qualified his statements more, Smith would not have become so famous, but his writing would have had a more salutary effect. There may be something to this.

A way to put the matter more sympathetically than Schumpeter does is to say that we, Smith's fellow mortals, have proved too much for him; we have outmaneuvered his good intentions. In his moral discourses Smith discusses at length the role he thinks our capacity for empathy plays in our behavior. He says we learn to think of what is best for others by exercising a wonderful gift, which a benevolent providence has provided to us, of putting ourselves in another's place. Then—quite legitimately I'd say— he doubles back, and says we spontaneously arrive at a correct sense of what our own behavior should be by trying to see ourselves through others' eyes—by imagining, that is, how different activities open to us would look to others. (Is there a shrewd anticipation of Kant's Categorical Imperative here? So it would seem, and of Sartre's reflections on the shame principle, too.)

This review of the nuances in Smith is needed, I believe, for an accurate assessment of what Smith intends in the canonical passage when he employs the word "interest." Smith does not speak of "selfishness," but he does speak of the "interest" of the individual human being. In Francis Ford Coppola's *Wall Street*, Gordon Gecko says, "Greed is good." Smith does not say, "Greed is good." He does however say the self-interest of the individual promotes the public good.

Our mistake has been to define this "interest" of his too narrowly. For Smith, a shoemaker's interest extends to having the customer walk out of the shop with a satisfying pair of shoes. If that does not happen, what pride can he or she take in being a shoemaker? If there are employees, a shoemaker's interest extends to having employees of high morale. A shoemaker's interest extends to maintaining a culture in which debts are paid on time and without fraud. Honesty is the best policy, not just because it will yield returning customers and promote word-of-mouth advertising and establish good credit against which the shoemaker can borrow, but because it provides the conditions under which the shoemaker can work with a sense of responsibility and predictability. Again, it's the shoemaker's interest to have a good walkway leading to the shoe shop, to have a good fire department to protect his place of business from burning down, to have a police force adequate for the security of the shop and the merchandise and the customers and the person of the shoemaker and for any employees of the shoemaker. A well-to-do society in which the people generally are decently educated and reasonably prosperous, and care about good-looking and reliable shoes, is also in the shoemaker's interest.

Unfortunately, when Puritan descendants of the late eighteenth century were ginning up the spirit of capitalism as a way of systematizing and maintaining momentum for their acquisitive activity, they were blind to much of the generous humanitarian concern that was taken for granted as context in Smith's presentation of an individual's "self-interest."

One of Weber's theoretical hurdles was to explain why he thought it proper that Benjamin Franklin should land smack in the middle of his—Weber's—exposition of the Protestant Ethic. Franklin was hardly a Protestant, much less a Puritan Protestant, in any conventional sense of the terms. He had a well earned reputation as a *bon vivant* during his days in Paris from 1776 to 1785 (where, incidentally, he met and conversed with Smith). When, however, Franklin was still in his proverb-writing days, he wrote eloquently and with a quasi-religious fervor of the virtues of living to generate income, and of living frugally and re-investing one's savings as one went along. These writings were immensely popular and much quoted here in the American colonies. Weber cites Franklin to make the point that, once the capitalist spirit was brought to a boiling point by Puritan anxiety, it acquired a self-sustaining character. Eventually a capitalist approach had restructured the human context sufficiently that capitalism was taken as a feature of the landscape. In the first fervor of American Puritanism, clerics writing on Puritan ascetic practice had often warned that the pursuit of worldly goods might become an end in itself. In successive generations from 1650 to the second half of the 1700s (a period, say, of more than a hundred years), this seems in many cases to have been accomplished. By the end of that process an ethos of virtue-by-acquisition was rooted in the South as well as in the North. Yet even amid that secularizing of Puritanism, humans needed a sustaining story. They required some sense that the lifestyle they led had a meaning that stretched beyond themselves and ministered to some larger good. They needed to believe that in some way they were acting in harmony with the universe and conformed to its destiny. For this, Adam Smith could prove useful.

To utilize him in our evolving American society would require tinkering. As has been argued—for anything some words of Smith may suggest to the contrary—Smith is presupposing a contextualizing decency and good will in the individual upon whom his prescriptive economics is based. He is innocent of any Puritan fear of "fellow feeling" as a potential distraction from God's work; rather he calls such feeling "empathy," sees it as coming from God, and he views our human gregariousness with Enlightenment optimism. Empathy of one human for another is a victory for the divine plan. Perhaps a too-optimistic agent of the Enlightenment, Smith is presupposing in his "individual" an internalized context in which law is respected, adulteration of content in a good or service is a disgrace, contracts are honored, and honesty is more the rule than the exception. (Until recently, and maybe still, Japanese society in its *intra-national* relations has exemplified something of the manners Smith ascribes to Englishmen—who believe in doing what's "cricket"—and to people in general.) An ethos in which *caveat emptor*—let the buyer beware—is a ruling maxim (cited as it is today as an excuse for anything and everything) is unimaginable to Smith. Certainly, he never envisions a scenario in which individuals will routinely and unapologetically seek personal aggrandizement at the cost of the whole order they share with others; in his thinking, it's only within a context of honored routine decency that a focus on individual acquisition can ensure the emergence of "the greatest happiness for the greatest number."

So Smith's theory is not about getting away with things. That's a preoccupation of contemporary corporate lawyers, but it is not his preoccupation. He is far from advocating the emergence of a new mercantilism, one not of nations but of corporations. (Can we stipulate that our current corporatocracy engages in a new mercantilism—one antipathetic to the democratic principles Smith championed—and that the resemblance of this corporatocracy to the theocracy envisioned by our Puritan forefathers is neither accidental nor unimportant?) According to Smith's theory the market will act to reward self-interest only in those instances where the needs of consumers are being genuinely served. Consumers routinely deprived, he thought, will seek out other providers—or, in a monopolistic oligarchy, will eventually wither and die. Without consumers, there is no market. (Smith may still be right. If, today, we say the market no longer disciplines banks and corporations, we may be speaking too soon. Plausibly, the market may yet discipline banks and other corporations through responses and strategies of consumer disapproval, or by descending into catastrophic dysfunction and collapse. Something of the latter seems rumbling on the horizons of several national economies as I write.) To conclude: it's highly unlikely Smith would ever have endorsed a neo-mercantilism of corporations which nurtures many of the impositions on individual liberty he wrote to protest against.

Yet one can see how Smith's model could facilitate a gradually secularizing Puritan quest for justification by way of mission and success. One has only to strip away the civilizing context in which he wrote, and one can meld Smith's acceptance of individualism with a Puritan sense of isolation. Smith can be made to chime with the latter-day Calvinist Jonathan Edwards. Just as for Edwards, the "hands of an angry God" work toward a godly purpose, so too one can claim does the "invisible hand" of Smith. Being descendants of Puritan forefathers, many business people today seem to feel it makes no more sense to appeal against the workings of the stock market than it would make sense to their Puritan forefathers to appeal against God's eternal decrees.

(Of course this doesn't keep those same business people from doing all they can to manipulate our allegedly autonomous and self-governing market. A notion of fatalism about the stock market provides in fact a cover for all kinds of free-wheeling subterfuge. Virtually indestructible cockroaches are put to shame by the banksters and other financial manipulators who emerge from the gutters of America today bearing the flag of "too big to fail." As for a sense of those who currently fall by the wayside, the new Puritan is just as ready to regard them as damned by an invisible hand as were earlier Puritans to find desperate and defeated Indians doomed by the hand of an angry God. No less than our forefathers, our contemporary Puritans are ready to regard those who suffer as having no just claims on the successful. That this was not Smith's attitude—nor, for that matter, the attitude of Benjamin Franklin in his maturity—is of no interest in our latter-day capitalism. Smith's readiness to decrease the role of government has been adopted and reformulated by a Puritan sense that this world's governments belong more to Satan than to God—and we've now come to regard it as the task of the godly to restrict the power of government to the service of our self-aggrandizement.)

So the Enlightenment thinking of Adam Smith was co-opted by the narrower and less humane thinking of secularizing Puritans. Though Smith's schematization and prescription was intended benignly and rooted in wholesome sensibility, when the model he offered was further schematized and reconfigured to merge with a Puritan mission to seek worldly success, it was felt that a license for selfishness had been granted—indeed that an obligation to aggrandize oneself had been decreed. A door opened widely to a world-wasting reduction that destroys not only forest and animal, but great swaths of the working poor both here and abroad, and which tends toward an incremental dissolution of social bonds in general. It's a reduction that tends to leave the world a wrecking ground for the richly demented.

Introducing Milton Friedman

While a reduced and distorted version of Adam Smith had become a standard feature of American thinking well before Milton Friedman, it took Friedman to endow it with that character of the "one true faith" that's a trademark of Puritanism. If the business schools of America today teach a bottom-line scorched-earth approach to economics, he more than anyone else can claim the credit.

The late Friedman, of the University of Chicago, and later of the Hoover Institute at Stanford University, is regarded by some as America's foremost expositor of "the conservative philosophy." His position is called "conservative" because its controlling concern is said to be to clarify and promote the laissez-faire principle set forth in Smith which says government should leave the marketplace free of its intrusion. Friedman himself then is called "a conservative" as one thought to be dedicated to conserving this principle—a principle he thinks modern-day liberals have a terrible habit of diluting or betraying.

One can catch the flavor of his conservatism in an article Friedman published in the *New York Times* in 1970. Chastising some business men, Friedman writes:

> The businessmen believe they are defending free enterprise when they declaim that business is not concerned "merely" with profit but also with promoting desirable "social" ends; that business has a "social conscience" and takes seriously its responsibilities for providing employment, eliminating discrimination, avoiding pollution and whatever else may be the catchwords of the contemporary crop of reformers. In fact they are—or would be if anyone else took them seriously—preaching pure and unadulterated socialism. Businessmen who talk this way are unwitting puppets of the intellectual forces that have been undermining the basis of a free society these past decades.[8]

---

8. Milton Friedman, "The Social Responsibility of Business is to Increase its Profits," *New York Times Magazine*, September 13, 1970, 32–33.

What Friedman objects to is the doubleness of vision that a concern for social goals introduces into the thinking and behavior of a businessman. Sitting in a classroom a couple hundred yards from the Hoover Institute during Friedman's residence there, I remember hearing a very orthodox Friedmanite economist warn us that, in the event we become businessmen, we must not sentimentalize the workforce; rather we must remember always to regard "it" purely and simply as "a factor of production." If, by laying off half our employees, we can increase the profits of our company, it is our duty to the stockholders to do so. Not to do so would be an act of theft—of stealing from the stockholders. (And if there are no stockholders? No doubt then, it would be a crime against ourselves to spend more money on the workforce than we had to.)

I remember thinking how sublimely surgical this was. Two thousand five hundred years of Hellenic and Judaic humanism out the window with a single toss! In its place: "Always treat a fellow human being as a mere means; never allow fellow feeling or a regard for the person to confuse your thinking; realize always that for all practical purposes the employee is a thing."

Years later I was in a college workroom running off handouts for an ethics class I was teaching when an economics teacher came upon me. He asked what I was up to. When I said I was preparing for an ethics class, he replied that ethics was good for Sunday afternoons but that the rest of the week was controlled by the discipline he taught. I loved him for his unvarnished arrogance. I reflected how completely Friedman's sense of what was central and what was peripheral had prevailed—with this instructor at least (but probably, in truth, with a majority of the students to whom I was attempting to teach ethics).

Friedman's sense, to be sure, of "reformers" and their "catchwords" (catchwords about providing jobs, working to diminish gender and race discrimination, attempting to reduce pollution of the environment) is not—for all the ease with which he pretends to dismiss them—a sense that these constitute a harmless Sunday-afternoon diversion. Rather he's afraid people are genuinely paying attention to these catchwords and these false prophets—else why the essay? At the end of the short excerpt above, he says that those businessmen who listen to the reformers are "unwitting puppets of the intellectual forces that have been undermining the basis of a free society these past decades." In Friedman's view, we're not talking about pleasant ways to spend Sunday afternoons. Anyone, he's saying, who attempts to introduce into the workplace an ethics distinct from the discipline of the free market itself, as elaborated by Friedman, is undermining America. In fact, his free market *is* ethics. Those attempting reforms betray our free way of life (betray, presumably what we send our young overseas to die for). Images of executions of "traitors" Julius and Ethel Rosenberg were not a distant memory as Friedman was writing. They're context here, and Friedman's use of the phrase "intellectual forces" was meant to convey that some intellectuals (people like the Rosenbergs and other fellow-travelers) were the agents of forces out to ruin us all.

Friedman was serious toward his political opposition; for this reason Friedman—notwithstanding an inclination to smirk disarmingly—should be taken seriously. Today when we hear echoes of his rhetoric on Fox News and talk radio, we shouldn't dismiss these voices as mere chatter; according to the argument I'm building, they express beliefs in which our tradition is rooted. In exposition of this tradition, a few paragraphs later comes Friedman's effort to elucidate how the profit motive provides the one and only responsibility of a corporate executive in a typical business:

> In a free-enterprise, private property system, a corporate executive is an employee of the owners of the business. He has direct responsibility to his employers. That responsibility is to conduct the business in accordance with their desires, which generally will be to make as much money as possible while conforming to the basic rules of society, both those embodied in law and those embodied in ethical custom. Of course in some cases his employers may have a different objective. A group of persons might establish a corporation for an eleemosynary purpose—for example, a hospital or a school. The manager of such a corporation will not have money profit as his objectives but the rendering of certain services.

The two passages here candidly place Friedman's cards on the table. His candor shouldn't disarm us but rather engage us to examine critically the game he is playing.[9]

1. Doesn't it seem a bit quaint, even if charming, to describe a CEO as an employee of the stockholders? It suggests that CEOs are like assembly-line workers, spending their days in carrying out the orders of their managers. Or again, it suggests CEOs relate to stockholders like a maid to the mistress of the house—a mistress who might say: "Today, Hilda, I want you to dust the windowsills."

2. Doesn't some of this quaintness reside in Friedman's implication that the CEO spends his or her day consulting with stockholders in order to do their bidding? Friedman might counter: "The CEO doesn't have to consult his employers; he already knows what they want. They want—as I said—as much money from their stocks as they can get."

3. Again, though, one wonders about the accuracy of characterization. In the name of schematization, has Friedman perhaps reconfigured and oversimplified?

4. Corporations get started for purposes. There's a rationale for the corporation before there is any rationale for stockholders. Unless one's an out-and-out scam artist, one doesn't just say: "I'd like to make a lot of money; I think I'll get a lot of people to invest in a corporation."

5. Isn't what really happens more likely to be that, say, a Theodore Judah—living in the 1850s in a promising but remarkably isolated new state of California—comes along and says: "There ought to be a transcontinental railroad"?

---

9. For the seminal ideas here, I'm indebted to a brilliant article by Christopher Stone ("Why Shouldn't Corporations Be Socially Responsible?" from *Where the Law Ends* (New York: Harper & Row, 1975), 80–87). I hope I have not stolen his very phrases.

Only when that's been said does Judah venture forth in search of investors.

6. One might counter: "Well, the motivations of the investors can be very different from the motivations of the visionary." Suppose though Judah had lived to become—as he'd hoped—the CEO of the Central Pacific. Would his motivation have been simply to make money for his investors, or would it have been to construct and run an excellent railroad? Quite probably his original vision would have carried through into his career as CEO.

7. Would he then have been defrauding his investors as he attempted to find the best steel, lay the best track, and provide the finest service he could? His answer would probably have been: "How so?" He'd say they must have known the purpose of the man and project they'd invested in.

8. The cynics may reply this didn't happen—not in Judah's case. But Judah puts us in mind of how money—in the best cases—is facilitator and consequence of well considered projects.

9. So it's partly Friedman's reduction of everything to money that one finds uncritical. It is this which disqualifies him as a disciple of Adam Smith. Smith understood the function of money was to facilitate life. This understanding runs through his thousands of anecdotes and arguments. Friedman on the other hand seems to take it for granted that people invest simply to make money. He doesn't take seriously the possibility they invest in things they believe in—that they invest to make particular things happen. When they do, he seems inclined to say, as in the second half of the second excerpt: "Well, this is no longer actually business we're talking of; now we're talking about hobbies."

10. To structure things thus—to turn things around in the way he does—converts his model of what business is into a Procrustean bed. To protect this model, he's willing to

lop off the areas of human endeavor and human interest the model cannot neatly accommodate, implying there's something about them that's un-businesslike.

11. To consider an example: surely Pope Julius II did not invest in Michelangelo in order to make money. Nor was Michelangelo's aesthetic sense dictated to by some compulsion to see that his patron got a maximum return of profit. Friedman's objection is predictable. He'd say: "I'm not talking about THAT!" He might add: "See, the word 'profit' doesn't even come up in such transactions!" Exactly.

12. And that should alert one to be thoughtful about how long a list one could generate of other "THATs" about which Friedman isn't talking.

13. Friedman speaks of the executive as making for his bosses as much money as possible "while conforming to the basic rules of society, both those embodied in the law and those embodied in ethical custom." This seems like a good and necessary concession—surely a concession that was the very context for Adam Smith's reflections on how free markets would operate to produce the greatest good. But one has to wonder what weight Friedman can actually allow this concession. After all, he's arguing that business motivated by the profit-motive is sufficiently disciplined by the free market. The role of government and presumably of government law is to leave it alone. He tells us the executive should not worry, for instance, about pollution of our habitat. Either Friedman's position is that there is no ethical custom of taking care of the environment, or—if he finds that unpalatable—that to attend to it and make it normative would be nonetheless to advocate "pure unadulterated socialism" and would be to enter among the ranks of "the unwitting puppets of the intellectual forces that have been undermining the basis a free society these past decades." So much for ethical custom.

14. We arrive then at one of Friedman's more troubled moments. The government issues a charter for a corporation. This

charter confers on a corporation a fictitious personhood, and the government endows this "person" with certain privileges so it can achieve goals which the government approves as conducive to the general welfare. Yet government should not, according to Friedman, intrude upon the operations of that which its law has created.

15. The reason for thinking Friedman's intentions about conforming to law and ethical custom are so vague as to dwindle to a null set—to a category that contains no instances—is that, taken seriously, they work against the rest of Friedman's argument.

16. The article is titled: "The Social Responsibility of Business is to Increase its Profits." But corporations are not chartered to increase their profits; governments charter them to build bridges, mine coal, feed the hungry, cure the sick.

17. Friedman then is in a bind. For in terms of contractual obligation and responsibility, the CEO has not simply to look over his or her shoulder to stockholder-bosses, but to look back before that to the particular purposes for which the corporation was chartered. Yet in Friedman's presentation of his model, this dimension of corporate concern would seem to have dissolved with the issuing of the license; once it exists, the purpose of the corporation seems to have become totally internalized.

18. This is not good even for the corporation. For it moves thereby toward the world of the schizophrenic. Enron, on the eve of its implosion, was such a totally internalized corporation. So was the enterprise of Bernie Madoff.

19. One cannot claim the endorsement of Adam Smith for a doctrine of unfettered corporations. Unlike Friedman, Smith sees the chartering government as there at the creation, and as responsible therefore for outcomes. This incites in Smith a cautionary concern. He regards with apprehension the special privileges government confers in

chartering and licensing things and sees how these privileges act as a restraint on the freedoms of those outside the grant. It would not have occurred to him to claim as Friedman does that once such privileges are in place, government has no responsibility for the impact their exercise has on the freedoms of those who have no share in them. While Friedman is concerned for the freedom of fictitious persons called corporations, Smith is concerned for the freedom of actual persons.

20. Friedman's corporation is a corporation born of Friedman's capacity to abstract. It's not connected to things outside itself by real-world relations. It's not beholden to the fire department or the police department for its safety. It's not beholden to a public water supply. It doesn't use roads. It makes no demands for protection against foreign invasion. It owes nothing to ends for which it was instituted. The educational system that has provided it with qualified workers is not entitled to its support. Only on such assumptions is Friedman able to find that the corporation is without social responsibility other than to increase the profits of it stockholders.

21. In other words, Friedman's corporation is a fantasy. He is serious in claiming benefits and opportunities for it, but when you ask him of its corresponding responsibilities, he wanders off into a denunciation of socialism. It's especially noteworthy how, in the earlier of the two excerpts above, Friedman dismisses "avoiding pollution" as among "the catchwords of the contemporary crop of reformers." Grown-up businessmen, he seems to say, don't concern themselves with avoiding pollution; avoiding pollution is not their responsibility. In tribute to Friedman and the tradition for which he speaks, one can't help but be impressed at how thoroughly this lesson has become imbedded. Whether Friedman is teaching this lesson because it's simply the rule in play, or whether it's the rule in play because he and like-minded economists have taught it is, I suppose, subject to debate.

22. My hunch is that the dispensation granted here by Friedman and "conservative" predecessors and current disciples contributes hugely to our current problems.

23. A couple years ago, uncalculated amounts of oil were pouring into northern waters of the Gulf of Mexico from a pipe in the water below a structure called Deep Horizon where British Petroleum drilled for oil. At that time a guest-expert on the *PBS NewsHour* cautioned watchers of the show against "hysterical reactions." From the general tendency of his remarks, it was clear it would *not* be an "hysterical reaction" to be deeply concerned about the future of BP. All adult persons know BP is important and must, at all costs, be preserved. What would be "hysterical" would be to so worry about the Gulf as to put the future of BP in jeopardy.

24. To recast the expert's sentiment in the vocabulary of Friedman: It had never been the function of BP to "protect the Gulf"—a "catchphrase" if ever there was one. The function of BP was—and is—to deliver oil. Yet even that is perhaps too romantic a description. The real function of BP has always been to deliver money to stockholders. That is why BP is right not only to drill for oil, but right to drill for it in as quick and cost-cutting a way as it can get away with. (The PBS-expert must feel happy; we've recovered from hysteria, and the future of off-shore drilling remains bright.)

25. One can hear Friedman muttering from his grave: "That's just the way it is. If you're looking for someone to blame, this looking about is itself a sign of your childishness—for this is the lifestyle you've been lucky enough to get born into. To think otherwise—to load BP with concerns about the environment and attempt to shame it for not living up to those concerns—is to be among the "unwitting puppets of the intellectual forces that have been undermining the basis of a free society."

26. As we've seen, Friedman does acknowledge this isn't the whole picture. He speaks of "eleemosynary" pursuits. That the adjective is rare enough to function as a stumper in a spelling bee is instructive. Friedman registers by its use that we pass at this point outside the purview of serious business. Earlier we looked at relations between Pope Julius and Michelangelo. Examples Friedman gives are hospitals and schools. He acknowledges that here the purpose may be other than to maximize profits. He makes a conscientious concession that not everything fits his model.

27. What he's not about to consider is that these business enterprises may actually be excellent models for reconfiguring our thinking on business in general. Notice the attributes of what we consider here. Both for hospitals and for schools there's a fairly undeniable need. In both there is organization to meet the need. Both require funds to operate. But the purpose of neither is reducible to the making of a profit. What if one were to take hospitals and schools as a paradigm for businesses in general? Let us say legitimate institutions in general are founded to fulfill some wholesome function. Well and good. Yet income in excess of daily expenses is necessary if these institutions are to survive. Again, well and good. The "profit" if you want to call it that goes toward maintenance and renovation. It is "instrumental," not goal setting. (For just this reason, Friedmanites are presently doing all they can to convert schools, hospitals, prisons, and all health care into for-profit enterprises.)

28. Recently I complimented a doctor working in the emergency room of a public hospital for bringing my son back from a coma that could have ended in death. I added to my remark—thinking perhaps like Friedman—"but you don't get paid adequately for the work you do!" She replied: "Oh, I get paid enough." I persisted, "How so?" She said: "What I get paid permits me do the job I live for."

29. The doctor declared a truth. The contented doctor (who may today be an endangered species) does not go into medicine to make a lot of money; she/he goes into it to cure people. The happy lawyer (if there is such today) goes into law to protect rights, curb wrongdoing, secure justice. The happy teacher is sustained by the experience of seeing people learn.

30. Aristotle, who perhaps would have gotten an F in any economics course taught by Friedman, endorses what my son's doctor said. As mentioned earlier, Aristotle insists "money is means" and adds: "One who lives for money lives the life of a slave." Finally he says: "Happiness is in doing—is achieved in action performed in accord with virtue." The doctor exemplified this. (Many an ethics student, feeling things have gotten a bit mystical with Aristotle, wants at this point to return to "money," but having declared it "pure instrumentality," Aristotle's not about to back down.)

31. As a consequence of simplifying and schematizing, the world with which Friedman ends is schizoid. He'd have the father of children feel affection for those children and concern that they live well in times to come; yet Friedman would have that same father go off to work and labor each day simply to increase the return to stockholders without exercising any regard for the impact his corporation might have on the society his son is to live in. True, Friedman might respond: "Well, that's just the way people behave." But he complains rather that they don't behave this way enough. He wants this schizoid behavior—has done his best to dictate it to the business schools of the land, and thinks people are behaving unethically when they don't practice it. More insistently than Adam Smith, he's a missionary. It turns out after all that Friedman is not just about money; he's about his doctrine about money. And this is what makes him a Puritan. Not only is the world that's generated by his thinking an alienated one, but he insists we enter that world as a destiny—as our ticket into adulthood. To our misfortune we often do.

There is nothing in nature that requires a businessman to shed his responsibilities as citizen when becoming a CEO. Somehow though, Friedman feels a businessman can and should do this—should suspend his humanity on the ground that he is owned by stockholders.

Further, while Friedman speaks of the restraints of law, there's nothing in his system to keep corporations from using their money to buy law-makers and insist they provide a maximum of privileges for corporations and a minimum of responsibilities. (Some were surprised when Friedman offered himself as a tutor to General Pinochet, the dictator in Chile, after President Salvador Allende was, with assistance from our CIA, ousted and then assassinated in 1973. No one should have been surprised that Friedman pitched in. Fully provided for in Friedman's conception of freedom is the freedom of a dictator to control all the laws and to be accountable to none of them. He had already done what he could to secure that kind of freedom for American corporations. In this way have we extended the reach of our Puritanism to Latin America.)

To be fair though, in asking us to join his world, Friedman is—as I've tried to show earlier—playing to some of the most deeply entrenched tendencies of our history and culture. (This is why "liberal" Democrats are such lame critics of "hard-line" Republicans. The Democrats emerge from the same history and culture, and have the same values.) Routinely, when it's been a matter of actual practice, our Puritan heritage has trumped our Enlightenment heritage. When we want to feel noble about ourselves, we put on the rhetoric of the Enlightenment; but when it's time to act, we regress to the behavior of forefathers earlier than Washington and Hamilton. Before moving on to discuss what these tendencies mean for our attitude toward the use of force, and for our attitude toward habitat (both already touched on), let's try to draw our observations on the ascendency of the rich to a close.

When bankers, stockbrokers, and laissez-faire economists find themselves confronted by ethicists or by people whom these financiers' policies have impoverished, the financiers tend to lapse into "don't blame me; I'm just telling you how it's done" mode. They'll claim their economics is merely descriptive. They'll say in defense of some action they're taking: "The stock market requires this of me." Or they may say of a past action: "Had I not acted as I did, I'd have been fired—and someone else would been brought in to do exactly the thing I wouldn't do. I had to do what I did. It was inevitable."

Such talk is instructive. With a good ear, one can hear echoes of Calvinist predestination. In place of an inscrutable God-Who is often angry, we have here a stock market whose decrees are absolute and predictably unpredictable—its decrees are beyond appeal. It's a fool's business to complain about this stock market; one can only attend to it closely and do what one can to accommodate to it. Any suggestion the "free market" is actually a market that humans freely manipulate is heresy. This somehow remains true in the face of contrary evidence coming in from all corners. A charge that the free market is a game rigged to serve the interests of its major players, the privileged rich, is not only blasphemous, it's subversive blasphemy, bordering on treason. For it fosters "class warfare" and unpatriotically is "undermining the basis of a free society." One who makes charges disrespectful to the market can be assumed to be an infantile person, isolated, aberrational—one who rejects reality. (Such a one is by no means entitled to chat with Charlie Rose, or be interviewed on the *PBS NewsHour*.)

This is instructive. The angry God in whose hands we found ourselves at the beginning of America's story was a God who had at once agents who could be depended on to dispense His wrath (the Puritans, for instance) and had also objects of His wrath (the "savages," for instance). Agents of His wrath could be presumed to be destined for heaven; objects of His wrath were all destined for hell. One of the best ways to reassure oneself one wasn't destined for hell was to enlist definitively as one of God's avenging agents against the objects of His wrath.

Something similar has happened in the twenty-first-century update to our story. The path to security and prosperity is to accept the ultimacy of the free market and its oracular decrees as the stock market reveals them—and then to respond in obedience—by engaging in the market, serving it, preserving it. This is true, whether one is by ethnicity "majority born" or "minority born," and whether one is born a U.S. citizen or is an immigrant. Regardless of which category you are in, the inclination is to sell out. This is so whether you are president, or secretary of state, or law professor, or justice on the Supreme Court, or journalist, or pundit, or portfolio analyst. If you wish to avoid being a target of the agents of wrath, your best course of action is to join their ranks.

Short of this maneuver, one remains among the market's more vulnerable. People living in other countries run special risks. If for instance in Central America, people don't show respect for the market in the manner and form in which we've shaped it, their country can be invaded, their leaders can be executed, and their land can be destroyed.

Yet even here at home, in ways that irritate those who insist on the profit motive, we find that the doctor, the lawyer, and the teacher are likely to perform at their best when outside our paradigm of orthodox bottom-line market economics. So also do other providers of public service—our police officers and fire fighters, our paramedics and nurses. It shouldn't surprise us therefore that some politicians win popularity by waging campaigns against such people. The strategy for a true-believer and wannabe-victor in today's economic world is, it seems, to move as far from these fuzzy-statused do-gooder types as one can— and to tame such do-gooders in the process by constricting their funding and belittling their dedication. (Sure, there's room for legitimate criticism of people in the fields of public service; but there are popular recent political campaigns against them as a class that can hardly be explained except by envy and resentment for the example they give.)

The newest discovery of the economic realist is in fact that in seeking a profit, no genuine good or service need be provided. One can make money off of money. Manufacturing can be shipped overseas. Service industries can go too. Sustained for years by influxes of loans from China and from our apparently inexhaustible federal reserve, financiers can play among themselves ruinous games with other people's savings—and be rescued with funds and rewarded by bonuses paid out against future taxes when it seems their failures might otherwise bring the entire money system crashing down.

The world we enter thereby is not altogether as alien and unprecedented as we sometimes protest. Puritans and Friedman – no mere icons of the past, but living mentors—have labored hard to bring this world to birth. The bleak model they've perfected for us tends toward a self-reinforcing and enduring efficacy. Today the elites among us see no real boundaries to profit-taking; nor do they see any real alternatives to it. They see it as the one landscape into which we all are born. Righteously, and with Jesus well domesticated, they march us forward. It's God's plan: to the extent we can make it happen, and though the heavens may fall, our acquisitions and opportunities must be maximized.

Hermann Gossen (a German economist of the nineteenth century deeply impressed by what he saw as a connection between God and laissez-faire economics), wondering that anyone should be seeking an alternative to this principle of self-aggrandizement, asked: "How can a creature be so arrogant as to want to frustrate totally or partially the purpose of his Creator?" Gossen meant God had sentenced us to pursue riches, and our duty was to do so. A majority of us in America today subscribe to this; and as we do, our rich grow richer, our poor grow poorer, our debts grow bigger, our use of habitat becomes more unrestricted, our infrastructure crumbles, and our society tumbles in the direction of terminal incoherence.

3 | Our Tenaciously Expanding Belief in Force

When the Japanese bombed Pearl Harbor in 1941, I was seven years old. In the early years after World War II, it became a part of American folklore to say: "We're a peaceful people, slow to take up arms—but once we're aroused, look out!" I think statements along those lines accurately capture both the mood of us Americans at the moment Pearl Harbor was bombed and the lesson we took from the way hostilities ended some three years and eight months later.

I remember my parents were isolationist on the issue of the war up to the very day of Pearl Harbor. Their generation had been children at the time of the First World War; and as they grew older, they and most all of their generation in America had come to a collective judgment, endorsed by their own parents, that it had been a mistake for Americans to participate in the First World War.

To say as much leaves questions open of how isolationist regarding economics we had been in 1941 as we approached December 7, and questions also of whether our government had ever been genuinely isolationist even politically in the years between the Treaty of Versailles and Pearl Harbor. Putting on hold these complicating issues, it remains fact that we Americans by and large had no desire to enter the Second World War up to December 7. With regard to whether, once aroused, we committed ourselves to victory, there can be no doubt. Everyone living through those days has vivid memories of how hostilities were abruptly concluded less than four years later with gigantic clouds over Hiroshima and Nagasaki, followed by the unconditional surrender of Japan.

Hence, the generalization: Americans are a peaceful people, but dangerous when attacked.

The problem with taking this generalization as a paradigm by which to view the American character in general is there's so much in our history that won't fit. (Historian John Toland, among others, has argued that the lead-up to World War II itself doesn't fit very well; and historian William Appleman Williams titles his discussion of American participation in the Second World War as "the War for the American Frontier."[1])

In fact, to accommodate the paradigm that finds us a peaceful people, we've had to forget huge chunks of our earlier history, and retain in memory to fill its place a story we began to nurture near the earliest days of our arriving here. In this devised story, the Puritans who arrived at Massachusetts Bay in 1630 were a peace-loving people who wished simply to be left at liberty to worship God according to their conscience. While they themselves were tolerant, back in England their English neighbors had been intolerant toward them. (Here there may be some memory-conflation of Plymouth Rock Pilgrim Separatists with Massachusetts Bay Colony Puritans. While one can accurately see the two groups as "cousins," there were significant differences between them.)

The facts on record for Puritans tell us that Charles the First, who gave the Puritans a charter to colonize New England, was desperate to be rid of them. He gave them their charter in 1629; and twenty years later, their fellow Puritans in England—with some New England Puritans returning as reinforcements—beheaded Charles. In the view of Puritans, King Charles had become an impediment to God's kingdom, so it was appropriate he be removed.

Similarly, as mentioned earlier, when Indians in the New World proved resistant to conversion and to Puritan governance, they too had to be removed. In 1637, about seven years after the Puritans arrived, when Puritans looked upon the Connecticut

---

1. John Toland, *The Rising Sun: The Decline and Fall of the Japanese Empire, 1936–1945*, 2 vols. (New York: Random House, 1970); William Appleman Williams, *The Tragedy of American Diplomacy* (Cleveland: World Publishing Company, 1959), chapter 5.

River Valley and saw its rich agricultural possibilities and saw also that it was native habitat for Pequot Indians, they did what they could to persuade the Pequots to become a "protectorate," a people protected by the Bay Colony and subservient to it. When the Pequots made clear they had scant interest in letting the Puritans control their lives and land, the Puritans did what they thought natural for those serving in God's army. After much mutual denunciatory interpretation of each others' motives, and following upon bloody skirmish, a rumor, and a Pequot refusal to accept a Puritan ultimatum, as noted earlier the Puritans conducted a surprise attack on the offending Pequot village at Mystic Fort:

> Thus were they [the Pequots] now at their wits end, who not many hours before exalted themselves in their great pride, threatening and resolving the utter ruin and destruction of all the English, exulting and rejoicing with songs and dances. But God was above them, who laughed his enemies and the enemies of his people to scorn, making them as a fiery oven: Thus were the stout-hearted spoiled, having slept their last sleep, and none of their men could find their hands. Thus did the Lord judge among the heathen, filling the place with dead bodies.[2]

As recounted in the chapter on wealth, the Puritans killed all the Pequot men, women, and children they could lay hands on. Later they sought out the survivors—Pequots who had not been living at the massacred village—who were seeking to hide themselves, and—with few exceptions—killed them too. Subsequently, if some other Indian tribe found a straggler from among the Pequots and took in that straggler, this was regarded by the Puritans as a hostile act against themselves, and body parts were required by the Puritans as proof the straggler had been executed.

The mindset portrayed here is worth pondering. It must have gone something like this. "Here we are, good Christians,

---

2. John Mason, commander of the Puritan forces, qtd. in Segal and Stineback, *Puritans, Indians & Manifest Destiny*, 111.

attempting to establish God's Kingdom. In God's Kingdom, to be sure, everyone is free—for the truth will set you free. But these Pequots are resisting the advent of God's Kingdom. If they would behave as we tell them to, we would treat them with the full measure of charity that it behooves a Christian people to exercise; but they will not behave. Therefore, resolute in defiance, they have sealed their doom."

John Mason's account helps us see that by the time the Puritans got around to attempting genocidal action toward the Pequots, Puritans had reconfigured the scene to see their act as defensive. They saw themselves as potential victims. Though historical evidence provides good grounds for thinking it was Puritan land-greed and desire for control that led to bad feelings between the two groups, the sleeping Indians were seen by Puritans as "threatening and resolving the utter ruin and destruction of all the English." It seems in fact it was this ability to reconfigure the attacking Puritan as victim that was needed to make their act influential—that is, to turn it into a precedent. Had the killing of Pequots been viewed as aberrational rampage or gross surrender to greed on the part of the Puritans, its importance for America's development and for the souls of future Americans would have been negligible. As actually retained in Puritan memory (that is, in our memory) as something unrepented and celebrated, it's been able to become a template for like action in a long series of later encounters.

In my youth in the thirties of the twentieth century, we romanticized the nineteenth-century imperiled homestead on the prairie in our story of westward development. Our version ran along these lines. Here, as they founded western outposts of civilization, our people were domesticating the land, attending church on Sunday, and conducting folk dances and pie-baking contests at the time of harvest. What more sacred image of Christians at peace could one ever hope to see? Yet all was in jeopardy. For savages, half-naked and godless, lurked in the vicinity. These were savages bent on desecration. They were encroaching. Once the harvest party was over, and the happy and celebrating crowd of friendly settlers had dispersed to their several homes, each little house would stand in isolation, defenseless against an immoral and near-invisible enemy—and, yes, the enemy was closer and more menacing than the industrious settlers might think. Suddenly came the unprovoked and maniacal attack. Thankfully, in the eleventh hour of our romance—in the last chapter or the last reel—our cavalry would arrive, federal guardians of law and order. The savages would be shot down, and civilization could take one further courageous step westward.

That little westward house requires study. I was nearly an adult before it ceased for me to be a symbol of peace and became instead a symbol of violence. I was slow to acknowledge any Indian right to a land they loved as their land of the free and the home of their braves.

Making that acknowledgement, one need not be arguing to "give the land back to the Indians"—nor be claiming immigrants from across the Atlantic should never have ventured here—in order to cast about for an alternative to what we did. Both Roger Williams and the Quakers had in fact conceived an alternative.

Let's consider again the beginnings. In 1635, a few years after the earliest encounters between Puritans and Indians, Roger Williams was banished from Massachusetts Bay Colony. As mentioned, he was banished in part for insisting Puritans had no warrant to appropriate land from Indians just because they wanted it or just because England's king had granted it to them; he insisted colonists were bound rather to negotiate in good faith with Indians for it, and to abide by agreements made. This meant the Puritans, as newcomers, were morally bound to seek an honest accommodation with those already using the land—were obliged to recognize Indians as people holding prior title.

To Williams' fellow Puritans this seemed an extravagantly troublesome position. It wouldn't just bring Puritans down to the level of Indians, as equals dealing with equals; it would—in a sense—place them lower than Indians. The Puritans would be the petitioners; and it would be in the competence of Indians to grant or deny.

Williams' appraisal of the facts was rejected by the Puritan leadership; and we can assume a majority of the Puritan community shared in rejecting it. While Massachusetts Colony did require that land purchases from Indians be recorded, the way the matter played out suggests this was more to determine which

Puritan had title to which land than it was a measure to protect Indian rights.

A half century later, in Pennsylvania, Quakers—despised and even hanged in Massachusetts Bay Colony—would take up a position close to the position Williams had taken. While William Penn's successors in Pennsylvania often ignored the policy he'd laid down, one has to wonder what the history of America (and of the world) would look like if the attitudes of Roger Williams and of William Penn had prevailed. The objection is that the development of the West would have been greatly retarded. As it was, two years after Williams was banished from Massachusetts Bay Colony, the Pequots were massacred. One must ask, would it have been some kind of catastrophe for America's future if the tempo had been less frantic—if time to reach accommodation for mutual benefit had been allowed.

Rather than allow for organic maturation, what was taken to be an efficient template for dealing with Indians was established. The Puritans regarded their action as defensive. They were defending the right of God's people to live in God's country. This Puritan perspective of entitlement became, through repetition, so well installed that two centuries later, when a house was raised on a prairie, there was no question about whether the house was entitled to be there, and no question either as to the criminal violence and savagery of anyone who would attack it. (In terms of current vocabulary, it was clear for all to see which party were the terrorists.)

Two habits of mind became embedded. First, in dealings between us innocent, purified and god-serving Americans and other people, what ought to set the premise for the dealing was the plan of us, the servants of God. The other party revealed itself as good, indifferent, or bad depending on how they responded to our plan. Second, in cases where our plan was rejected or disregarded, it became a premise that we descendants of Puritans were right to think ourselves the injured party. Our plan became The Plan, self-evidently just; it became in fact the very standard of Justice, incarnated and brought down to earth by us. From then on, its defense and promotion have not needed justification. An obstructing party should know better than to oppose it; one who does oppose comes to deserve whatever the god-serving defenders of peace deal out.

This psychological aspect needs underscoring. In later times, as we legitimate offspring of Puritans employed force, it became practically invisible to us in its character as violence. It wasn't we who acted aggressively; ours was action in the service of law.

Remarkable is the habituation to unacknowledged violence that ensues. One regrets this habituation not simply for havoc it visited on others; one regrets what it did to us. Let's trace this expanding process of habituation throughout the nineteenth century (leaving, for a time, events closer at hand to speak for themselves).

The Revolutionary War in the last quarter of the eighteenth century deserves perhaps a pass. Fought against a force deemed a superior power, let's grant to the Patriots who fought it their sense that it was defensive. Even though an interest in moving into Indian lands in the Ohio Valley was among Patriot motives, and even though Canadian relations with Britain present an interesting counterexample to feisty American relations to Britain, let's say the Revolutionary War was mostly motivated by a desire to resist the mercantilist policies, provided for in British law, that the British had unwisely decided to impose more fully in the aftermath of the French and Indian War. Let then the war's character as defensive stand. (Its negative value lay, paradoxically, in the way its success has resounded among us. With its David-and-Goliath aspect, once won, the Revolutionary war nurtured among us a celebratory regard for war. Every American-born American has been raised on legends from it which tend to legitimize and dignify wars—at least those in which we find ourselves engaged.)

In addition to the Revolutionary War of the eighteenth century, there were two wars in the nineteenth century, one minor and the other momentous, which don't readily lend support to a case that we are a war-prone people. One was the War of 1812; the other was the Civil War.

Though existence of American "War Hawks" complicates the issue, the War of 1812 can be explained as resulting from an ill-advised British effort to re-impose a modified form of mercantilism on an American people who had already irreversibly shaken off British control. At war with France, the British seemed to think they could require their former colony to forgo its own economic interests and act economically as Britain's ally against the

French. The choice they offered us was either to do that, or retire from trade on the high seas altogether. (The latter choice was something the Francophile Jefferson—to his credit—attempted, but which only postponed the war till Madison was president.) True, there were side issues—ones the ever-thoughtful historian Herbert Agar says in fact were controlling issues.[3] Among some Americans was a desire to annex Canada. Contributing to American restlessness too was a desire of some to move more rapidly into westward territory still comfortably held by Indians, and to do so unencumbered by Canadian land claims. Writing about 1812 though, Henry Adams comes to the conclusion we Americans were at this time generally pacifist, documenting at length that, once war was declared, we seemed woefully unprepared to wage it. Theodore Roosevelt, in a book he wrote on the war while he was a student at Harvard, writes along similar lines. Let's concede then that the War of 1812 doesn't offer much that reveals us as an aggressive people.

As for the Civil War, Lincoln never wanted it to be a raw matter of the North imposing its will on the South. He had enough roots in Southern ancestry, and his wife had even more, to sense how the South viewed the war as a monumental overreaching by the North. While Lincoln's consistent sense of the war was that the North's motivation was to save the Union, what had made him a viable candidate for the presidency was his speech at Cooper Union in which he declared the institution of slavery should not be permitted to move westward. Significantly, he left it to the South therefore to "draw first blood" at Fort Sumter; and when eventually he issued an Emancipation Proclamation, he did not see it as providing the war's motive, but issued it rather as a measure he hoped would give the North an advantage in ending the war. Once the war's end was in view, it's true he hoped the terrible loss of life on both sides could achieve something more than a restoration of the status quo at the war's start. He wanted an end to slavery, but saw this as possible only through an act of Congress—not as something he could do as commander-in-chief. Famously, he rejected the consolation many on the Northern side

---

3. Herbert Agar, *The People's Choice: From Washington to Harding* (Safety Harbor, Fla.: Simon Publications, 2001), 76–77.

offered him that "God's on your side," and replaced it with a wistful expression of hope that he and the Union army might be on God's side. This seemed to be—was in fact—an un-Puritan way to think. For these reasons (no doubt with many Southerners dissenting on this), it's problematic to use the Civil War as evidence for a case we are an aggressive people. All things considered, and while allowing room for a pacifist dissent, let's concede a defensive—or at least "unchosen" character—to the Civil War, not only from the Southern perspective, but from the Northern as well.[4]

Taking the War of 1812 and the Civil War off the board (while acknowledging this may seem quite arbitrary to some), there remain, among others, four representative and instructive uses of force in the nineteenth century deserving our attention. Each use has the double character of being (1) highly deliberate (chosen rather than imposed), but (2) deliberate in such a manner that our collective opting for violence goes almost unacknowledged. Because these cases seem not to have been logged into collective memory in an accurate way, it would seem they continue to fester like an undetected virus within the body politic. They are: (1) the removal westward to Oklahoma of the Cherokee Indians of Georgia; (2) the Mexican War; (3) the War on the Plains; and (4) the war that ended with American hegemony over Cuba and with the bloody annexation of the Philippines—a war we rather inaccurately call the Spanish-American War.

---

4. I admit this may be seeing the war too much through Northern eyes. What makes the Civil War such a difficult case is its aftermath. Viewing the war from its aftermath, it's no easy matter to provide a coherent account of what the root of Northern motivation was. As remarks by Howard Zinn suggest, the mayhem and the wounds inflicted on the spirits of Northerners and Southerners alike, and the vitriolic hatred that ensued among defeated Southern whites toward "emancipated" blacks makes one wonder if the matter of slavery could not have been ended better by slave insurrections, relentless shaming of the South by abolitionists, and by economic factors and the general inconvenience of holding in bondage a huge population—rather than by full-scale federal invasion of the South by the North. Howard Zinn, *A People's History of the United States* (New York: HarperPerennial Modern Classics, 2005), 186–89, 198.

Cherokee Removal

In the War of 1812, some Cherokee led by John Ross had fought on the American side against the British. Among his eight great grandparents, Ross seems to have had only one Indian, so his sense of himself as affiliated with white plantation culture is perhaps not surprising. What is remarkable is that the Cherokee among whom Ross was a chief seem largely to have shared Ross's sense of affiliation. These were Cherokee who wrote and read in a Cherokee script of their own invention, who printed a newspaper in Cherokee and English, who imitated white landowners in the cotton plantation economy, slaves and all. Also they set up schools as a path toward further assimilation into the surrounding white society, and they welcomed Christian missionaries into their midst and welcomed intermarriage of their women with whites.

At times, whites had said to Indians: if you would be like us, there would be no problem, and we could live together in harmony. Here was a test case of that olive branch.

Unfortunately for them, the Cherokee lived in a northeastern section of Georgia where gold was discovered. To fortify themselves against the acquisitive interests of their neighbors, the Cherokee wrote themselves a constitution modeled on ours; and they passed a law that no one of their citizens could sell any land to a non-Cherokee without the consent of their Cherokee government.

Their thriving ways stuck in the craw of white neighbors. Not only did Cherokee presume to do as whites did, but they did so so well as to become envied rivals. The Cherokee constitution was itself an affront; they seemed thereby to present themselves as the equals of whites. Clearly though, most obnoxious of all was simply that Cherokee lived on lands the whites wanted.

The great champion of white enterprise was Andrew Jackson. No one in America could rival Jackson's well-earned celebrity as a killer of Indians. That John Ross had fought in 1812 under Jackson's command was no matter. When Jackson was not killing Indians, he was negotiating with them for their land. He was very accomplished at it. As early as 1817, he'd written to President Monroe: "I have long viewed treaties with the Indians an absurdity not to be reconciled to the principles of our government." An elegant turn of phrase. Indians were not to be taken seriously. As a negotiator, Jackson felt free to beguile them, lie to them, intimidate them. He behaved in full accord with the convenient maxim adopted by earlier Puritans: "there's no treating with Indians above board."

Wiley though and stubborn as Jackson was, not all Indians succumbed. Having failed as government agent to remove the Cherokee through negotiation, once Jackson was president he withdrew federal protection from them, leaving them to the mercy of the State of Georgia. He then used the vulnerability of the Cherokee as a pretext. In his first State of the Union message, Jackson observed disingenuously that since it wasn't likely their neighbors would leave at peace such Indians as lived east of the Mississippi, it should be the policy of the federal government to do what it could to protect Indians by moving them to a territory west of the Mississippi "to be guarantied [*sic*] to the Indian tribes, as long as they shall occupy it."

In response, Congress passed the Removal Act of 1830. In 1832, in the case of *Worcester v. Georgia*, John Marshall wrote for the Supreme Court an opinion upholding the Cherokee as "having territorial boundaries, within which their authority is exclusive," and Marshall said these were boundaries "in which the laws of Georgia can have no force, and which the citizens of Georgia have no right to enter, but with the assent of Cherokees themselves, or in conformity with treaties, and with the acts of Congress."

Perhaps Jackson felt the Removal Act, as an act of Congress, blunted the force of Marshall's decision. At any rate, he despised Marshall's assertion of Indian rights, and pushed ahead with the policy of removal. In practice this meant Georgia was licensed to use every means of bribery and harassment to force the Cherokee off Cherokee land, while the federal government did what it could to negotiate new treaties to nullify old ones. Even then, many Cherokee stood resolute in principled resistance. Finally, in 1837 Martin Van Buren, Jackson's successor, sent General Winfield Scott to remove the Cherokee by force:

> Families at dinner were startled by the sudden gleam of bayonets in the doorway and rose to be driven with blows

and oaths along the weary miles of trail that led to the stockade. Men were seized in their fields, or going along the road, women were taken from their [spinning] wheels and children from their play. In many cases, on turning for one last look as they crossed the ridge they saw their homes in flames, fired by the lawless rabble that followed on the heels of the soldiers to loot and pillage.[5]

Why is this episode significant? Its significance is in how little it's been noticed. Three weeks before Christmas in 1838, on December 3, President Van Buren informed Congress:

The measures [for Cherokee removal] authorized by Congress at its last session have had the happiest effects....The Cherokees have emigrated without any apparent reluctance.[6]

The use of force was invisible. Certainly, that was as Van Buren wanted, and the atrocity hasn't left a discernible mark on the reputation of Jackson. The memory entertained of Jackson's proneness to violence is not that it was cruel but that it was effective. It cleared southern land of Indians, and rendered that land available for the righteous spread of plantations and slavery. We remember Jackson as one of the great American presidents — as one who

---

5. Quoted in Gary B. Nash, Julie Roy Jeffrey, et al., eds., *The American People: Creating a Nation and a Society*, 2nd ed. (New York: Harper & Row, 1990), 417. This may strike us as an eerie foreshadowing of the internment of Japanese residing legally in America — many of them American citizens — during the Second World War. In the case of the Cherokee, though, the extenuating circumstance of an America reacting in shock and irrational fear was not a factor. The Cherokee case bears a closer resemblance to the rounding up of Jews by Nazis. In both cases the legitimation was simple racism, and in both cases the outcome for many was death. We have no neat census of the Cherokee dead. Estimates suggest that about 14,000 were coerced onto the "Trail of Tears, and that of these about 4,000 — somewhere between one-fourth and one-third — died along the way.
6. Cited in John Collier, *The Indians of the Americas* (New York: W.W. Norton, 1947), 123.

opened the West to the uses of democracy. Only in the second decade of the twenty-first century have there been rumblings of criticism concerning the long-standing custom of the Democratic Party to gather yearly in the separate states for Jefferson-Jackson Day dinners during which Democrats commemorate "the good old days" and nerve themselves to meet the challenges of the present in the same splendid spirit these men met challenges of the past. Howard Zinn remarks that in historian Arthur Schlesinger Jr.'s prize-winning salute to "the Age of Jackson," one finds no mention of the Trail of Tears.[7]

One must wonder what logical consequence such complacency should have for our claim to be "the land of the free and the home of the brave." Surely our complacency requires us to contract Francis Scott Key's sparkling phrases to mean: "we're a land for the right kind of people to be free," and "for those of the brave who have white skins we've become a home." It doesn't scan as well as the original, but cuts closer to the truth. When we pledge allegiance to our "one nation, under God, with liberty and justice for all," we have to understand that, while we may aspire to be such a nation, what our past has achieved so far is a less perfect union, one in which the liberty of some has meant—in the gestures and lifestyle modeled by Jefferson and Jackson— the freedom to trample on the liberty of others. When we lose awareness of this poignant disservice to principle, we reduce the aspiration of our truly beautiful phrases down to the level of mere propaganda and cant.

The Mexican War

It would be impossible to find another presidential administration to match the record of James Polk. He entered the presidency to fulfill four goals during what he said would be a one-term presidency. In one term, he achieved those goals, after which he left the White House, went home, and died.

In the course of his time in office, Polk added, by reason of the Mexican Cession, two-thirds as much land to the U.S. as

---

7. Zinn, *People's History*, 130.

Jefferson had by the Louisiana Purchase; and if one counts Texas (added in response to Polk's election) and the Oregon Territory (whose boundary he settled), he added considerably more land than Jefferson had. If one rates presidents by how much real estate they acquired for their fellow Americans, Polk comes out at the top of the list.

When they hear such things, students ask: "Well, if he did all that, why isn't he famous?" Polk is overdue for a close look.

He was a man of moderate height and prickly disposition. He was thought to have neither charisma—the ability to command spontaneous devotion—nor a capacity to intimidate. What he had was his Presbyterian/Methodist faith, and a stubborn sense of personal mission. He was a protégé of Andrew Jackson, whom he sought to imitate. The four goals he brought to his presidency were: (1) to settle the boundary with England over the Oregon Territory; (2) to lower the tariff; (3) to institute a new banking system for the federal treasury; and (4) to acquire California from Mexico. The first three he achieved with relative ease during the first half of his one term. The fourth required a war.

In early May 1846, after a year and two months in the White House, Polk addressed Congress requesting that Congress acknowledge existence of a state of war between the United States and Mexico. Polk wrote:

> The cup of forbearance had been exhausted even before the recent information from the frontier of the Del Norte [the Rio Grande]. But now, after reiterated menaces, Mexico has passed the boundary of the United States, has invaded our territory and shed American blood upon the American soil. She has proclaimed that hostilities have commenced, and that the two nations are now at war. As war exists, and, notwithstanding all our efforts to avoid it, exists by the act of Mexico herself, we are called upon by every consideration of duty and patriotism to vindicate with decision the honor, the rights, and the interests of our country.

The United States, Polk was insisting, was the victim. Mexico was the relentless invader. It was more or less on this premise that for almost twenty-two months, and at the cost of some 13,000 American men and a greater but not well counted number of

Mexicans, that the United States invaded Mexico, took control of its capital, and wrested from it the cession of "Alta California" and the larger area sometimes called "New Mexico."

That we were the defending party was—as we saw—Polk's story. To an extent, he may have taught himself to believe it. It's possible he never let himself regard the war as an exercise in conquest. If one squints one's eyes, stands on one's head, and looks at the whole thing just right, one may catch a glimpse of Polk's angle. For one thing, the territory at issue—California and "New Mexico"—was sparsely populated and barely governed. After having won independence from Spain, Mexico had spun into a swirl of shifting governments; amid the turmoil, outlying northern districts were often given little or no direction from Mexico City. In these circumstances, perhaps Polk was able to conduct a self-persuasion; he may have persuaded himself his policy was a mere effort to occupy vacant territory and settle boundary issues.

In the case of the Oregon Territory, in truth it was an issue about boundaries that Polk's diplomacy addressed. In this case, after some fairly standard threats, counterthreats, and near-ultimatums, the issue with Britain was settled peacefully, and the settlement produced no lasting discord.

The case of California was different. Conflicted as Mexico was, we can be sure there resided in the back of the minds of Mexico's contending parties the notion that Mexico was a nation of vast land-wealth—that Mexico was rich in northward prospects for prosperity in the not-distant future. Who would manage such prospects was in fact a significant part of what the Mexican factions were squabbling about. Events leading to the de facto loss of Texas had to seem a naïve mistake to Mexicans, and only quickened the sense of urgency among Mexican officials not to repeat such mistakes at the threshold of Polk's administration. Polk may have thought however that, having lost Texas, surely Mexicans realized they must also lose California. He may not have understood how the loss of Texas enhanced for Mexicans the preciousness of what northern land remained.

As to Mexico's title to California, Polk did not really have genuine doubts. He'd sent Thomas Slidell to Mexico City for the express purpose of buying California. Understanding the purpose of Slidell's mission, no Mexican official would meet with Slidell. Reaching for any excuse handy, Polk was getting ready to treat this diplomatic snub as itself a "casus belli"—a violation of American rights sufficient to justify war. Such a pretext was, however, transparently weak—as if nations have some obligation under international law to meet with others whenever those others wish to make a purchase of their land. So Polk sent General Zachary Taylor south through Texas to stake out a position on territory just north of the Rio Grande about which there was a running boundary dispute. (We claimed that Texas extended south to the Rio Grande whereas Mexicans claimed it was bounded by a river to the north.) Polk's hope was that Taylor's presence in disputed territory would provoke an incident with Mexican forces situated on the Rio Grande's southern bank.

It did; and the consensus of commentators then and now is that Polk was greatly relieved when it did.

Therefore, when Polk said in his request for a declaration of war that the war had come "notwithstanding all our efforts to avoid it," he was lying. He had to be aware of his own efforts to provoke the war. From then on, an issue that continued to divide Congress and ordinary people as well all through the war was between those who were content to allow the lie as being in a good cause, and those who weren't.

The fact the lie "succeeded" and the U.S. gained immense real estate as a consequence has had two effects. First, Polk and the actual war have sunk below the visible horizon for most Americans. Since the war ended in "success," we haven't needed to think about it. Secondly, for those who do think about such things, the war allowed one more experience from which to argue that force used in the service of America's destiny can be a good thing.

The harm in this is hard for most Americans to discern. A truly masterful book on the Polk administration, *A Country of Vast Designs* by Robert W. Merry (of the Wall Street Journal and the Congressional Quarterly), after it provides a fascinating record of the to-and-fro-ing, the conflicts, manipulations, and duplicities of the war effort, concludes with the following exoneration of Polk:

> The moralistic impulse, when applied to the Mexican War, misses a fundamental reality of history: it doesn't turn on moralistic pivots but on differentials of power, will, organization, and population. History moves forward with

a crushing force and does not stop for niceties of moral suasion or concepts of political virtue. Mexico was a dysfunctional, unstable, weak nation whose population wasn't sufficient to control all the lands within its domain. The United States by contrast was a vibrant, expanding, exuberant experiment in democracy whose burgeoning population thrilled to the notion that it was engaging in something big and historically momentous.[8]

As an expression of what was the general sense among politically conscious Americans (at least once the treaty ending the war was in place and memories of the dead had begun to recede), the passage cited above may be accurate. It has however obvious inconveniences. When, in the mid-1930s, Japan looked again to the Asian mainland (having already stationed itself in Korea), no doubt what the leaders of Japan beheld in China was a "dysfunctional, unstable, weak nation" unable "to control all the lands within its domain." When these same Japanese leaders looked to their own country, no doubt they beheld "a vibrant, exuberant experiment" (if not in democracy, at least in something that had far-reaching patriotic endorsement—the Emperor, after all, was divine) by a "burgeoning population thrilled to the notion that it was engaging in something big and historically momentous." One might say Japan paid the United States a compliment—a kind of homage to the Monroe Doctrine[9]—by proclaiming as its ambition a "Greater Asian Co-Prosperity Sphere."

Simultaneously, when Hitler was looking to the east of Germany for *Lebensraum* for the German people, what he saw were Slavic countries, ill-governed and dysfunctional. Looking to the German and Austrian people, he saw a "vibrant, exuberant, experiment"—in a kind of populist democracy—by a "burgeoning population thrilled to the notion that it was engaging in

8. Robert W. Merry, *A Country of Vast Designs* (New York: Simon & Schuster, 2009), 476.

9. The Monroe Doctrine, penned by the always sagacious J.Q. Adams, was intended as an instrument of peace, taking the Western Hemisphere out of the turmoil of European politics and allowing the U.S. to live in separate harmony with itself and its neighbors. Already by the time of Polk's administration, it had been flipped and rendered toxic.

something big and historically momentous." He would entirely have agreed with Wall Street Journal writer Merry's contention that history "doesn't turn on moral pivots but on differentials of power, will, organization, and population." Further he'd have claimed no one believed more firmly than he that "history moves forward with a crushing force and does not stop for niceties of moral suasion or concepts of political virtue." The point being argued here isn't that the Mexican War caused these other aggressions, but that it forfeited in advance the moral ground from which we professed to criticize Japan and Germany. Though I can still recall the outraged denunciations of Japan and Germany I heard as a boy during the Second World War, I came to see as I grew older how opportunistic they were. Our premise for the Mexican War and Merry's rationalization for it made it clear we would not be restrained by the principles we demanded of others.

That we Americans found ourselves inconvenienced in the twentieth century by these might-is-right agendas of other countries, is moral karma. We vigorously denounced "imperialist behavior" in the most moralistic terms, but the actions against which we protested (and went on to reverse by war) were actions for which we'd provided paradigm and advertisement. Our Mexican war was a "success," and we've never repudiated it. If one wants to, one can say that the Japanese and Germans didn't need our example for their attempt to grab other peoples' land—but to do so misses the point. If the actions of Japan and Germany were so contemptible, what then of ours?[10]

Surely, the principle of expansion, as internalized by Americans and accurately expressed by Merry, was self-contradictory and deeply damaging to our internal accounting system. As noted earlier, in our American formulation, the case for expansion has routinely invoked the notion we were expanding the domain of democracy. We've presented Democracy as our sterling goal; its goodness was that it enlarged the domain of human

10. In the case of the Japanese, I think there are in fact plausible historical reasons suggesting our example toward Mexico and the rest of Latin America *was* a motivating factor in the development of their Greater Asian Co-Prosperity Sphere.

rights. To trample on human rights in the interest of enlarging their domain involves no minor instance of cognitive dissonance; one needs to shut down one's mind to pull it off.

It adds to the irony of things that in this pell-mell effort supposedly to maximize opportunities for human freedom, we've often portrayed ourselves as having no choice. We were acting as servants of Manifest Destiny. Held in its grip, we could do no other. So in our mission to bring human freedom to an ever wider sphere, it seems the denial of our own freedom—made when we said: "The matter is out of our hands!"—was a price we were willing to pay.

I've mentioned Polk as partly Presbyterian; his father was one. Of the Christian sects, Presbyterians were the most directly descended from Puritans and were the most enduring of Protestant sects in maintaining a Calvinist sense of things that resonated echoes of predestination. We've noted earlier how the Puritan sense of an obligatory American mission to promote God's reign could transform itself into a mere secular impulse to pursue goods compulsively. It could do this without undergoing a loss of momentum or foregoing any of Puritanism's constraining demands for aesthetic deprivation, deferred gratification, or bigotry toward others. (Weber invites his reader to find particularly the first two demands in Ben Franklin's days of producing aphorisms by "Poor Richard.") The vivid presence of such Puritan demands on us as we waged the Mexican War manifests that Puritanism was alive and well as we fought.

Beyond other evils consequent upon this war though is this one that can be invisible—enabled therefore to be enduring and potent. It's the hidden evil implicit in Merry's eloquent rationalization: The Mexican War "worked" and therefore inquiries into the means by which it worked are irrelevant. To believe that is to believe in evil—to believe in entrenched evil of the kind Jesus may have had in mind when he said "sins against the light" are satanically tenacious.

The War on the Plains

There's really no name for this war. That makes it easier to dismiss. Perhaps it was no war at all, we're inclined to say. We've re-cast it in our folklore as "the Winning of the West." As I suggest, typically the folklore memorializes valiant efforts on the part of white settlers and the federal troops who protected them to subdue mindless acts of domestic violence by those resisting the westward march of civilization. It confuses things, we tend to think, to call this activity a war; it was a policing operation. It was law enforcement of duly negotiated treaties—made necessary by faithless Indians who refused to abide by these treaties. It was action—to use a term popular in my youth—necessitated by "Indian-givers."

Such at least we have preferred to think, and so—until recently—many of our teachers would have us believe.

The heroes of this campaign in the West counted among their ranks some of the foremost heroes of the Civil War. Recall that right up into 1865, federal soldiers were marching courageously into hostile territory, risking their lives—losing their lives in great numbers—to liberate blacks held in bondage on the slave-labor camps that were the "peculiar institution" of the South. No sooner had these soldiers succeeded in their selfless venture than they turned their faces westward and marched out across the plains in a new effort at liberation—this time in an effort to liberate the lands of the West from the bondage of non-use or imperfect-use imposed by the savages who inhabited them.

The story won't work, will it? It ends in anticlimax. Yet it's true that many of the protagonists in this War on the Plains were from the victorious northern ranks of our Civil War. Some three years after the Civil War, General William Tecumseh Sherman wrote John Sherman (a brother, and a future secretary of state): "The more [of Indians] we can kill this year, the less will have to be killed in the next war, for the more I see of these Indians the more convinced I am that they all have to be killed or be maintained as a species of paupers." In January of the next year, 1869, another great hero of the North's liberating army, General Philip Henry Sheridan, is reported to have said at Fort Cobb: "The only good Indians I ever saw were dead."

Until recently there have been writers who admired the candor of such words, seeing Sherman and Sheridan as realists willing, surgically, to make the task of Indian extermination as quick and painless as possible. They were men who manned up—saddled up, John Wayne might say—to do the dirty work that needed doing. They acted as mercy killers.

It's a defense few can now stomach. But then we find ourselves re-directed to an issue we addressed earlier. If these once-honored soldiers were not humanitarians, what are we to make of that Civil War which brought them to the forefront of our affairs?

(Before the Civil War, back in the 1850s, politicians and citizens had spoken of "Free Soil" in the West. California and John C. Fremont were prominent in the Free-Soil movement. When one first hears the phrase "Free Soil," one is likely to conclude— since the phrase clearly intended to exclude slavery from the West—that the phrase envisioned a West where blacks, among others, could work the land in freedom. Yet after the war, the West did not soon see any large migration of blacks. Looked at more closely, the phrase "Free Soil" seems not to have intended a West that was free for blacks, but a West that was free from blacks. Envisioned by the victorious North was a West in which whites would be free to seek their fortunes without competition either from the institution of slavery or from the people once afflicted by that institution.)

Even though America was convulsed in the middle of the nineteenth century over the issue of slavery, one should be slow to conclude slavery was the century's central theme. The readiness after the war with which Reconstruction was shunted to the side demonstrates it was not. The organizing focus of mainstream America in the nineteenth century was, as the Mexican War suggests, the expansion westward of our white and Christian way of life. How to accommodate emancipated blacks in that expansion was given little attention—even by Lincoln. As for Indians, there really was no interest at all in how to accommodate them. In language of today, what expansion meant for American Indians is that, indiscriminately, they'd be discounted as its collateral damage.

Once one had chosen to persist—by adopting this accounting system—in denying personhood to Indians, once one had risen to the heights of Merry's "big and historically momentous" forces, one may have felt in a safe position (as some writers still do) to shrug and re-personalize as it were—and to do so on behalf of both sides. One can say: "Well, we must be fair; just as it was wrong in the nineteenth century to say all the wrong was on the side of the Indians, so today it would be wrong to romanticize the Indians and say all the wrong was on the side of the whites; the truth is, there was good and bad behavior on both sides."

How we love that kind of thinking. It seems to excuse us from ever making sense of anything. Writing as recently as 1995, Charles M. Robinson III, after describing the white/Indian encounter as a "basic conflict between a technologically-advanced society and a primitive, tribal society," informs us: "In such a situation, where both occupy—or wish to occupy—the same area, the less advanced society must yield."[11]

To posit this is an adroit maneuver. It abstracts from the context of oppressor and victim, and of moral evaluation. Social problems reduce thereby to merely technical ones—a kind of extension of Newtonian physics. "He with the most technology wins." The account-giver is thereby freed to recount the War on the Plains as a kind of sporting event—one in which some on each side showed valor and agility in tactics, while others on each side showed the lack thereof. Morality isn't at issue—and the outcome is foreseeable by anyone with common sense.

Trouble is, such "balanced treatment" requires a near total suspension of aesthetic sensibility and empathy. The Nazi holocaust can be defended by one willing to argue this way; the Nazi Party had more technological competence in hand than had the Jews of Germany. We recognize spontaneously how banal and empty the argument is. In the War on the Plains, on the one side, the contestants were soldiers invading lands to which their most plausible claim was, "We bought this land from Napoleon!" On the other side, the contestants were husbands and fathers fighting to protect wives, children, and a place in the sun. An observer genuinely free from bias cannot see the issue here as one in which the merits and grievances on one side are more or less matched by those on the other—cannot use the type of "balanced" historical commentary one will still find commentators attempting who nonetheless regard themselves as fair-minded and liberal.

---

11. Charles M. Robinson III, *A Good Year to Die: The Story of the Great Sioux War* (New York: Random House, 1995), ix.

To achieve the resetting of scales needed to provide this comforting sense of equilibrium (to give, that is, a measure of legitimacy to federal soldiers and the settlers on whose behalf they fought and killed), one has no option but to continue with our traditional undocumented and unhistorical demeaning of Indian husbands and fathers. This balancing act requires that Indian husbands and fathers be viewed as devoid of dignity. Unless they can be found unworthy of respect, there can be no balancing act. The phrases for the un-dignifying of Indian braves have been ready-to-hand for generations now. "See how they hang about the trading posts and agency offices!" "Look at them: alcoholic, suicidal, shiftless, waiting for handouts, quarreling pointlessly among themselves." "Red devils, snakes, vermin, half-naked savages!" "Altogether untrustworthy!"

In the good old days, this denial of status was relentless and uncriticized—indispensable in fact to maintain the morale of us Puritans. Even today, if one is somehow out to sanitize God's Elect for their attempt to exterminate their rivals, these notions are needed as a thumb on the scale.

One demeaned these husbands and fathers so one could view their destruction with equanimity. An alternative to destroying them—that of reaching an accommodation—was always regarded as too inconvenient to be taken seriously. It would have placed intolerable restraints on white liberty. It would have meant we were no longer the land of the free. We were free to fight Indians because Indians were worthless.

A tortured argument for sure; for both whites and Indians fully understood that the point in fighting Indians was to *render* them worthless. It was not alcoholic, suicidal, shiftless, impotent Indians against whom the War on the Plains was fought.

Was this genocide? The question perhaps is just semantic. If "genocide" looks to extermination of the last member of a race, perhaps not; for the intent was to move Indians out of the way. If however one means by "genocide" a systematic effort to deprive a people once and finally of all agency, I'd say this effort of our recent ancestors was as good an example of genocide as anything history offers. The influence of Indians on white purposes—the agency of Indians to influence and impede white purposes—was to be annihilated. We settlers shouldn't have to worry about Indians any more. As the legitimate children of white Puritans, we intended to secure total security by withholding all security of free action from our Indian predecessors and rivals.

Effective federal efforts to stop the sun dance and the ghost dance, and to take Indian children into Christian schools so as to extinguish in them the beliefs of their parents were as totalitarian and intolerant as anything the Chinese government has done in the twentieth and twenty-first centuries against Tibetan Buddhists or the Falun Gong. The successful attack on the buffalo herds—the staple and focus of Indian life on the plains—sets some kind of record in the annals total war.

Among the events in this war, the most famous was the campaign toward the end against some Lakota, a resistant federation led by the Sioux among whom Sitting Bull emerged as the paramount leader. One should be mindful of course that this episode, sometimes given recognition as "the Great Sioux War," doesn't name an initiation of hostilities between whites and Indians; as we've seen, hostilities date back nearly to first encounters. Further, without conceding "moral equivalence," it can be conceded there'd been acts of cruel violence perpetrated by both Indians and whites in the long chain of bitter relations that preceded this final episode on the plains. (Both then and now, whites found barbaric and reprehensible the Indian custom of mutilating the dead bodies of their opponents—yet some whites engaged in it too, and some local white governments paid bounties for Indian body parts.)

So, yes, grievances and outrages on both sides provide context. If though one wants to use the words "massacre" and "terrorism," it seems one shouldn't reserve them simply for the deeds of one's opponents. Further, use of such special terms should be warranted by special circumstances.

To refer to an episode on December 21, 1866, at the start of the Great Sioux War, as "the massacre of Fetterman's party" seems unwarranted. A group of seventy-nine federal soldiers and two civilians, led by William Fetterman, had intended to pacify (whatever that entailed) a band of Oglala Sioux but instead were outmaneuvered and killed by them.

Sherman used the phrase "the massacre of Fetterman's party" in a letter to Grant (not yet president), and then Sherman added: "We must act with vindictive earnestness against the Sioux, even to their extermination, men, women, and children.

Nothing less will ever reach the root of the case." In a more conscientious use of words, it would seem what the Sioux accomplished in the Fetterman incident was the ambush of a pursuing force; it was what Sherman advocated by way of retaliation that can properly be called a massacre.

"Massacre" and "terrorism" are terms which share each others' connotations. In the case of a "massacre," a large number of non-combatant people — "innocent civilians" if you will (though Sherman, with his concept of "total war," seemed to deny civilians can be innocent) — are indiscriminately killed. This is a condition that general usage seems to imply by use of the term "massacre." Similarly, it is annihilation of non-combatants for the purpose of sending a message, that can meaningfully be called "terrorism." To shrug off these constraints in the use of terms seems then to leave these terms in the category of mere name calling.

In the subject-matter under consideration here, even in looking to the issue of civilian innocence, one can argue there was in the Indian/settler comparison, a lack of moral equivalence between the two sets of civilians. One population, as we noted, was an intruding and expanding population, instigating an ever-renewed breach of treaties; the other population was a population residing in traditional habitat. The argument made then and now by apologists for our side has been that the second population, being the weaker of the two and making the less intrusive and exhaustive use of the land, had no genuine right to live in any place where we whites wished to live instead.

To strengthen their case, some partisans for our inherited sense of entitlement have added: "Surely these very Sioux had themselves displaced other native populations in earlier generations." To attempt though in this way to dismiss justice from the discussion is to make an argument that's clearly a bridge too far. Alleged injustices among native Americans can't exempt white Americans from all obligation to treat native Americans justly. To say otherwise is to make a mugger's argument. (The argument goes like this: "No doubt there have been times when you've acted unjustly; therefore I have no obligation to treat you justly. Give me your watch and your wallet.") Also, there's a matter of scale. Native Americans had engaged in skirmishes with each other; we whites intended a war whose only limit was extinction.

The immediate circumstances leading to the Great Sioux War had to do with transportation, and involved a trespass on land occupied by Indians traditionally and guaranteed to them by treaty. Federal troops tried to defend whites who, trespassing through this Indian territory, were building a trail to connect white mining operations near the towns of Bozeman and Virginia City to the Oregon Trail. Some Sioux who were guided by Red Cloud and Crazy Horse recognized that this intrusion could lead to much greater intrusions, and they found the means to create endless trouble for the road-builders and their protectors. This can be regarded as the beginning of the Great Sioux War. The killing of the party led by Fetterman — sent to subdue Sioux troublemakers — was an early and important episode in this conflict. Since the conflict had started with white trespass on land guaranteed to Indians, our federal government thought a good remedy following the killing of Fetterman and his troops was to revise and contract our guarantees to Indians. A federal invitation was sent out for all parties to meet and negotiate at Fort Laramie in 1868. In light of what Sherman wrote Grant, one can judge of the degree of good faith our side would bring to the meeting.

The negotiations were problematic. For one thing, Indians had only fragmentary knowledge of the language in which conclusions were written down. Another problem was that such Indians as were present were not empowered to speak for all their fellow tribes-people. Still another is that Red Cloud and many other chiefs boycotted the meeting. Far and away the most serious problem was (as earlier we saw both early Puritans and Andrew Jackson admit) whites wouldn't feel bound by any agreements they negotiated.

Negotiations at Fort Laramie ended with a treaty-signing on April 29, 1868. Red Cloud didn't come to Fort Laramie to sign the treaty until November 6. By then, treaty provisions regarding a removal of federal forts had been implemented as an indication of federal good intentions. Red Cloud and one hundred twenty-five other chiefs signed; but Red Cloud remained suspicious of federal intentions.

The treaty itself contained clauses sounding very beneficial to the Lakota-Sioux. Noteworthy was Article 16: "The United States hereby agrees and stipulates that the country north of the North

Platte River and east of the summits of the Big Horn Mountains shall be held and considered to be unceded Indian territory, and also stipulates and agrees that no white person or persons shall be permitted to settle upon or occupy any portion of the same . . ."[12]

Article 2 listed, significantly, most of the Black Hills (regarded by the Sioux as particularly sacred ground) as an integral part of the Sioux reservation. This meant this territory would remain under complete control of the Sioux.

But Red Cloud was rightly suspicious. Less than seven months after the day Red Cloud signed, Sherman issued a general order saying Indians found on the "unceded lands" mentioned as Indian territory in Article 16, "as a rule will be considered hostile"— which meant they were subject to being captured or, if prudence suggested it was safer, shot. This annulled Article 16.

Further, when the economy dipped five years later (due in part to mismanagement, corruption, and greed in the Grant administration), whites began to lust for the gold rumored to be in the Black Hills. Yielding to temptation, in 1874 the federal government authorized Civil War hero George Armstrong Custer to conduct a "scientific" expedition into the Black Hills—an expedition joined by two professional prospectors. The next year, after exculpatory words about the importance of observing the 1868 treaty with the Lakota, President Grant wrote, "Efforts are now being made for the extinguishment of the Indian title, and all proper means will be used to accomplish that end."

If a presidential wink had been needed, it was given; "all proper means" were intended to be along lines of an offer one could not refuse. The door was opened to the second and terminal stage of the Great Sioux War.

What could have been done here? Most writers falter in answering; they end by deferring to Merry's and Robinson's (and Calvin's) "irresistible" laws of history. Suppose though the gold had been just north of the border with Canada. Suppose Canadian Mounted Police—Canada's warriors—had been on the border and had attempted to push trespassing American prospectors back onto U.S. territory. Would American federal troops then

---

12. Treaty of Fort Laramie (1868), available at https://www.ourdocuments.gov/doc.php?flash=true&doc=42.

have taken up a war to the death against the Canadian Mounted Police? It's unimaginable. Having a treaty-line with Canada, American troops would—had they been engaged at all—have been engaged to hold back the American prospectors.

Perhaps it's too much to ask of us white and profoundly purified Americans, even in the twenty-first century, to imagine our federal soldiers joining forces with the Sioux to protect a federally guaranteed Sioux right to some Sioux territory. (As the event made clear, when push comes to shove, we leave "equal justice for all" to the "impractical" among us—the Roger Williamses, the Thoreaus, the Martin Luther Kings. Once we recover our breath from the insolence of an "outsider" who claims rights, we tend to shout as one man: "What about us? Don't we have rights?"—as if any recognition of others' rights diminishes our own.)

Consider then a lesser case. Is it really outlandish to think, in this matter of Sioux land, that U.S. federal troops, feeling disinclined to block white trespassers from entering Sioux territory, might have just stood to one side and told the trespassers that the risk of entry was all theirs? Could not American soldiers have honored the clear implication of the Laramie Treaty that the Sioux were within their rights to defend land the treaty had guaranteed as theirs? (Federalists of honor like Alexander Hamilton and John Marshall would have understood this.)

Had we honored our promises, perhaps federal coffers, squandered in the greedy days of the Grant administration, wouldn't have been replenished quite so quickly for further squandering. Were gold-mining profits and fresh land so indispensable to our prosperity that a more legal and accommodating method and tempo would have been an unsustainable national loss? (That to this day, white writers' imaginations frequently draw a blank at this point tells us much about the damage such episodes have done to us and why our diplomacy continues to be such a farrago of contradictions today. What kind of "success" was it that it required us to violate our own word so starkly?)

As it was, our readiness to overstep negotiated boundaries led, first to an effort on the part of federal commissioners to insist that the Sioux sell the Black Hills; then, when the Sioux simply said no, the Department of the Interior demanded that all Indians who still roamed freely on territory the Treaty of Laramie had guaranteed as theirs must report to the Indian agencies by January 31, 1876. When some Indians—looking increasingly to Sitting Bull for leadership—refused, our government officially declared them "hostiles." Federal expeditions against the Lakota-Sioux intensified; and the Great Sioux War moved toward what proved its climax and end.

There was an inconclusive battle at the river Rosebud on June 17, 1876—one from which General George Crook and his command were thought lucky to escape alive. A week and a day later, entering the valley of the Little Bighorn, George Armstrong Custer—famous for his dashing spirit in the Civil War, and encouraged by what now seems in hindsight a string of gambler's luck—broke ranks from an elaborate, multi-pronged battle plan, and led an entire cavalry contingent to their death.

Departure from the battle plan may not have been intended; yet it seems most everyone in the federal command had seen it coming. Custer had moved with great speed. General Gibbon, the commander of a major prong, had been delayed. In Gibbon's absence, General Terry, commander of the Seventh Cavalry, was to move with a large contingent from north of the Sioux's expected encampment, and Custer was to come up from the south; together they were to catch the Sioux in an inescapable pincher.

On June 25, once Custer surmised that scouts of the Lakota Sioux had discovered his presence, he seems to have decided he had no alternative but to engage—whatever might be the whereabouts of Terry. It seems he did so with no proper estimate of the size of the intended victim. While he may have intended a massacre at the immense camping ground of Lakota-Sioux and other Indians assembled near the Little Bighorn, he and all two hundred and ten men under his direct command were outnumbered in direct combat by one or two thousand Indian warriors and destroyed.

This was not a massacre. It was defense against massacre—a defense only temporarily successful. Too many Indians were killed or wounded in the event for it to be celebrated at length among those who survived. As for white Americans, the year 1876 was our nation's first centennial; and the shock of such a reversal at the hands of "savages" was almost more than we whites could take in. (One wonders what we whites expected. Did we think the thousands of Indians present should have just lain on the ground while Custer and his troops executed them one-by-one?) The press was full of cries for retribution and vengeance and for a final solution to the Indian problem. The reconfiguration of Custer into a martyr for the American way tells us a great deal, not just about Custer's skills as a showman, but about ourselves and our romantic tendency toward necrophilia.

With intensified effort on the part of the federal government, and with virtually unlimited authority now granted to Sherman to deal with Indians as he saw fit, what remained was a mopping up. Indian resistance continued but with ever-diminishing hope and confidence during this period when exhausted and resource-less Indians were being corralled into reservations hardly distinguishable from prison grounds. High percentages perished in federal custody.

How relentless the white will was to destroy all remnants of Indian life can perhaps be comprehended by the event at Wounded Knee, twelve years after Custer's death, when two hundred or more Sioux men, women, and children were slaughtered—with the help of Hotchkiss repeating guns—after they came together to celebrate the Ghost Dance. Twenty medals of honor were awarded to federal troops who participated in the slayings. At least two medals seem to have been awarded for outstanding conduct in searching out and killing those who were hiding in ravines to escape the massacre.

One might continue from here, and go on to attempt the story of Chief Joseph. If ever in the nineteenth century a man evolved toward becoming a kind of American Gandhi, it was Chief Joseph. The tragic story of his long effort to hold the Nez Perce together against relentless persecution distinguishes him as one of the noblest heroes of our history. (It's ironic that so many Americans are taught the story of Gandhi's heroic resistance to the English, and so few Americans are taught the story of Chief's Joseph's heroic resistance to white Americans. Do we commemorate Chief Joseph on the Fourth of July? Why we don't might provide an interesting reflection for that day—perhaps a welcome relief from the predictable romancing of violence that precedes our firecrackers.)

Enough though may have been said of the War on the Plains. Finally, let's turn to what we call the Spanish-American

War—which occurs a decade after the Massacre at Wounded Knee.[13]

War Against Spaniards (and Cubans?) and Filipinos

From early on, our "successful" way of treating Indians had accustomed us to deal with others from a sense that the moral high ground was permanently ours. When we'd reached out in the 1840s to take Northern Mexico from Mexico, such dealing was one to which our continuing seizures of Indian land had habituated us and had anesthetized us to intrusions of ethical concern; the issue of Northern Mexico had seemed much like business as usual.

That's to say, the seizure of Mexican land had had much in common with earlier land seizures: (1) in this confrontation with Mexico too the land was contiguous with "the land God had given us"; (2) it was land within the westward trajectory of our Manifest Destiny—manifest that is when looking out to that huge rectangular plot of real estate that a glance at any map clearly showed God meant us to have; (3) this Mexican land was but sparsely settled by the people claiming title; (4) our U.S. citizens were already settling there (in the case of Texas, and to a lesser extent in California, good white Anglo-Saxon Protestants, cleansed in the fires of Puritanism, were already in possession of land deeds); (5) we knew much of the indigenous population of the other party, less pure than us, was contaminated by Indian ancestry; (6) an added aspect was that, though this land had slipped from Spain's control, it had an Hispanic and Catholic culture in a hemisphere the Monroe Doctrine had already unimpeachably declared to be in the keeping of us Americans—a

---

13. My concern as we move on from this is that those among us who are non-Indians and who fancy ourselves decent participants in the American mainstream continue to speak of "the Winning of the West," and in the confused complacency of that phrase, conceal from ourselves an addiction to force that makes it difficult for us to get our bearings and find our balance in all the years that have followed. We've been wounded by that "Winning" more than we imagine. The untended infection from that wound continues to fester.

people with an enduring, if increasingly subterranean, purified brand of Christianity. Romanism was something against which we were maintaining a principled stand.

Later then, some fifty years following the Treaty of Guadalupe-Hidalgo and the Mexican Cession of 1848, when the West had been "won" and continental expansion westward had been achieved, our mindset was firmly defined and was in control; American settlement reached from sea to sea, and we were ready for fresh adventure. The first episode of this adventure is routinely called "the Spanish-American War." Revisionist historians think it might more properly be called "the War to Thwart Cuban Independence and to Gain a Foothold off the Shores of Asia." Not surprisingly, the shorter label has prevailed.

To dispense with the tone of sarcasm though, when I speak here of an "adventure," I hardly take the measure of the urgencies besetting us amid our successes as the nineteenth century drew toward a close. We must look to those urgencies; and we should proceed in an awareness that the interaction and proper weighing of the factors in play at the time remain at issue today. There remains much murkiness as to details, and we should be tentative and cautious.

Still, were we able to look on from outer space, it might seem our next move was well prepared by our past. Just off our southeastern shores was Cuba, a holdout in the Western Hemisphere of what we regarded an anachronistic and dying Spanish Empire. In words John Quincy Adams wrote as secretary of state in 1823, Cuba was "a ripe fruit"—waiting to fall into American hands. The words fit well the spirit of J.Q.'s Monroe Doctrine. While we'd grandfathered Spain's western colonies into our conception, we should be the arbiter of order in the Western hemisphere. Spanish administration of Cuba had always been mercantilist: it had been organized for deliberate, full-scale exploitation of Cuban resources and labor, and had been reliant on slavery and cruel measures from its earliest days.

In the 1890s, by no means for the first time, Spain's rule was being challenged by local Cubans. As had been the case in prior instances, Spain sought to control such opposition by brute force. Though slavery had been officially abolished in the 1880s, the blacks of Cuba didn't live in the status of a free people; and as part of a fresh crack-down, much of the workforce of Cuba—black and black-Hispanic—were now being herded into *reconcentrados* by Spain's General Weyler. In these concentration camps it's estimated a third of Cuba's population died of hunger and disease. Predictably, much of the Cuban population became resolute for independence. Was there not, then, an American opportunity—or rather, an American "obligation"—here?

The makeup of the rebel population may be beyond an accurate accounting by now. Without being tutored by archival research, let me share my conjectures as to how things stood. It's likely some in the ranks of the rebels were *peninsulares*—people born in Spain but critical of Spain's cruel management of Cuba. Less speculatively, we know some of the rebels (José Martí, at least from his father's side) were from the "Hispanic" or criollo class: native-born Cubans with a claim to pure Spanish descent (at least for a parent if not for oneself). In the manner that we American colonists in the century before had taken issue with England, many from the criollo class probably took issue with Spain's refusal to give Cubans official representation at Madrid. More than that, as people who prided themselves on being Spanish, one can assume many of them had to resent Spain's general and amorphous contempt for the human rights of Cubans. Criollos then were likely the yeast for the rise of revolutionary feeling. As for Cubans of mixed Spanish and African ancestry (anywhere from 25 to 50 percent of the population) and Cubans of pure African ancestry, they had suffered physically more than the criollos, and it's plausible to assume these groups were ready to be recruited by criollo revolutionaries when offered a promise of racial and economic equality in a liberated Cuba. Remaining groups can be assumed to be recruitable in like manner. As for Indian ancestry: in the course of the island's earlier history, it had been reduced by inhumane work and inhumane living conditions to the point it remained mostly as mere traces in the blood streams of some who were of mixed Spanish and African ancestry. Indian ancestry did survive more recognizably perhaps in some quite limited groups of people of Indian/European ancestry without an African component. Finally, it seems there remained some few small settlements of pure-blood Indians. I suspect that even a very talented and diligent Cuban ethnologist of today would have trouble with all this, in that issues of ancestry may have been delicate enough so that in many cases it was thought best to leave them unexamined.

To conclude this tentative consideration of parties, it's likely that by the late 1890s, a high majority of those who could legitimately be called Cubans were at least in spirit rebels against Spain, although there were, as in our revolution against England, no doubt some prominent loyalists who held out for continuing with the way things were.

As for us Americans, we were on all sides of this struggle between Cuban rebels and the Spanish. Present among us were fresh sponsors of the sugar economy of Cuba who wanted Cuba to enjoy good order for the sake of predictable production, trade, and profits. Some probably were of double minds: in support of a Spanish crackdown from business motives, but opposed to its actual brutality from humanitarian motives. More widely, celebration of our own official abolition of slavery three decades earlier was still fresh in the minds of abolitionists and of Republicans in general, and this inclined these people to a humanitarian concern for the blacks of Cuba—blacks whom they accurately saw as still deprived of freedom and, in fact, in current danger of extinction from abuse and starvation. Further, and probably extensively, we Americans felt that the struggle of Cubans against Spain paralleled our own struggle for independence from England in the previous century.

From the desire our business men had for the protection of American property rights and opportunities, we tended to balance our concern for freedom among Cubans with some wariness about Cuban independence. "If we don't control Cuba, who will?" was a question on American minds of those who anticipated an imminent end to Spanish rule—with the spiritual boundary, as suggested, between self-interest and humanitarian concern something of a blur. (This was the time when robber barons first came to the fore, and no doubt some of them wondered, "Why should the mercantilist Spanish exploit Cuba when our anti-mercantilist corporations can do the job so much better?")

Considerations of these sorts occupied our minds in 1898, with our yellow press—especially the Hearst side of the Hearst/Pulitzer competition—doing what it could to heat things up. Responding to this array, chroniclers have sometimes presented our eventual engagement against Spain as simply a matter of humanitarian concern, whipped to frenzy by the newspapers of Hearst and Pulitzer, finally overflowing into war when our battleship *Maine* exploded in Havana Harbor.

The trouble with leaving our war with Spain to such an explanation is that it leaves more general, strategic interests unattended. While the explosion of the *Maine*, for instance, was unquestionably an event of immense public interest in the United States, how one interpreted it depended on prior dispositions. The explosion of the *Maine* constituted for us Americans a kind of Rorschach test.

Some Americans seemed quite sure the Spanish government had done it. Their argument depended on circumstantial evidence: the whereabouts of the *Maine* when it exploded and the context of Spain's growing hostility toward the U.S. The major problem for those who took this view had to do with motivation. It was manifestly contrary to the interests of the Spanish government to have our battleship explode in "Spanish waters" at this delicate moment. Even the *Maine*'s captain, Charles Sigsbee—interested to show that no neglect of good order in the interior of his ship had led to the tragedy—nonetheless veered off away from Spain toward a notion the ship had been sabotaged by freelance terrorists.

Some, then, have come forward with "false-flag" theories. Such theories say that anti-Spanish agents who wished to provoke the U.S. into war with Spain blew up the battleship in the expectation that Spain would be blamed. The actual provocateurs could have been either Cuban rebels or interested Americans. But if it was Cubans, this would be cool treatment indeed toward a potential ally. The "interested American" part also faces this problem of who and why. It seems implausible such Americans could have been government agents. For one thing, the administration could have achieved a declaration of war from Congress without this loss of American lives and treasure. Secondly, in those days before the Cold War and the black ops of the CIA, it's a stretch to finger (even in the office of Assistant Secretary of the Navy Theodore Roosevelt) a sector of our government with the stomach for so treasonous an action. So if it was Americans, it's more plausible to think it was Americans acting on their own. Whether then one looks to Cubans or to Americans, one seems left with individuals, acting in the shadows and invisible, as one's explanation.

The major alternative to inconclusive saboteur hypotheses was the natural-combustion hypothesis. Stored coal could have ignited spontaneously, and the fire could have spread to a munitions magazine nearby which then exploded. Other accidents can also be imagined.

What's noteworthy for our purposes is that those who wanted war with Spain gravitated quickly to the interpretation that Spain was the culprit, whereas those concerned to avoid war were open to alternative explanations.

If so, this incident can't be seen as the decisive cause of the war. Predispositions each person brought to interpreting the incident played too large a role for that. Even factoring in an irresponsible use of the incident by the newspapers won't go the distance to explain why we declared war. One would need to explain why this journalism resonated as forcefully as it did. Still further, while acknowledging the intensity and legitimacy of humanitarian impulses, one can say when these are fully acknowledged and given due weight as context, we still lack a sufficient theory. Cruelty was happening in many places, near and far. Why did this particular instance of cruelty against Cubans lead to a war? Most important of all, why did this particular instance and the ensuing war have the aftermath it did? To explain the Spanish-American War we seem to need to add a backdrop of other, more strategic, considerations.

Let us look then for explanations in the wider context of America's situation at the time. Marx had said in the mid-1800s that capitalism has a tendency to implode. His argument was that, as the capitalists economized on labor costs to meet the requirements of their ideology (paying laborers the lowest possible wages in a kind of auction toward the bottom), capitalist enterprise would eventually outproduce the purchasing power of their own society—composed as it was mostly of laborers. At that point, the workers—if there still were any—would be stuffing the warehouses with manufactures and agricultural produce they were too poor to buy. Lacking domestic consumers, the market would collapse from surplus product unless—and here's the heart of the matter—the capitalists could unload the surplus abroad. (Marx presciently wrote of efforts to tear down Chinese walls.)

By the depression of 1893, this problem of surplus was not only being openly discussed by Marxists but by businessmen and politicians all over America—people whose reputations for being "sound" and patriotic were beyond reproach. To be sure, unlike a Marxist, a preponderance of these profit-oriented spokespersons did not focus on a need for a more equitable distribution of purchasing power in America (a concern of William Jennings Bryan and other populists) but rather, as Marx predicted, they focused on a concern to find purchasing power in the hands of non-Americans abroad. Even though we had reached our Pacific shoreline, we continued our tradition of looking westward. Predictably, it was there that we hoped to find that "larger pie" or that "rising tide" which would ensure the continuation of American prosperity.

It's not as if America had never before ventured beyond our western shoreline. We'd long been involved economically with a west beyond the border of our continent, and we'd become even more engaged there in acts of imagination. Secretary of State William Seward had persuaded Congress to purchase Alaska for the United States in 1867—envisioning Alaska as a bridge to Asia. Seward had also ambitioned a reciprocity treaty with the Hawaiian Islands; and this came to pass when, in 1875, a succeeding secretary of state, Hamilton Fish, negotiated a strong pact regarding mutual trade benefits between Hawaii and ourselves—a pact providing an American veto over any Hawaiian plan to cede territory to other countries. It's amid such predispositions we can hope to find what deeper roots there may have been for a war with Spain.

Introducing Turner, Mahan, Brooks Adams, Hay, Theodore Roosevelt, and McKinley

Each of these men was in some way an architect of our intervention against Spain and of the expansion which that intervention served. Without some grasp of the context for that intervention as reflected in their motives, the further development of American foreign policy into the twentieth century and up to the present is likely to be misunderstood. In particular, it seems helpful to identify here in 1898 the characteristic way an American reliance on force slips past us unacknowledged. It's helpful, that is, if we wish to arrive at a realistic understanding of who we are now, and of how we're currently perceived by others.

Let's start with the historian Frederick Jackson Turner. Turner didn't of course cause the closing of the American frontier with which his name is ever associated. And there are American historians who subsequently have argued that his announcement in 1893 of its closing was premature, or that the event was unidentifiable or at least less momentous than he claimed. A more basic criticism is one that questions whether his flattering assessment of the American character is accurate.

Such qualifications notwithstanding, in depression year 1893 Turner framed and explained our general sense of crisis in a way that resonated with prominent policymakers—contributing thereby toward a consensus about our predicament and its resolution. Even if his thesis was somewhat "unhistorical," it was historic—for it functioned to shape our future. The West, he said, had been the horizon of the American people. It was the repository of our hope. It was the cutting edge at which our democratic spirit had been honed. His thesis could be elaborated by a cluster of generally held notions. The West was where one had gone to give oneself a second chance. It was the room in which America's expanding population has been able to find a home, an escape valve for energies that might otherwise have turned rancid. "The Wilderness" had from the beginning provided our setting for The American Story: the story about the mission of God's people to plant God's kingdom here by taming a continent. The West was a storehouse of boundless resources. The challenges it offered had provided us with something we could mobilize against and come together over. It had been both an outlet for American feistiness and a motive for American union. It had been, Turner claimed by way of conclusion, a nurturing ground for the American spirit of independence, a test of manhood, a continuing inspiration for American ingenuity, a breeding ground for raw unspoiled instantiations of democratic spirit, and a source of national pride.

And indeed the popularity of the slogan "Manifest Destiny" demonstrates how central the movement westward was to our sense of identity. Turner saw the closing of the frontier as problematic since he took our westward momentum to be the conserver of our values, providing challenging experiences indispensible to the renewal of American character in each successive generation. This momentum had become indispensible to American coherence, for we could hold together only by moving forward. The urgent implication of his message was that America must find a fresh frontier if it was to go on being America.

Turner wasn't alone in his forebodings and his prescription. Brooks Adams, grandson of John Quincy Adams and great-grandson of John Adams, was—like his articulate and sardonic older brother Henry—convinced America was in trouble. Writing *The Law of Civilization and Decay*, Brooks Adams traced a path similar in some respects to the path suggested in earlier pages here. Adams saw "Imaginative Man"—poet and soldier, deeply motivated by religious conviction—as the builder of civilizations; he saw the success of this type leading dialectically to its own morphing and replacement—leading that is, eventually to the emergence of "Economic Man" as the new type at the center of things. Economic Man arranges everything for the enhancement of Economic Man, reducing his fellows to opportunities and victims in his arrangements. In so doing, he thereby guarantees the decay and collapse of the society that nurtured him. Economic Man is not unlike the protagonist in an Ayn Rand novel—only where Rand casts her protagonist as hero, Adams sees him as harbinger of pending disaster.

Written in Mark Twain's Gilded Age, Adams' account seemed an account that had abundant confirmatory evidence. The thing that marred the account—or at least was off-putting about it— was its easy acquiescence in a form of fatalism. Adams purported to be setting forth immutable laws of history. He'd have it that he was doing science; the pattern set forth was one for which he claimed inevitability. In the backdrop, one can hear echoes of Hegelian, Darwinian, and Marxist determinism. If one has a good ear, one hears the ghost of Calvin.

Were this all Adams had to say on the subject, he couldn't have been among the architects of expansionism. Even Adams himself however found his doctrine dreary beyond bearing; and, for at least a time—and when it counted—he seems to have allowed the possibility that heroic human agency might break free from the doom his theory foretold. Appalled at the vision of its own approaching decay, America could turn and invent itself once again after the model of Imaginative Man. Quickened by something of the religious sensibility of its forefathers, it could draw again from its heritage of poetic and soldierly qualities. (Martin Heidegger's thought takes a similar turn in the twentieth century, leading him into a romantic and uncritical sense of German destiny.) Bolstering such optimism, Adams had discovered an additional law, a kind of mystic blend of Isaac Newton and Frederick Jackson Turner: "civilization moves westward." If our nation could place its interests at the center of that westward movement, and if Americans could place national interest at the center of their individual lives, perhaps America could postpone or even escape the onset of decay.

Brooks Adams' acquaintance with Theodore Roosevelt (with whom Adams maintained an intermittent conversation for more than a decade, and at a time when it could make a difference) probably had much to do with the rejuvenation of Brooks Adams; it likely also had something to do with the phenomenon of Theodore Roosevelt. Specifically, in prescribing that we center ourselves in westward movement, Adams seems to have contributed toward our intervention against Spain and our acquisition (though Adams first opposed our use of force) of the Philippines.

Adams couldn't of course have played such a part were it not that he was giving definition to ideas already vaguely diffused across America. As Roosevelt wouldn't have been popular and able to exercise leadership had he not been representative of much that Americans were already feeling and thinking, so Adams' contributions to Roosevelt's thinking wouldn't have mattered had they occurred outside a generalized context—a spirit of the times—open to plans for expansion. (While it's become the fashion among many to view nations as moving according to supra-personal laws of their own, a less mystical alternative is, I think, to see society as a place shaped by interaction of multiple freedoms and ambitions overlapping and confirming each other.)

A more direct, quasi-physical impact upon policy came from Alfred Thayer Mahan. Mahan was a maverick in a profession that favored ordered and predictable behavior. In the heyday of his naval career he was never promoted beyond captain. Shining through his writing is an almost quaint desire to use language accurately, backed up by an engaging transparency of character. To employ a non-naval metaphor, Mahan marched to his own drum. Perhaps his disinclination toward typical careerist behavior (he seems not to have been a notable ship captain) explains how his mind was free for matters of theory. The paradox is that few American navy men have had more influence on practical matters than this man who seemed disengaged from them.

In Mahan's mental ramblings on the role of the navy in the big picture of America's future, he began at a conventional place. From the start he saw trade as important for America's wellbeing; and the role he first saw for the navy was a defensive one, protecting such trade from predatory action by foreigners. The predatory action could be anything from outright piracy to a long-term effort of some other nation to commandeer trade routes. To discourage such action and protect against it, coast-hugging cruisers, lightly armed, which could move and maneuver quickly, would seem the appropriate instrument.

As he continued to ponder these matters, however, Mahan's thinking developed along a line familiar to military theorists — namely, it embraced the logic that says one defends best who commands an offensive position. Gradually his reflections moved to a specific, but global, question: "Have those states which have been notably successful been possessed of more than ordinary sea power?" Once posed, the question practically answered itself. Though he considered himself more a theorist than an historian, Mahan presented an abundance of data suggesting the correlation between "success" and "sea power" was, in current jargon of statistics, remarkably robust. "Successful" nations turned out to be nations possessing superior sea power. Taking Britain and the British navy as his prime example, this is the case Mahan presented in 1890 in his widely read, much translated, very consequential *The Influence of Sea Power upon History*.

Self-evident as this thesis may seem for the long era before air-power, Mahan's thinking had undergone a notable stretch. His new thinking came to entail the principle that territory far from America's coasts must be secured if America's future was to be secured. While conquest was not an end in itself, control of land was necessary so that America's freighters could be, not just close to places where resources are, but close also to places where markets are. Short of that, America would be at a disadvantage in the great trade fair our globe was becoming. Further, if there were to be great freighters, there must be great battleships to protect them and to maintain the control of harbors and coaling stations—the infrastructure of naval system.

In a masterful paragraph, Warren Zimmermann sums up the vision in which Mahan's thinking culminated:

> For Mahan, there were many reasons why America had to abandon isolationist thinking and look outward: its growing production, public sentiment, a geographic position between two old worlds and two oceans, the growth of European colonies in the Pacific, the rise of Japan, and the peopling of the American West with men favoring a strong foreign policy. He was not a warmonger; in fact he had a highly sophisticated view of how to prevent war through deterrence. Preparing for war, he wrote, will help prevent it. He urged upon the United States a three-pronged naval policy: short-range warships to protect the chief American harbors, an offensive naval force to extend influence outward, and a national resolution that no foreign state should be allowed to acquire a base within three thousand miles of San Francisco. In his writings Mahan was introducing core concepts—deterrence, sufficiency, détente, globalism—that were to return as principles of American policy during the Cold War.[14]

Mahan had come to see in the Monroe Doctrine far more than a mere defense for present American security and influence; he saw it as a template for the future, the source of a forward-leaning strategy, a proclamation of unilateralist intent which could not be deduced as some mere corollary to international law. While it's by no means implicit in international law that the Monroe Doctrine should be reinterpreted as a global agenda, such an agenda was, in Mahan's view, a legitimate American agenda harnessed in the service of a decision for a strong international presence, one which could only be secured by extraordinary unilateralist

14. Warren Zimmerman, *First Great Triumph: How Five Americans Made Their Country a World Power* (New York: Farrar, Straus & Giroux, 2002), 115.

exertion—particularly, that is, by a strong navy. As such, Mahan's vision was irresistible to eventual Under-Secretary of the Navy, Theodore Roosevelt.

Mahan became a highly effective champion of a canal through the Isthmus of Panama, a champion of some form of control over Cuba as the eastern guardian of that canal, a champion for annexation of Hawaii as a westward station from which to protect and service the trade routes which the canal opened, and a champion for retaining ports in the Philippines as a stepping stone and westernmost base for our conduct of trade in Asia. (Mahan eventually joined the consensus position, that Providence had—in spite of ourselves—intended the whole of the Philippines to become our colony.)

As suggested, Mahan's vision owed much to his study of the British Empire. He envisioned however an improved version. He wanted a stripped down, bare-bones-and-muscle version—one which realized the benefits of empire but without its encumbering administrative responsibilities. What makes his vision so significant is that it reached out toward, and brought together, and became a point of convergence for the visions of many Americans—that of Brooks Adams included—and became the vision at the center of the Open Door Policy to be promulgated by John Hay, Roosevelt's secretary of state, after the conclusion of the Spanish-American War. (It is in fact the vision which endures to this day at the center of American foreign policy. Tactical dependence on the navy has somewhat yielded to air-power and rocketry, but the strategic vision is the same.)

Let us speak then of John Hay. In the sixty-six years and some months of his life, undoubtedly the most memorable and intense years were not those when he was secretary of state but those from 1861 to 1865 when, with John Nicolay, Hay served in the White House as one of Abraham Lincoln's two personal secretaries. Those years began when Hay was twenty-two. At that time, he was altogether unfamous, yet he lived in the shadow of Abraham and Mary Todd Lincoln, helped Nicolay manage Lincoln's appointments, penned correspondence in the president's name, romped with Lincoln's children, reluctantly accompanied Mary Todd on some of her manic buying expeditions, and was at the bedside of Lincoln throughout the long night as Lincoln lay dying.

Later, Hay said of Lincoln: "As republicanism…is the sole hope of a sick world, so Lincoln, with all his foibles, is the greatest character since Christ."[15] Hay never got over that encounter. You could say he never recovered from it. Some historians conjecture Hay became a kind of surrogate son to Lincoln, a consolation after the death in the White House of young Willie Lincoln. In Hay's later years, with a long string of accomplishments, well received writings, and illustrious friendships to his resume, it was remarked of Hay that he sometimes seemed inexplicably melancholy. This may have been largely due to temperament. It's plausible though to think some of it was the residue of the momentous four-year episode of his life in his mid-twenties when he was Lincoln's everyday gopher in the titanic struggle to hold the country together.

Hay never again felt so close to a center of absolute ethics as he had in the Lincoln years. The secret at the core of it all was not divulged, and the great task of the Lincoln years remained, as we know, unfinished—in fact, in some crucial aspects, it remained undefined. The reference to "republicanism" indicates the direction of Hay's mind. As Richard Hofstadter has remarked, the death of Lincoln spared Lincoln any participation in what, in the rest of the nineteenth century, evolved out of the republicanism Lincoln had helped bring to birth. Hay was not so spared; and he labored through his remaining four decades to salvage for the nation something of what he'd glimpsed in his youth.

If, as I and others think, the Civil War was primarily concerned with how the West was to be incorporated into the Union, it's useful to remark that Hay's career, initiated with such unique personal involvement in that bloody argument, reached its peak a third of a century later with notes he penned regarding the Far East—a Far East which had by then become in our imaginations the new West.

I've claimed an instructive way to look at the Open Door Policy is to see it as a corollary to the Monroe Doctrine. Like the Monroe Doctrine, it was a policy that enjoyed the tacit approval of England; and like the Monroe Doctrine it ambitioned a sphere

---

15. Zimmerman, *First Great Triumph*, 46.

of influence modeled on the British Empire while avoiding—so at least it intended—the inconveniences of colonialism.

The Monroe Doctrine had said in effect it would be regarded as action unfriendly to the United States if any European power were to attempt to curtail the influence of the United States in the Western Hemisphere.[16] Similarly the Open Door Notes said in effect it would be regarded as action unfriendly to the United States if any power—Japan and Russia included—were to attempt by colonization or spheres-of-influence in China to close markets there to the United States. While couched in diplomatic language (as was the Monroe Doctrine), and while actually encouraged by a British bureaucrat assigned to China, the underlying statement of the Open Door Policy was "Don't attempt to close doors in China to the United States." Moreover, what some foreigners surely discerned as implicit here would in subsequent decades be made explicit by action: that the name of any place in the world could be inserted for "China."[17]

On the surface, this policy may look benign and pro-Chinese. Just as the United States had presented itself as the natural and rightful protector of the nations of Latin America, so now we were stepping forth as the protector of China against the kind of division into colonial sections that Europe was already imposing on much of Africa.

If though one looks at the policy from, say, the position of Japan or Russia (or, for that matter, of China), it can look quite different. When, by the Monroe Doctrine, the United States claimed

---

16. I speak here and elsewhere of the Monroe Doctrine as it has functioned in American foreign policy. As actually written by J.Q. Adams, it is clear the intent was to keep the Western Hemisphere from being Europe's oyster; however, we soon came to interpret it as meaning the Western Hemisphere was America's oyster. (J.Q. was a man of peace, and even when he wrote of Cuba's falling into our hands as a ripe fruit, it now seems clear to me that he envisioned an organic and peaceful development.)

17. In his lecture on "American Diplomacy: 1900–1950," George Kennan correctly states that other nations—including Britain—paid little attention to the Notes when they were first circulated; what he merely glances at, and seems to sell short in some texts is the immense influence the notes had on us, the source country, as providing the framework in which future American policy was formulated.

Latin America as a kind of protectorate, it raised over that vast region an umbrella of hegemony—a vague claim of American sovereignty; it implied that throughout most of half the planet, our word was law.

Let's ruminate on this. Though the claim expressed by the Open Door Notes with regard to China was more nuanced and less strenuous, it wasn't lost on attentive and interested foreign parties that the scope claimed for the Monroe Doctrine was being significantly extended. Our sphere of national concerns had abruptly bulged westward to include the largest country in Asia. Implicitly, as just suggested, the Open Door Notes meant that in the view of us wilderness-conquering Americans, the legitimate and sovereign interests of America were unbounded.

Between the original announcement of the Monroe Doctrine early in the nineteenth century and the publishing and distribution of the Open Door Notes at its end, occurred the Spanish-American War. Without that war and the physical shift in power it achieved, the Open Door Notes would not have been noticed at all. Indeed, they would probably not have been written. So it may seem John Hay is being introduced too early in the story. It may seem he is less an architect of the war than an inheritor of opportunities it provided. Hay was after all across the Atlantic as Ambassador to England (and actually vacationing in the Middle East) at the time the war was coming on.

But this is to think unhistorically. Better to think as Aristotle invites that the end (in the sense of "goal") operates at the beginning. Throughout the early 1890s, at their adjacent homes in Lafayette Square—with Hay's home looking out at the White House—John Hay and Henry Adams were conducting on and off, as referenced earlier, an informal but influential seminar on American foreign policy. This was not what we usually call a conspiracy, for it wasn't clandestine. The ideas they discussed and criticized were the common coin of the realm; many of their sessions were no doubt paralleled by discussions in the barber shops and front parlors of quite ordinary people. But it happened that the attendants at this seminar had more access to the levers of power than most. The logic that emerged eventually as a statement of policy in the Open Door Notes was the logic emerging in this seminar; here, if you will, were mechanics who could manufacture a war with Spain as a means to advance that policy.[18]

What the Notes told the world at large — albeit *sotto voce* — is that we intended the "mission" of the United States to go forward unimpeded; we had banished longtime holdings of the Spanish empire from both hemispheres to show ourselves in earnest. From this larger context we can conclude then, regarding Hay, that — both before it was waged and afterward — this war with Spain had his attention, and that his sense of policy helped bring it about.

Beyond Hay however, our quest to understand why the Spanish-American War happened requires us to fix attention on Theodore Roosevelt. In him the previous strands come together and find a champion. It's not so much that each of these other strategists and planners endorsed Roosevelt (though, in some measure, they did) as that Roosevelt heartily endorsed relevant things from each of them, and took the sum of their work as a platform to be implemented — was the chief mechanic who regarded their aspirations and plans as something to make real.

Roosevelt had been writing his four-volume work *The Winning of the West* when Frederick Jackson Turner first put forth his thesis on the closing of the frontier. Roosevelt recognized immediately

---

18. Today, to elaborate an earlier point, some American historians and policy-makers dismiss, to their discredit, Hay's Notes as trivial and wishy-washy. Even the circumspect and articulate George Kennan seems at times to think the Notes were more in the order of window dressing and decoration than actual engines of policy, not recognizing that his own "containment policy" is the Open Door Policy up-dated and outfitted with a new name. Containment is neither more nor less than the other side of the coin to a policy for keeping the door open; those who would close the door must be contained and isolated; to quarantine them is a logical corollary to maintaining an open door. Equally lacking in insight are historians who say the rest of the world simply dismissed the Notes. It would be more accurate to say the British saw them as one strand in their own policy (one of maintaining Anglo-Saxon dominance in world affairs) while other countries held them at arm's length as something to be regarded with distrust. The hidden agenda of the Notes was never *very* hidden; indeed, to thoughtful people, it was likely transparent.

how Turner's view invited his own expansionism, and he wrote Turner offering enhancing arguments.

With regard to Brooks Adams, the connection has already been mentioned. Adams communicated to Roosevelt something of Adams' own dark sense of urgency (alarming Roosevelt sufficiently that at one point Roosevelt commented: "I wonder if Brooks is not quite mad").

Regarding Alfred Thayer Mahan, the connection with Roosevelt was very direct. Mahan had been impressed by that book Roosevelt wrote as a college student which described the navy's insufficiency in the War of 1812, and Mahan had incorporated Roosevelt's thinking into his own. In 1887 when Mahan was teaching at the Naval War College, he invited Roosevelt to come as a guest to lecture on the War of 1812. A few years later when Mahan published his own foundational work on sea power, Roosevelt strongly complimented Mahan in a letter, and also wrote a glowing review of the book for the *Atlantic Monthly*. Further, on occasions when either Mahan or the existence of the Naval War College seemed in jeopardy, Roosevelt volunteered to run interference. When Mahan was in Washington, he and Roosevelt would meet at the Metropolitan Club or at John Hay's house—where Brooks Adams, Henry Cabot Lodge, and Henry Adams were engaged in their intermittent but unending seminar on America's future.

With regard to John Hay, Roosevelt's connection went back to the days of his childhood. As a boy Roosevelt had been introduced by his father, the senior Theodore Roosevelt, to Hay. John Hay, along with Henry Adams, and Brooks Adams, had all become, from the time Roosevelt arrived in Washington as Civil Service Commissioner in 1889, informal tutors in Roosevelt's ongoing political education. Hay it's true maintained something of Henry Adams' amused detachment at the spectacle of Roosevelt's countless enthusiasms (even as Roosevelt, in private comments in later moments, had a tendency to downgrade Hay as more a dreamer than a man of action like himself). So while both Hay and Adams recognized in Roosevelt an agent more prone to action than they were, they worried—and in Adams' case sometimes complained starkly—about the form the action could take.

For all the currents and cross-currents, when Roosevelt became president after the assassination of McKinley, one of his first acts was to retain Hay as secretary of state. Roosevelt understood the aggressive dimension of Hay's Open Door Notes and kept Hay on as Secretary until, in Roosevelt's second term, Hay became exhausted and died. It's helpful for understanding Roosevelt's connection to Hay to remember it was the calm and sometimes melancholy Hay who referred to the Spanish-American War as "a splendid little war."

At the time the war broke out, Roosevelt was Assistant Secretary of the Navy. While others among the more economically motivated expansionists wondered whether the price of a war over Cuba was too great, Roosevelt—who seems never to have met an expansionist argument he didn't like—regarded the possibility of war as an enticing prospect. War, he thought, was good for people. It set them in motion; and if ever a human maintained equilibrium by moving forward, it was he.

His forward momentum was a trait well understood by those closest to him. During his life it was remarked that while Theodore fulminated and celebrated, his second wife Edith stood by, interested and helpful, but sustained in her own center-of-gravity. She was somehow insulated from being swept off her feet by each new gust. It seems it would've had to be that way if the marriage was to endure; while truly a friend, she was never merely a fan. The same can be said more emphatically for Roosevelt's first daughter, Alice. At once caustic and affectionate (and perhaps more caustic than affectionate), it was she who remarked that her father wished to be "the bride at every wedding, the corpse at every funeral."

Theodore's restlessness had no doubt many personal circumstances that help to explain it. Of more interest is why this restlessness made him so acceptable to America as a leader. He's like Stephen Leacock's knight who "jumped on his horse and rode off in all directions." We noted Henry Adams' misgivings; he spoke of Roosevelt as "pure act" (something like the medieval scholastic concept of God)—but Adams' intent was not particularly complimentary. Like an accomplished lawyer who could make a case for anything, Roosevelt could become a cheerleader for any cause. He performed as one celebrating the achievements of America's big businessmen, and as champion of the need to control them; as ardent seeker after world peace, and as one who could think of no higher exercise of the human spirit than to be engaged in war;

as a great believer in democracy and the equality of humans, and as one who saw nothing wrong with the resolute extermination of Indians in order to provide white men with a larger arena for the exercise of virtue.

Here, in fact, would seem the key to Roosevelt's popularity. Like Americans in general, he did not brood over inconsistencies. He was moving so fast that no keen awareness of inconsistency could overtake him. In this, he served and intensified our aspirations while he allayed our misgivings.

For there were at least two major fault lines in the American psyche. One had to do with the identification of our national mission with the purposes of God. Nothing seemed more natural. Our mission was imposed by God; therefore what served the mission, served God. Debates, newspaper articles, memoirs, sermons, letters, and diaries of the late nineteenth and early twentieth centuries are studded with references (as we still find often enough today) to "mission," "the destiny of America," "the fulfillment of America's promise,"—along with reference to America as "God's Country" and "the land of the free and the home of the brave."

One can say of course, this is a way of speaking. Of what though is it a way of speaking? What have we been talking about? Why could these phrases volley forth, over and over, as so self-evident as to render further discussion unnecessary? How did these phrases get to be "clinchers" in debates regarding national policy? While every society is held together by an ethos of sorts, ours seems to have been suspended in mid-air, held up by nothing more than our fervent say-so. There is latent anxiety in all of this. We protest too much.

The trouble with our Puritan ethos and shared dream of a New Eden in our New World is that, as noted, it immediately generated immense tension in the lives of those dedicated to it. We were, as we continue to be, bible-bearers. In 1899 we founded Gideons International with the purpose of making this book always accessible. Yet much of our activity seemed radically out of step with significant biblical teaching. The book of Job pictures a good man suffering. The weakest and most despised among us can be, the book of Job seems to teach, closer to God than all who criticize and despise him. Again, in the latter part of Isaiah, we find Isaiah describing a "Suffering Servant." The servant is regarded with contempt and cast out; but Isaiah seems to say this weak, vulnerable, and disfigured servant will be, quintessentially, the chosen instrument of God's redeeming love. At least this is the way Isaiah was interpreted in the four Christian gospels. In other places, the prophets had spoken of God's unwavering solicitude for the widow and the orphan, and had proclaimed our treatment of them as the test case of our relation to God. And all this comes to a culmination for Christians in the gospel portrayal of Jesus as the special patron of the poor, the orphaned, the diseased, the Samaritan. The New Testament story is about a man who accepted crucifixion in solidarity with outcasts.

If the purpose of the New Eden was to be a place where the spirit of Jesus would reign, clearly it could not be a place where might makes right. Unless, from its foundation, it was instituted as a place with a tender regard for the weaker party, it could not be anything like the Kingdom of God that Jesus proclaimed. Yet in the New World, who among all was more vulnerable—"savage" gestures and desperate stratagems notwithstanding—than the American Indian?

Unwillingness to entertain this question meant the mission carried forward by our Puritan ancestors could never be the mission they intended—could never be the justifying mission in imitation of Jesus by which they sought to live meaningfully. For all that—or perhaps because of it—there was a desperate need to find in such deeds as were actually being carried out a reassuring manifestation of God's approval. Great awakening followed great awakening. Our need to identify the lives we actually lived with some conception of divine will became the stronger and more compulsive as our brooding sense of our behavior's failure to measure up became more undeniable.

Tension was enhanced when this original fault line in our Puritan legacy was quickened from a second source of values. Perhaps we inherit this too from the Bible; but its more immediate history dates from the Enlightenment—from the thinking that surfaces in Rousseau and Kant, and closer to home, in Adam Smith and Thomas Paine. Here we find shining proclamation of the equality of persons and fervent witness to the unalienability of human rights. If America was to be the city on a hill envisioned by Puritan John Winthrop, it would—in the constituting ambitions of our political founders a century and a half later—achieve this exceptional place only by becoming the world's exemplary society where equality had become palpable and human rights were not only professed but were respected and manifest in the events of daily life.

The reason this enhanced our tensions was that it conflicted directly with our Puritan sense of being an Elect. The divinely endorsed self-aggrandizing of the Puritan was incompatible with the egalitarian ideals to be found in our Declaration of Independence, our Bill of Rights, and some other major amendments to our Constitution. Therefore, Puritan urgencies drew us away from Enlightenment thinking, and when push came to shove, it was routinely our Puritan urgencies that prevailed.

Startling is the degree to which, from the very start, the commitment to equality was diluted and ignored. Ironically and beyond all logic, Enlightenment waters were quickly contaminated by a convenient sense that we who understood human equality so well were, by that very fact, superior to other people. Readily we came to see ourselves as better than those we thought incapable of our inspired insights. This mindset characterized frequently enough the leaders among our best and brightest— those whom we honored as architects and inheritors of Enlightenment thinking. In affirming human equality, we violated it; and the enthusiasms of the Enlightenment were redirected into Puritan channels. Enlightenment came to be regarded as a source of prestige—as a distinction and claim to privilege among the Elect.

So co-option of Enlightenment rhetoric was successful, and the doctrine of the Elect survived advocacy of egalitarianism and secularization. To state the irony as starkly as possible: we Americans were entitled to treat others inhumanely because our sense of humanity was more enlightened than theirs.

It's in embodying this contradiction that Roosevelt strides forth in the 1890s as an ideal leader for the generation of our great-grandparents. In the third volume of *The Winning of the West* Roosevelt tells us:

> The conquest and settlement by the whites of the Indian lands was necessary to the greatness of the race and the well being of civilized mankind.... Such conquests are

sure to come when a masterful people, still in its raw bar-
barian prime, finds itself face to face with a weaker and
wholly alien race which holds a coveted prize in its feeble
grasp.[19]

Note the word "necessary." In it sounds that theme of Mission—of
a divine calling—which resonates through all our history.

That Roosevelt is deliberately thinking in racist terms is made
still more evident from an earlier passage in the same volume:

The most ultimately righteous of all wars is a war with savages, though it is apt to be also the most terrible and inhuman. The rude, fierce settler who drives the savage from
the land lays all civilized mankind under a debt to him.[20]

Here the paradox smacks one in the face. The "most terrible
and inhuman" behavior is entitled to receive praise and honor
from "all civilized mankind."

Even a moment's pause here—as it were to take a breath—
provides the opportunity to wonder how such a dreadful means
can be conducive to such a glorious end. Neither Roosevelt nor
the American people had the appetite for such a pause.

Lest I seem to be wrenching his words out of Roosevelt's context, here's a passage from a page just before the last citation:

Whether the whites won the land by treaty, by armed conflict, or...by a mixture of both, mattered comparatively
little so long as the land was won. It was all-important
that it should be won, for the benefit of civilization and in
the interests of mankind.[21]

All of this is the language of the Elect. It is language poisoned
by the bigotry of the Elect. It coats the poison over with silvery

---

19. Theodore Roosevelt, *The Winning of the West*, vol. 3 (New York: G.P.
Putnam's Sons, 1889), 174–75.

20. Roosevelt, *Winning of the West*, vol. 3, 45.

21. Roosevelt, *Winning of the West*, vol. 3, 44.

phrases from the Enlightenment such as "the benefit of civilization" and "the interests of mankind."

As suggested earlier, war against the Indians required a
demonizing of the Indians if whites were to kill Indians with
a good conscience. Warren Zimmermann, who culled together
the passages cited above, writes of Roosevelt's attitude toward
Indians:

> Roosevelt's picture of Indians was a stereotype of inferior-
> ity. They were "filthy, cruel, lecherous, and faithless," and
> their life was "but a few degrees less meaningless, squalid,
> and ferocious than that of the wild beasts with whom
> they held joint ownership." In describing them, Roosevelt
> habitually used words like ferocious, treacherous, blood-
> thirsty, duplicitous, and skulking.[22]

One thinks of Indian-killers as having the status in Roosevelt's
imagination that we assign to Walter Reed and those other heroes
who drained fever-bearing mosquitoes from the swamps of Cuba
and Central America. Indians were there to be exterminated. (So
too, evidently, were "wild beasts" whom Roosevelt visited other
countries in order to put down by the crate-load.) In celebrating
racism, Roosevelt writes with a purity and eloquence not even
Jefferson could match.

With perfect candor Roosevelt helps us to situate the place the
Spanish-American War had in his thinking. A year after the war,
in a new forward to his four-volume work on the West, Roosevelt
writes:

> The whole western movement of our people was simply
> the most vital part of that great movement of expansion
> which has been the central and all-important feature of
> our history—a feature far more important than any other
> since we became a nation, save only the preservation of
> the Union itself. It was expansion that made us a great
> power.... At bottom the question of expansion in 1898

22. Zimmerman, *First Great Triumph*, 219 (citing Roosevelt, *Winning of
the West*, vol. 2, 147–48).

was simply but a variant of the problem we had to solve at every stage of the great western movement.[23]

Regarding Roosevelt's important, on-the-ground, real-time contribution to the war with Spain, we must look away from his cowboy performance in Cuba to the time immediately preceding when he functioned in Washington as Assistant Secretary of the Navy. There, he was an indefatigable member of the McKinley administration and a vociferous participant in meetings with cabinet members, arguing at every opportunity that there was no alternative to war. He proceeded from at least three mutually-reinforcing premises: (1) the United States needed to expand; (2) War would be good for the character and morale of the American people; and (3) the Spaniards did not deserve an empire.

When the *Maine* exploded, Roosevelt went on public record as certain the Spanish had done it, and questioned the patriotism of those who presented theories to the contrary. When McKinley wavered as to whether war was necessary, Roosevelt was bluntly pro-war to McKinley's face, and was even more blunt, adding sarcasm about McKinley's wavering, behind his back. Of most importance: when his immediate boss John Long took a half-day off on Friday afternoon, February 25, 1898, Roosevelt sent a cable to Hong Kong to his crony Commodore Dewey that included the words: "In the event of declaration of war Spain, your duty will be...offensive operations in Philippine Islands." This was a startling usurpation of power on Roosevelt's part. That this cable was not countermanded by McKinley when he caught wind of it is instructive. The act had a rash character; but the mindset behind it had to have been generally shared, had to be within the bounds of the consensus that was forming.

So, finally, we must turn to McKinley to see how the consensus forming at that time led finally to war with Spain. McKinley has sometimes been seen as weak and vacillating. When he's viewed from a distance, this appraisal can appear plausible. Viewed closer up, he comes across more positively. Career politicians who dealt with him at close quarters seem mostly to have found him kind and straightforward. He seems not to have been inclined

---

23. Roosevelt, *Winning of the West*, vol. 2, xxxiv–xxxv.

to nurture grievances, and in the tumbling free-for-all of Ohio politics, those who were his rivals at one turn often emerged as friends at the next. He was conscientiously devoted to American prosperity, and throughout most of his official career tried to promote it by promoting high tariffs. The booster spirit Sinclair Lewis would later portray in his character Babbitt seems to have come naturally to McKinley, but in McKinley's case it seems it was free from pettiness. Perhaps he left the more sordid details of backroom deals to his self-designated manager Mark Hanna. It can be reckoned a part of his constancy that, in his pursuit of prosperity for the nation, he'd always aligned himself with the business class and had kept its interests at the fore of his attention as he wended his way through the complexities of foreign policy. For just this reason, promotion of business can't fairly be charged against him as a hidden agenda. In matters of personality, he was attentive to his invalid wife, and seems to have been unburdened by narcissism or undo sensitivity. It may be that from the start of his career he'd spontaneously and genuinely thought of himself as a mediator, a smoother of ruffled feelings, a builder of consensus. This might help explain why rivals did not often turn themselves into enemies. This was so predictable that even in defeat he seemed to float upward. Having acquitted himself bravely and with distinction in the Civil War, he'd seen the carnage of war and had conceived a visceral repugnance for it. Humane feeling figured in his rhetoric about Cubans, and there's no reason to doubt the concern he expressed for them was authentic. A man whose life was guided by uncriticized platitudes, in the inner circle of officials forming policy prior to the war with Spain, he may well have been the least (explicitly anyway) ideological and dogmatic. Later, as he lay wounded from a bullet he'd received while trying to shake hands with his assassin, he's reported to have said of him: "Poor man; I'm sure he had no idea what he was doing."

In most of the three months and some days in 1898 that led to his April 11 request for a declaration of war, McKinley should be called consistent rather than vacillating in his desire to find a peaceful end to the turmoil in Cuba. If he can nonetheless be seen as vacillating during those days, the vacillation was more about means than purposes. Could the U.S. buy Cuba from Spain? If so, let that be the end of the crisis. Could the U.S.

intimidate Spain into granting Cuba a kind of autonomy (similar to that for instance which the British were in the process of granting Canada)? If so, let that be the end. Could the Cuban insurgents against Spain prevail in battle and win their independence? If so, well then, more power to them—though here there were to be sure reservations and forebodings among his advisors and within the business community, and these probably entered into his calculus.

The trouble for McKinley was that each of these courses seemed a dead end. That may not actually have been the case; but this probably was the way McKinley saw things. The Spanish government, fragile in Spain itself, was unwilling to enter negotiations for the sale of its colony, knowing how unpopular such a sale would be in Madrid and among the Spanish people. Secondly, "autonomy," while it had all the nice-sounding attractions of a compromise, was not actually acceptable either to the Spanish government or to the Cuban revolutionaries. It was unacceptable to the Spanish government for the same reason the sale of Cuba was: the home front—including the military—wouldn't abide it. But—at least by the start of 1898—it was unacceptable also to the Cuban revolutionaries: their sufferings had led them past the point where they could regard even the best of reconciliations with Spain as tolerable; independence had become the goal that held them together as a revolutionary force. Further, to tell the truth, we weren't ourselves sure how we would adjust to autonomy. Finally, leaving the Cubans to win independence on their own didn't seem a realistic policy. Weak as Spain was, it had dedicated over two hundred thousand Spanish soldiers to suppressing the Cuban insurrection. It had suppressed Cuban insurrections before. Perhaps Spain had the power and quite possibly the will to annihilate all Cubans who opposed it sooner than grant Cuban independence. And, anyway, were Cubans really ready for Cuban independence? And were we?

Along such lines, one more gambit, short of all-out war, seemed open to an American administration burdened by genuine concern for the Cuban people. This was to play a part similar to the part France had played in the American Revolution. The United States could recognize the Cuban revolutionaries as the legitimate government of Cuba, and then do what it could as an ally to protect that government.

Perhaps this kind of tightrope walking could have worked; but in fact it was probably the least discussed of the options available. Not only was there a high likelihood it would provoke a conflict with Spain rather than avoid it, but—more importantly—this option didn't fit the prevailing ethos of the American expansionist movement. It was outside the architecture of American political thought. The Monroe Doctrine wasn't a principle of international law; it was, as clarified by Mahan's advocacy of a strong navy, a proclamation of American intention—saying in effect America's word was law in the western hemisphere. While Spain's hold on Cuba had been, one might say, "grandfathered" into the American proclamation, clearly the writ permitting that unruly exception was running out. It was widely felt it was time for America to take Spain in hand. Further, had the United States enrolled itself merely as the ally of a Cuban struggle for independence, the tactical consequences would have been unacceptable to American policy-makers and military leaders. Our military maneuvers would have needed to coordinate with, and be subject to, initiatives of Cuban revolutionaries whom we knew very imperfectly—persons whose motives were anything but transparent to us. These were "untried" leaders, often squabbling among themselves. For all we knew, some were quite hostile to our ever-expanding participation in Cuba's economy. For tactical as well as strategic reasons therefore, one can assume this particular alternative had few backers in Washington.

I've argued that McKinley's vacillations concerned means to avoid war. Even in most of March 1898 (following the explosion of the *Maine* in February), McKinley seems to have been consistent rather than vacillating in his search for a peaceful resolution; it's only when the moment arrives when he's convinced that things he does want can't be obtained without the war he doesn't want, that he yields.

And only at that point, when he came to see war as inevitable, does it seem the real vacillation of McKinley came front and center. It wasn't clear, even by the time McKinley requested war on April 11, what kind of Cuba he envisioned as the outcome of the war. He requested war because he became convinced it was necessary for his larger plans regarding American commerce abroad, and because he had been persuaded by Elihu Root and others that if he did not request it, his administration would fall apart.

Probably he hadn't decided what he intended for the future of Cuba. On the surface at least, he left the matter to Congress. With its Teller Amendment (foreswearing annexation of Cuba), Congress attempted to clarify American intentions as it declared war. Even then, the matter remained ambiguous. (One can see why some Cubans have said with sardonic humor that Cuba lost the war for independence not to Spain, as some feared it would, but to the United States, as all Cubans should have feared it would.)

Regarding McKinley's decision to ask for war, a fair summary statement is Warren Zimmermann's: "McKinley was driven by inertia rather than design." The inertia, to be sure, wasn't that of immobility but of Newtonian forward momentum. While Hearst and (to a lesser extent) Pulitzer, and the *Maine*, and humanitarian sensibility are not by themselves sufficient to explain the decision for war, nonetheless when these are seen as forces drawn up into the groundswell of American expansionism, the war acquires an aspect of inevitability. While the expansionism itself was, one ought to conclude, a product of our collective freedom as people enjoying a form of self-rule, we preferred to see the matter differently. The war came to seem unavoidable as a step toward implementation of a destiny somehow imposed upon us. In this context as mentioned, McKinley came to feel—as both Henry Cabot Lodge and Elihu Root had warned him and as Roosevelt had relentlessly insisted—that if he wanted to maintain a measure of control over events (if, that is, he didn't want to lose all public support and all confidence in his administration and in its plans to rescue our economy through an expansion of trade), he would have to opt for war.

In retrospect, both the critics of the decision and the defenders of the decision have tended to emphasize its novelty. I think they would do better to notice how unoriginal it was—how totally in keeping it was (as Theodore Roosevelt claimed) with the overall flow and momentum of American history. That we maintained this momentum in denial that it was we who were maintaining it was, we should notice, something that reinforced our continuity with our Puritan past. Manifest Destiny made us do it.

In the case of our Indian wars, it's true we'd had on our side a kind of legal fiction in international law. This helped us feel our forward march was in the path of justice. Jefferson, for instance, had bought the Louisiana Territory from Napoleon; therefore Indians who encumbered that territory and interfered with our plans for its development could be seen as infringing on our rights; they could, in effect, be cited as "trespassers." In the case of Cuba, we lacked that legal cover.

Yet even a moment's reflection on the Indian case must reveal how shallow that cover was. When, in the case of Cuba, we couldn't claim even that legitimacy, the Monroe Doctrine supplied the lack. Here too though the stubborn problem remained. Neither could kingly grants nor could Monroe Doctrine really serve to anchor our policy. An axiomatic conviction, expressed eventually in that slogan "manifest destiny," had been operating all along. It was our ethereal sense of privileged assignment—our sense of a divinely-directed mission—that gave the Monroe Doctrine its authority in our eyes. The mere fact Cuba (unlike, say, California) was not contiguous land was hardly a sufficient reason to require, beyond such exalted doctrine and destiny, any further invention of legal principle.

Thus did Cuba, in the anticipation of the war, and in the course of it, and in its aftermath, become, unofficially, something analogous to an American state. While the Teller Amendment had renounced annexation, the Platt Amendment (which declared an American right to intervene in Cuban affairs) effectively countered the sovereignty the Teller Amendment seemingly guaranteed. We mandated that the Platt Amendment be recognized in the Cuban constitution. The amendment provided to our federal government a veto power analogous to the power our federal government has exercised over our states (especially since the end of the Civil War)—a federal power, that is, to annul or restrict state laws when it finds them in conflict with American federal law and purpose. Garry Wills examines this evolution of federal supremacy in his work on the Gettysburg Address.[24]

---

24. Garry Wills, *Lincoln at Gettysburg: The Words that Remade America* (New York: Simon & Schuster, 1992). The special relationship thereby established with Cuba goes a long way toward explaining something that can be puzzling to non-Americans: the outrage felt by many Americans over the seizure of power in Cuba by Fidel Castro—a man who surprised us by resolutely turning his back on Washington. Many an American has felt toward Castro something similar to what the typical northerner may have felt toward Jefferson Davis at the outbreak of the Civil War.

In coming so far, we've surveyed the complex motivations for the Spanish-American War. What remains for further discussion is examination of what motives led to the annexation of the Philippines.

Here too let me suggest there's less mystery than meets the eye. If one is asking simply why the seizure of the Philippines got "added" to our effort to establish stability on the island of Cuba, the problem may appear beyond solution. But the wrong question has been asked. The Philippines was never just an add-on. It was, from before the war with Spain, a key piece in the scaffolding of our strategy.

That Roosevelt was not countermanded in his Friday telegram to Dewey is a clue. Unlikely as it seems, from early in McKinley's first term there had been lengthy afternoon carriage-rides of President McKinley with his irrepressible and insubordinate young Assistant Secretary of the Navy, Theodore Roosevelt. What did they talk about? It's likely they talked about Manila among other things. They talked of Mahan's grand scheme, in which America could not thrive without foreign trade (foreign trade being, as noted, a subject McKinley had concerned himself with throughout his whole career); and it seems likely, at Roosevelt's instigation, they talked of how, in accord with Mahan's scheme, trade required (1) pacification of Cuba, (2) a canal through the Isthmus, (3) annexation of Hawaii, and (4) possession of a far-east port like Manila.

We've noted it was the lure of Chinese markets (and our wish to settle the Cuban issue quickly so we could address this "larger" issue) that generated urgency and impatience in the last days of

---

Castro, they have felt, is a secessionist and impostor, a violator of American sovereignty—one whose usurpation should not stand. This in turn helps explain, among other things, the extreme animosity toward John F. Kennedy—the sense in fact of sacrilege—felt by some in America's high command and in the CIA over Kennedy's alleged failure, first during the Bay of Pigs Fiasco and then during the Cuban Missile Crisis, to reaffirm our traditional jurisdiction where Cuba was concerned. Kennedy, they would have it, was the un-Lincoln—was in fact a traitor who let secession go forward. (James Douglass among others has regarded this high-level outrage at Kennedy—who had seemed in his campaign to promise he would do something about Castro—as an important factor in motivating the assassination of Kennedy.)

our negotiations with Spain, and that led McKinley finally to terminate discussion and issue an ultimatum that led to war.

Once we'd terminated Spain's military hold on the Philippines, the expansionists (Roosevelt, Mahan, Hay, McKinley, etc.) could ask critics in America who opposed them (critics sometimes called "anti-imperialists") what was to be done with the Philippines other than to hang onto it. The anti-imperialists had no good answer. We seemed to have a hot potato in hand. Were we to drop the potato and run, it seemed there would be massive confusion and lethal civil unrest in the Philippines; and it seemed likely the islanders would soon become the victims of new European powers and/or Japan. We'd shattered what order there'd been for the people of the Philippines, and the responsible thing was to remain and do what we could to establish new order in its place.

But to have framed the discussion this way seems to have been to pretend the acquisition of the Philippines was accidental—was something that happened to us. It takes up the annexation after the fact, which as I've said above is a mistake. Granted soon after in the early 1900s, the Philippines and our urgent desire to maintain and increase our share in the "China market" slackened some; yet it's in just such matters that time, with its shifting frames of reference, can trick us. In 1898 the desire to take the Philippines and hold it can't accurately be judged to have been a minor concern. That would be to ignore history as it was being made, and to note it only as it settles into a fixed place in the past.

McKinley may have given a group of Methodist clergymen to understand the Philippines had fallen into our lap from heaven, but that's not how it happened; an administration is more than one man. What happened is that within a week of our declaration of war, Commodore Dewey (acting in accord with Roosevelt's pre-war telegram) entered Manila Bay and altogether destroyed the Spanish fleet. This was no act of God or gods. Though we subsequently came to regard our acquisition as something of a liability, the logic of our program in 1898 seemed to require this acquisition. Without it, the Open Door Policy (which, as I argue, has provided us with our sense of what we're about ever since) would most likely never have become the charter for American foreign policy it did. The assertion of a right to an open avenue of trade with China would have been abstract and meaningless had we not been fore-positioned in the Philippines to exercise it.

If anywhere, it is in the Philippines that our reliance on naked force for the achievement of our "destiny" should have become evident. Many Filipinos simply did not acquiesce in our assertion that we were their new masters. Yet it wasn't possible to portray the local freedom-fighter Emilio Aguinaldo, and the *insurrectos* whom he led, as aggressors against the people of the United States. With some pushing and pulling and blinking, we'd managed to do that with American Indians—had done it with the likes of John Ross, Sitting Bull and Chief Joseph. Here though the vast geographical separation of the two peoples left that psychological maneuver out of bounds. Instead, the whole context had to be reconfigured mentally (and without aid of some manifest geometric rectangularity to feed our imaginations) to make our cruel war against Filipinos palatable.

The new configuration in our thinking was along these lines: "Here are us Americans—selflessly attempting to provide the Filipinos with a share of those blessings with which God has abundantly blessed us. In their benighted and un-Christianized [!] state however, many of the Filipinos lack the wisdom to grasp the motives that inspire us. Unfortunately therefore it's necessary to fight a goodly number of Filipinos to the death—until such time as a majority of the survivors come to see the light. At that point, we can begin to treat Filipinos as a people possessing all those rights of human beings which our traditional values require us to respect."

For all that, not surprisingly, our government preferred not to be too explicit regarding the particulars of what was taking place.

Five years after we'd managed in 1901 to capture our former ally Aguinaldo through a pretense of having been captured by his troops, and long after Roosevelt's proclamation of general amnesty in 1902 that was supposed to end hostilities, there was under General Leonard Wood (buddy of T.R. during the campaign in Cuba) a massacre of roughly 600 Moro Filipinos. These were Muslims, and it was thought, because of their recalcitrant ways, to be a kind of economy of energy to kill them all when the opportunity presented itself. That's what the American soldiers under Wood's command did.

We're told in the official report to Washington that every man, woman, and child of these Moro villagers, trapped in the crater of a volcano to which they'd fled, was killed by Wood's well-armed American troops shooting from the crater's rim.

On Monday, March 12, 1906, three days after reports of this incident had been published in American newspapers, Mark Twain attempted to dictate a satirical reaction to it. He resumed the effort two days later on March 14. One can say of this writing endeavor that it was one of those rare occasions when Twain's voice deserted him. Later in the year when Twain was marking writings for inclusion in his autobiography, excerpts of which were being published in the *North American Review*, he marked this dictated material on the Philippines "not usable yet."

Twain's problem was he couldn't maintain the satirical distance which might have made the piece work. He gave it his best shot, speaking with mocking praise of "the brilliancy of the victory" and referencing the official report as registering the "heroism" and "gallantry" of our troops as they murdered the helpless Moros. But Twain was altogether unable to harness his despondency and outrage into a disciplined work of satire. When he remarked on a commendation of the incident by President Roosevelt, Twain bluntly said:

> His whole utterance is merely a convention. Not a word of what he said came out of his heart. He knew perfectly well that to pen six hundred helpless and weaponless savages in a hole like rats in a trap and massacre them in detail during a stretch of a day and a half, from a safe position on the heights above, was no brilliant feat of arms—and would not have been a brilliant feat of arms even if Christian America, represented by its salaried soldiers, had shot them down with bibles and the Golden Rule instead of bullets.[25]

---

25. Mark Twain, *The Autobiography of Mark Twain, Vol. 1* (Berkeley: University of California Press, 2010), 405.

You can hear Twain reaching back toward a tone of irony as he approaches the end of that long third sentence; but it's too late. His temper is already lost, and the piece has simply the flat character of a white-hot denunciation. The gross necrophilia of TR is too much for Twain's stomach. A further two days later, recounting a going-away party of the previous day for his friend George Harvey, Twain remarks how all the guests were condemning the behavior of Wood and company. Twain comments:

> Harvey said he believed that the shock and shame of this episode would eat down deeper and deeper into the hearts of the nation and fester there and produce results. He believed it would destroy the Republican party and President Roosevelt. I cannot believe that the prediction will come true, for the reason that prophesies which promise valuable things, desirable things, good things, worthy things, never come true. Prophecies of this kind are like wars fought in a good cause—they are so rare that they don't count.[26]

Again, one can see Twain reach for wit and irony, but the character of the whole is bleak anger.

One can imagine history teachers encouraging their students to write essays about heroic Patriots holding off the British at Bunker (or Breed's) Hill. One can't imagine any history teacher ever inviting students to write essays about how we heroically killed Philippine Moros in 1906. (Surely no teacher has ever given such an assignment; instead the incident has been let gently disappear from The American Story and from American memory.)

The question those insisting on annexation asked anti-imperialists in 1899 and 1900 was: "How do you propose we handle with honor our current predicament of being the only source of order in the Philippines today?"

It was, again, the wrong question. It's like the fellow whose loving and trusting wife has found him in a compromising relation to another woman. Suppose he asks you, his friend, how he's

---

26. Twain, *Autobiography*, 407.

to extricate himself from the situation with honor. The error of the question is that it presupposes there's a way to come out of such a situation with honor.

There was no answer to the question about the Philippines once the question was so framed. The condition we were in was dishonorable. To treat it subsequently as something destiny had dropped on us from the sky (as even the realist Mahan tried to do) was simply to compound our guilt by adding denial. It was quite in the Puritan mold: we don't do things; God does them through us.

Honor would have been not to present ourselves as a conqueror in the first place. Once we'd compromised ourselves thus, it wasn't incumbent upon those who'd opposed the project to come up with an honorable way out.[27]

There was no honor in staying; and there was no honor in leaving. We should simply have extricated ourselves. An apology might have helped.[28]

The argument that we felt Filipinos were not ready to govern themselves should have had no traction. There were people all over the world whom we felt were not ready to govern themselves (as there continue to be to the present moment). And the argument that "if we don't rule the Filipinos, some other power will," seems specious too — even if touched by realism. For if, as

---

27. Brooks Adams became so confused on this point that even though he'd opposed the conquest, regarding annexation as the wrong way to expand, he nonetheless reversed himself once the Filipinos engaged in lethal resistance, saying, "Now our honor requires that we fight them to the finish.")

28. While Roosevelt lusted for the Philippines and acted coolly and cruelly toward Filipinos, the portly presence of William Howard Taft as a benign administrator there in the opening years of the twentieth century provided some Filipinos a cushion against the sense of being oppressed. A generation later a romantic with an off-the-scale ego to rival Roosevelt's, Douglas MacArthur (perhaps in an effort to expiate the cruelty towards Filipinos of his own father) seems to have forged a lifelong bond with the Phillipine people which went far toward assuaging the insult of annexation. Whatever the faults of this later man, clearly he had gifts of intelligence and empathy that exceeded Roosevelt's.

it pretends, the argument looks to the interest of Filipinos, surely that was their risk to take. Had they wished to dodge that risk, they could have invited us to protect them. Their fierce resistance showed they did not so wish. If the argument for annexation looked to *our* interest (and this is where the real argument resided), its premise was that we were entitled—at whatever cost to others—to do whatever we thought would secure us advantages or protect us from disadvantages. On such a pretext, all men can become robbers.

Conclusion Of Discussion On Force

My purpose in this survey focusing on four uses of force (against the Cherokee, Mexicans, Plains Indians, and, lastly, against—or to the disadvantage of—former subjects of Spain) has been an attempt at demonstrating how our uses of force are typically invisible to us. We tend to think all our wars have been defensive, or at least humanitarian. Thus, when the internal logic of capitalism ("pay the laborer as little as possible") began to contract our market, and we began to feel a more urgent need for markets abroad, we simultaneously came to feel that anyone in the world who didn't serve as a means for advancing that purpose of ours was, by that fact, a self-designated enemy—deserving whatever retribution we saw fit to mete out. Such people were no more than obstacles to a rightful ordering of the planet. For the sake of order, we would punish and incapacitate them. Repugnant as the task might be, God or destiny had assigned it. Once those others submitted, they could begin to participate in the benefits of the order we were establishing. History would justify us.

The special convenience of the "Open Door" is that its humanitarian aura was ideal for blinding us to the brute force required by our method. We said we wished only to set in place the rightful rules of the road. We wished only to take our place among the nations of the world—to stake out, among the peoples of the world, our place in the sun. We wished to be a city on a hill, and to exercise from there our God-given right to compete on equal terms for the opportunities and riches the world had to offer.

Doing so, we would be a beacon of light to all, and humankind's last best hope.[29]

Lest it seem I've gratuitously ascribed to the Spanish-American War a selfishness and racism which weren't really a part of the picture, it might be helpful to grant the last word to Senator Albert Beveridge. While his was not the only voice in the long debate over acquisition of the Philippines, his was a voice of the party that prevailed. On January 9, 1900, speaking in favor of the majority consensus in the Senate, Senator Beveridge proclaimed:

> Mr. President: the times call for candor. The Philippines are ours forever.... And just beyond the Philippines are China's illimitable markets. We will not retreat from either....We will not renounce our part in the mission of our race, trustee, under God, of the civilization of the world....The Pacific is our ocean....Where shall we turn for consumers of our surplus? Geography answers the question. China is our natural customer....The Philippines give us a base at the door of all the East....My own belief is that there is not 100 men among them [the Filipinos] who comprehend what Anglo-Saxon self-government even means, and there are over 5,000,000 people to be governed. It has been charged that our conduct of the war has been cruel. Senators, it has been the reverse....Senators must remember that we are not dealing with Americans or Europeans. We are dealing with Orientals.[30]

---

29. Surely this kind of Puritan acquisitiveness proceeding under the umbrella of Enlightenment rhetoric has only grown in the century and more since the Spanish American War, and is very much with us today— relying on ever more lethal technology, and ever more sophisticated means of monitoring and intruding, to smooth its path.

30. Quoted in Howard Zinn, *A People's History of the United States* (New York: HarperPerennial Modern Classics, 2005), 313–14.

4 | The Sense That Nature Can Take Whatever We Dish Out

We've looked at signs of accelerating incoherence with regard to disinvestment in education, with regard to ascendant greed and growing inequality in our accumulation and distribution of wealth, and with regard to our increasing reliance on force to serve an expanding mission. Let's now turn our attention to our treatment of nature.

As Americans we hold as a generalized truth that humans can't fundamentally harm nature. The belief must be deeply rooted; it seems more an axiom than a conclusion drawn from observation and experiment. If we position ourselves as a mere observer, we see for instance that a major deforestation has occurred across North America. We see that cod fishing has fallen off along the northeastern United States. Along the northwest, we see that salmon are going the way of cod.

If we look to lumberjacks and fishermen however, we find a curious response. At least until very recently, they've been less likely to complain that their fathers and grandfathers have cut down too many trees or caught too many fish than they have been to complain of government regulations that are meant to restrain them from acting as their fathers and grandfathers did.

In the midst of their complaints, they've been likely to call themselves "conservatives." What they've wanted to conserve is a lifestyle, and as seems clear, the attitudes that would preserve this lifestyle have deep roots. It's a lifestyle of freedom—one in which one has generally felt free to engage nature without inhibiting restraints from government. If our lumberjacking activities were making a profit, we were doing God's work. Let us be honest here. This lifestyle has tasted good, and these complaining lumberjacks and fishermen are genuinely engaged in trying to continue it and pass it on. So their claim to be conservatives is not unintelligible.

This is so true, that those who wish, instead, to conserve the actual trees and cod and salmon have had to move over and call themselves by a different name. They call themselves "conservationists." There are few things conservatives are more likely to find pesky and not worth saving than conservationists.

If we consider, say, the case of salmon, we can anticipate how the position of the conservative plays out. As the salmon become fewer, the demand for salmon either remains steady, or quite possibly rises. This means that as salmon become harder to find, and the supply dwindles, the price of each catch increases. As the supply dwindles, so presumably do the suppliers—at least over time. But the incentive for true stalwarts to continue fishing for salmon—if left unharnessed by government regulation and fines—can hold steady or even rise as a function of the increasing scarcity and rising price of salmon. I call them "stalwarts" because the expenditure of labor per salmon increases.

Those who catch the last salmon are likely to find those salmon command a higher price than any salmon ancestors in history. Because of this, the run towards extinction may in fact accelerate as extinction approaches. In the real world of course, the actual end of the industry probably won't be reached with a "last salmon" but rather at a point when there are so few salmon left, and the trouble of finding them is so considerable, that only demented billionaires will be able to pay for what a continuation of salmon fishing would cost, and they too will pass. (Also, there may be a critical mass necessary for salmon to continue to breed, and when the number of salmon fall below that, they may go extinct. Further, to be sure, the insult of our industrial wastes to the nurturing seas may render the seas no longer fit for salmon.)

What we observe among fishermen and lumberjacks still caught up in this economy—and here we can, for good measure, throw in oil-personnel with regard to petroleum products—is that most aren't much interested in contemplating some imaginable extinction point down the road. Rather they focus on the very real trees, fish, and oil still out there waiting to be "harvested."[1]

If, for all that, one insists on engaging in an argument with these enthusiasts for full utilization of forest, fish, and geology, and insists of pushing this process of depletion in a mental experiment to its predictable conclusion, the conservative fishermen, lumberjacks, and oil producers aren't bereft of all response. Those among them given to theoretical thinking may respond that once the resources run out, there awaits in nature a malleability and provision for substitution that's limited only by the imagination and ingenuity of humans. If Africans hunt elephants to extinction for the sake of their ivory, well, that's no big deal. We will find a substitute for ivory. We will engineer from nature an "ivory" far better than any "raw" ivory nature has provided on its own. If the polar ice caps melt, and take the polar bears and penguins with them, well, we will create in air-conditioned studios animations of bears and penguins more engaging for our children than any bear or penguin behaviors we or our parents ever observed. Likewise, if we deplete our fishing waters of salmon, we will create "salmon meat," pinked over by the magic of science, every bit as tasty as the antiquated salmon that delighted the palates of ancestors; and because we will control the process from start to finish, this new salmon will be easier to harvest. We can't lose for winning. And of course, if petroleum products ever *really* run out, we can always go solar.

As I say, such optimism roots itself in a sense of the indestructibility and infinite plasticity of nature. Our easy taking for granted here betokens our confidence that this mistress we take for granted won't run out on us. Our complacency about Mother Earth is firmed up in part by our observation of the miracles of

---

1. People in petrol-industry in particular try to tamp down any alternative developments of energy while they engage in increasingly desperate captures of petroleum resources; they seem haunted by a fear that access to alternatives, coupled with public concern over climate change, may bring their enterprises to a premature and untimely end. They seem to be genuinely in the grip of a conviction it would be a crime against nature if their industry were tapered toward a shut down before the last accessible petroleum was converted to carbon dioxide.

the industrial revolution. And anyway, aren't people living longer than ever? Who says Progress is a myth?

Let's concede this sense is not peculiar to Americans but is to be found today among entrepreneurs all around the world. It's around the world however partly because we've exported it there.

I'm inclined to look back beyond steamships, and skyscrapers, and computers in search of a basis for our easy complacency. As Americans, we may tend to think we're too practical to owe much to philosophy. I've argued however that ideological convictions are often more powerful when we don't reflect on them. Some claim to find our attitude toward nature rooted in the Bible. In the Bible however (if only we can stop quoting it long enough to read it thoughtfully) we will find notions of human dominance of nature tempered significantly by notions that nature is precious and that we are meant to care for it and learn from it. Francis Bacon, with his ambition as it were to put nature on the rack and tear from her her secrets, seems a closer-to-hand and less ambiguous source for that attitude toward nature we find embedded among us.

In the generation after Bacon came Descartes. If Descartes was not the sole source of "Cartesian dualism" (the dualism of Descartes), he was at least a highly persuasive promulgator of it. Descartes saw us humans as containing souls (genuine instances of an immaterial principle), and was inclined to think everything else on the face of the earth was soulless. We are spirit and therefore immortal, he insisted; but he seemed ready to posit the rest of the world was sheer matter (sheer stuff extended in space and time, lacking any dimension of subjectivity or consciousness). Compensating for such radical emptiness in matter (the *en soi* that Sartre portrays as nauseating) was its endless pliability. In the footsteps of the Greek originator of atomic theory, Democritus, and in company with Galileo, Descartes affirmed that matter was without color, sound, scent, or taste. These traits, he taught, were mere creatures of our consciousness, products of our way of sensing and thinking.

The world-devaluing scope of Descartes' conception may take a moment to sink in. Even in the case of animals—your pet dog or cat, the dolphins, the bonobos—Descartes seemed to doubt there was any actual interiority, any capacity for sensation, much less any capacity for affection or decision-making.

In the fifth part of his *Discourse on Method*, he floats the notion that if God designed "automata" (we would say "robots") having all the operations we observe in a monkey, we humans would not know these monkeys were mere machines. He finds it plausible to think the whole animal world may be a clever array of interacting machines. He could thereby strategically eliminate a "middle case" that would otherwise have blurred his system's neat dualism; for if a tiger had a "tiger soul," it would seem it must have a tiger-immortality to match—souls being, in Descartes' conception, incorruptible; and similar consequences would follow for snails and cockroaches. To populate heaven with the souls of dead tigers, snails, and cockroaches seemed unimaginable. Cartesian tidiness invited the conclusion that tigers feel nothing at all. Why complicate things by positing an "inner tiger" beneath the fur? Why not settle for mere levers, pulleys, and connectors?

John Locke, while criticizing Descartes' rationalism, accepted Descartes' dualism with its denatured nature—colorless, soundless, tasteless, and odorless. Locke declared material substance an "ignotum x"—and passed on Descartes' impoverishing dualism to those who were colonizing America.

If we contrast this approach with the approach of American Indians, and with the approach of almost all our own non-Indian ancestors, we get some sense of how original and radical it is—indeed, how idiosyncratic and surgical. Yet Descartes' soulless animal seems a comfortable premise for the factory farming whereby we supply our tables with meat today. And Cartesian Dualism may supply a clue when we try to understand the ease with which we slip into spectator mode as we watch so many species approach the threshold of extinction and see others cross the threshold and glide irretrievably into extinction by reason of our habits of encroachment and consumption.

In humble mode people will say: "Humans are too puny to have any real impact on nature." This is said though the loss and threat of loss of species is empirically evident everywhere. What perhaps enables our indifference to the endangered species list is an underlying sense that the loss of one or another contrived automaton is no big deal. In the magnitude of our humility we believe we can engineer other automata to replace whatever we do in.

Cartesian impoverishment of nature opens the door to a kind of Baconian utilitarianism that situates all things in the service of our need and wants. Nature, it conceives, is neither more nor less than a storehouse of resources for us to dispose of. The value of things other than ourselves is their value to us as consumables. What's the point, we come to ask ourselves, of elephants? Unless we can eat them, or ride and tame them to our service, or clothe ourselves with their skins, entertain ourselves by watching them, or make figurines from their tusks, they have no point at all.

Still, some may reply: "Why blame us Americans? The world at large thinks this way." This is true; and it seems increasingly the case. Let's concede that Cartesianism—and the industrial revolution that hitched its wagon to it—did not begin on American soil. It is however in our interest to discover why a uniquely thoroughgoing, spontaneous, and uncriticized form of optimism about the plasticity and pliability of nature has so captured our hearts and found among us its purest expression. The question opens a realm for speculation comparatively new; one ventures into such relatively unexplored territory at one's risk.

Puritans and Nature

Fortified with awareness how speculative this is, let me offer three topics toward providing some kind of answer. I begin with the apparent vastness of our continent when our Puritan forefathers first came to settle it. My second topic is the Christian tendency—particularly as Christianity was taken up by Puritans—to observe nature through the lens of sacred scripture. And my third topic, which is something of an outcome of the first and second, is the Puritan tendency, which came to be incorporated into our national consciousness, to see the continent as an unredeemed wilderness.

We begin with the vastness of the American continent. The following speculations seem plausible.

The Puritan sense that the "new world" was, for all practical purposes, inexhaustible must have been compelling. Its message was that God intended through them—the purified Christians—to start the world anew. Cost was no consideration towards achieving God's aim. Creating things is no trouble for

God. Providence had made provision in "a new world" for a new edition of humankind. In response to this unparalleled opportunity, we see in the early days of New England, a continuing flow of immigration from England. Later, when this flow decreased some, there was the hardy natural increase of God's people that made necessary a continuing movement into fresh territory. Within the lifetimes of some of the first settlers, New England Puritans had stopped looking eastward—back to cramped and contaminated England—and had focused their eyes on the open west. The "errand in the wilderness" transformed into the manifest destiny of a people.

Inevitably, every move westward involved encroachment on habitat. Tragically for native Americans, this encroachment was Puritan encroachment on their habitat. As noted earlier, it would be a mistake to think such encroachment took place without deliberation. Book was kept; entries were made; in a sense then, the Indian counted. What it may have taken a while for the Indian to figure out is that he or she counted as a Canaanite— one whom the Lord God had created in order to destroy. The loss of an Indian would not be recorded in red ink, but in black. His or her death was a liability canceled. The Indian was being identified with nature as nature was conceived by Cartesians: nature was object, something to be conquered or disciplined or discarded. Indeed Indians' inability to share this Puritan perspective on nature is what made them "savages."

In what was regarded as a part of their benighted state, Indians thought of themselves and nature as alive, conscious, and rich in purpose. As for encroachments on other living species: such encroachments were, we can surmise, regarded as incremental and negligible. Theoretically, animals that were not eaten or skinned or domesticated could retreat westward. As for vegetation, it seemed extravagantly supplied. It would have to have been a very eccentric settler who factored in its cost. When, well into the nineteenth century, Thoreau began factoring in the loss of a grove of trees as a deduction from Progress, he was regarded as odd.

This last consideration is telling for the mindset we explore. Puritans weren't notably prodigal or careless; if anything, they were the opposite. But it would truly have been a rare settler who'd feel compunction or trepidation about uprooting a tree or plowing over of a field of flowers. Done for the sake of a New Eden, such things were a necessary and trifling cost. The redundancy and generosity of nature impeded a sense of its preciousness.

Admittedly, these reflections are speculative. They embody reasonable hunches as to how the vastness of the new world registered on Puritan sensibility.

Secondly, while Catholic theologian and ecologist Thomas Berry does not precisely cite the Bible as a source for devaluation of nature, he has said there's been a strong tendency among our Christian ancestors to seek their bearings from their reading of the Bible, and then assign to nature the place and character their scriptural interpretations permit. It would be healthier, Berry suggests, to take our bearings from nature and then, guided by these empirical observations, take up the Bible and read it in the context our acquaintance with nature offers. For the Bible, Berry says, draws on what our observations of nature yield. The psalms, for instance, are rich in passages that presuppose we're alive to the mystery and beauty of our habitat.

The Renaissance was an effort to achieve the break-out Berry describes and advocates. We can see this in the case of Galileo: telescope first, Bible second. Actually, if we look alertly, we can find this in the cases of Michelangelo, Leonardo, and Raphael— and running all through the Italian initiations of what we call the Renaissance. We find there the rebirth of pagan enthusiasm for the human body and the human scene; and this aesthetic shift re-configured the way people looked at the Old and New Testaments.

Beginning in Italy, the Renaissance spread westward and northward. It was sponsored more often than hindered by the popes of the time. When however the Renaissance effort to rebuild St. Peter's led to the selling of indulgences and the revolt of Martin Luther, the Renaissance in the North took on in fundamental ways the character of a rejection of the Renaissance in the South. In fact a new label had to be minted for it: the Reformation.

The North strongly reaffirmed the primacy of scripture. Reaffirming the primacy of scripture, the rebirth or Re-formation in the North found many un-scriptural elements to complain about both in the contemporary Catholic South and in the Catholic past. There was the strong monocratic doctrinal and political power of the Roman pope. There were all those sacraments. There was the High Mass from the Middle Ages—with a metaphysical doctrine of "transubstantiation"—along with incense, Gregorian Chant, mammoth cathedrals, and stained-glass windows. And the return of a pagan Greek celebration of the human body was one more troublesome encumbrance marring the shining face of scripture—one more impurity. The North was sure one did not look to nature for the right way to read scripture; one righteously read scripture for a way to hold nature in check.

Even among so many protestors, Puritan Protestants dissenting from the Anglican Church distinguished themselves as a people who would have nothing to do with "Roman" accretions and dilutions of Christian faith. Because these Puritans have been a parental influence on every subsequent generation of Americans, one can ask whether, in rejecting so much that brings aesthetic sensibility into play, they didn't successfully put their children's and their children's descendants' capacity for appreciation of nature under constraints that tended to sap its vigor.

Our third topic regarding Puritan aesthetic sensibility continues the first and the second. We consider the Puritan reaction to wilderness. Wilderness was a place of wildness, a place of unpredictability. As New Englander Robert Frost says in later times to his neighbor: "Something there is that doesn't love a wall." For the Puritan, this "something" had to be addressed, dealt with, brought to heel. The wild and the free was the devil's playground.

Here however we must be especially tentative. Puritans were capable of spontaneous response to natural beauty. Rich in written culture, and profoundly introspective, some demonstrated warn emotional engagement with this world. Anne Bradstreet, who lived from 1612 to 1672 (belonging therefore to the first generation of American Puritans) could write a letter to her husband in the form of a poem, and could begin by addressing him:

> My head, my heart, mine eyes, my life—nay more,
> My joy, my magazine of earthly store...[2]

---

2. Anne Bradstreet, "A Letter to Her Husband, Absent upon Public Employment," in *The American Puritans: Their Prose and Poetry*, ed. Perry Miller (New York: Columbia University Press, 1956), 271.

There's conjugal compatibility celebrated here; but surely there's tribute to conjugal sexuality as well. This is but a sample of much in her poetry showing a lively sense of the good things present here and now; and her poetry tells us something not just about herself but about her community, for it seems her poetry was well regarded by fellow Puritans.

In the next century, there's Jonathan Edwards. In a notebook of personal jottings, Edwards reflects on natural beauty:

> The works of God are but a kind of voice or language of God to instruct intelligent beings in things pertaining to Himself.... The immense magnificence of the visible world in inconceivable vastness, the incomprehensible height of the heavens, etc., is but a type of the infinite magnificence, height and glory of God's work in the spiritual world.[3]

The first sentiment can be paralleled in the notes, life, and work of Michelangelo. The second is something one could say anticipates the message of Van Gogh's *Starry Night* (the favorite one).

Here's more from Edwards:

> It is very probable that the wonderful suitableness of green for the grass and plants, the blue of the skie, the white of the clouds, the colours of flowers, consists in a complicated proportion that these colours make with one another.... The gentle motions of waves, of the lily, etc., [seemed designed to be agreeable] to other things that represent calmness, gentleness and benevolence, etc.; the fields and woods seem to rejoice, and how joyful the birds seem in it....
>
> Those beauties, how lovely is the green of the face of the earth in all manner of colours, in flowers, the colour of the skies, and lovely tinctures of the morning and evening.[4]

---

3. Ola Elizabeth Winslow, ed., *Jonathan Edwards: Basic Writings* (New York: New American Library, 1966), 250–51.

4. Winslow, *Jonathan Edwards*, 252–53.

Here is a much richer sense of nature than the sterile sense of the world projected in Cartesian dualism. And this continues in Edwards. One might think one was reading John Muir. (Edwards belonged to the tradition out of which Muir came; Edwards was an American-born Scotch-Presbyterian-Puritan. His differences with other Puritans over church structure shouldn't disqualify him as a representative of Puritanism. The breakout toward exuberant sense experience in Edwards becomes full blown in Muir.)

What remains noteworthy though is that these Puritan tributes to nature come from the same pen that wrote the sermon "Sinners in the Hands of an Angry God." In this sermon we're not concerned with journal jottings. This was a sermon Edwards put out there for the world at large to ponder. Here we're told that the very charms and god-revealing beauty of nature may lure the unsuspecting Christian into false complacency. When all things are going well, such a Christian may say to himself or herself that eternal damnation is an unlikely prospect, and this for Edwards places that soul in jeopardy.

In his sermon Edwards goes to great lengths to shatter one's workaday trust, and make the case that the natural world in which we live and move is a thin crust over the flames of hell. How close are the excruciatingly painful fires of hell, and how eternally they will burn! Speaking of those who have succumbed to human emotion and begun to live trustingly in the world, Edwards preaches:

> The wrath of God burns against them, their damnation does not slumber; the pit is prepared, the fire is made ready, the furnace is now hot, ready to receive them; the flames do now rage and glow. The glittering sword is whet, and held over them, and the pit hath opened its mouth under them.[5]

The sermon, powerfully written, has provided an example for evangelical preaching ever since. Its relevance to our inquiry is that it argues we'd be making a dangerous mistake were we simply to surrender ourselves to the harmony and beauty of things

---

5. Winslow, *Jonathan Edwards*, 153.

as they now present themselves. We must regard earthly beauty with what Puritans have elsewhere called "weaned affections." Howsoever nature may still deck herself in innocent beauty left over from Eden before the Fall, she stands now—due to the sin of humankind—in need of redemption. An acute Augustinian sense, further refined by Calvinism, had come to qualify, and all but erase, that passage we find in Genesis: "And God saw everything that He had made, and behold, it was very good."

Augustine, writing *The City of God*, depicted the present world—perhaps with deliberate rhetoric and hyperbole—as "the city of Satan." What Augustine may have intended for dramatic contrast was literal truth for Puritans: this world is Satan's domain. Between Augustine and the Puritans had come Calvin. With his doctrines regarding the fewness of the elect and the predestined damnation of most humans, Calvin had limned in dark shadows a version of Christianity which became gospel truth for Puritans. Those shadows are brought to the foreground in the writings of Hawthorne, a deliberate anti-Puritan; they shade and color each page of *The Scarlet Letter*. Similar shadows linger in misgivings that haunt the meditations of Melville. One can find these shadows still in the much later homey poems of Robert Frost.

The beauty of nature became provisional—a hypothetical beauty. The only world that could be trusted was a redeemed world, and it would obviously be premature in the Puritan understanding of things to say the wilderness that confronted them was such a world. Rather the world as it presented itself to the Puritan was the domain of the trickster; it was Satan's domain, and one put oneself in jeopardy who trusted in its beauty.

Only through completion of the God-given mission we have now mentioned at length could that wilderness be redeemed. Until then, if one was to regard nature's beauty, it must be with "weaned affections." Dedication to the mission armored one. An encounter with nature could be safe only for one held tight by the discipline of our godly mission.

Rejection by Puritans of the Renaissance in its Italian and Catholic forms of celebration of human nature was a good predictor of how Puritans would regard American Indians. When Puritans were pushing the notion that they had come into a *vacuum domicilium*, an unoccupied territory, they would often remember (how could they forget?) that Indians did after all live here. That's when it was convenient to call the Indian a "savage," suggesting thereby he was a part of unredeemed nature; the implication of the term was that the Indian was altogether too much at home in his body and in nature, a condition certifying him as satanic.

The issue then of Puritan aesthetics is richly complicated—complicated by its rejection of "Catholic paganism," and by resistance to the beauty and dignity of nature. Moreover the Italian Renaissance itself was a truncated project. In rejecting it—in rejecting the celebration of human beauty so evident in Renaissance painting and sculpture (and really in its literature and architecture as well)—the Puritans rejected what was an imperfect recovery by Italian Renaissance Catholics of that love of nature we find in classical Greece. From the perspective of ecologists today, the Catholics of the fifteenth and sixteenth centuries didn't go far enough. While reclaiming the Greek sense of human beauty, these Renaissance Catholics fell short of a general reopening of their eyes to nature. The Council of Trent and other features of the Catholic Counter-Reformation acted as agents to cool such paganizing tendencies toward nature among European Catholics.

If we look to the Greeks of pagan times, we see their celebration of the human form was just one part. They celebrated ocean and sky, sun, earth, and time itself. The forms they sculpted, and the stories—often erotic—they told of gods and goddesses, provide intimations of sublime and awesome powers rippling everywhere. Even at the beginning, leaders of the Catholic Renaissance may have held back from a fear of idolatry were they too confidently to follow the Greeks in such a direction. (We know for instance that both Botticelli and Michelangelo, stirred by warnings from Savonarola, feared at times their preoccupation with beauty was putting their souls in jeopardy.) Also, perhaps even in Italy, it could be that with the emergence of the Scientific Revolution and Cartesian thinking, these freshly "re-born" Catholics came to regard celebration of nature as a step backward. The bleak landscapes that backdrop some of Leonardo's most graceful paintings of saintly humans are enigmatic; they provoke curiosity, and are perhaps instructive anticipations of Cartesian thinking. Perhaps Leonardo was registering a sense that humans are the one bright spot in an otherwise desolate world.

Be that as it may, Puritans in general seem to have guarded themselves from even the threshold of any spontaneous veneration for nature. When Arthur Miller writes *The Crucible*, he has the Salem witch trials originate from news that young girls were dancing scantily clad or naked in the forest. Whether this was really the beginning of that multilayered episode, is probably impossible to say. What makes it at least plausible is that two elements, both of which were regarded with Puritan suspicion, come together: the human body and the wilderness. To a Puritan imagination, conjunction of these two may have been proof enough that Satan was alive and well and about to take over Salem.

In general, American Indians, like the pagan Greeks, seem to have taken joy both in their bodies and in the natural surroundings that nurtured them in body and spirit. While nature had fearful aspects for them as well as for Puritans, Indian cunning and spiritual technology were usually deemed adequate to placate and supplicate malignant spirits. Nature seems for the majority of tribes to have been a "familiar"—a dazzling ever-present counterpart to life. But that's too weak. Nature was the wellspring of life and resting place of ancestors, the source of being and a matter of constant interest—a richness far more to be met with gratitude than suspicion. Had Frost been writing of Indians, he'd have done well to have them say: "Before the land was ours, we were the land's."

We can hypothesize that in rejecting and killing Indians, Puritans did immense damage to their own souls. In the course of their long project of violence to wrest the land from Indians, one can imagine cases in which large numbers of them throttled what vestiges of aesthetic sensibility Calvin had left them. That some became murderous toward their own at Salem, as many had been murderous toward Indians, is not surprising. Freud might find in such violence something like a "return of the repressed"—the karma-like price one pays for despising what is natural. As Descartes had devalued nature, so Puritans despised those who recognized themselves as nature's children.

If ever anyone thought "an idle mind is the Devil's workshop," Puritans did. It seems, "an idle mind" came to mean for them a mind that was at rest contemplating. One can speculate that this attitude became a widespread source of American anti-intellectualism. Contemplation was especially dangerous, they thought, when this idle mind was reveling in natural beauty. To sanitize and purify one's attention to nature, it was important that it be dealt out only under the constraints of duty. Pleasure in nature was legitimate only when it served the Mission.

Max Weber writes:

> The idea of a man's duty to his possessions, to which he subordinates himself as an obedient steward, or even as an acquisitive machine, bears with chilling weight on his life. The greater his possessions the heavier—if the ascetic attitude toward life stands the test—the feeling of responsibility for them, for holding them undiminished for the glory of God and increasing them by restless effort. The origin of this type of life also extends in certain roots...back into the Middle Ages. But it was in the ethic of ascetic Protestantism that it first found a consistent ethical foundation.[6]

Weber goes on to say this ethic "acted powerfully against the spontaneous enjoyment of possessions," but then immediately he adds:

> On the other hand, it had the psychological effect of freeing the acquisition of goods from the inhibitions of traditionalist ethics. It broke the bonds of [restraint on] the impulse of acquisition in that it not only legalized it, but (in the sense discussed) looked upon it as directly willed by God.[7]

And so the Puritan Mission, begun as "an errand into the Wilderness" (phrase cited by Perry Miller from a Puritan pastor), transformed itself into—became in time the informing spirit of—the Monroe Doctrine, Manifest Destiny, the Open Door, and (to bring things into the twentieth and twenty-first centuries) the War to Make the World Safe for Democracy—i.e.,

---

6. Weber, *The Protestant Ethic*, 170.
7. Weber, *The Protestant Ethic*, 171.

make the globe safe for American-style economic activity every-where. In the course of the transformation, "the wilderness" became the whole world, and the Mission became a permanent crusade—whose latest instantiation can be seen in our seeming war-without-end on terrorism.

This at least is Weber's and my schematized version of how the pursuit of happiness came to be replaced among us by a compulsive effort to acquire goods and stabilize the process that makes their acquisition and secure retention possible. It's a version that predicts what we actually experience: the commercialization of almost all aspects of our life—so that it seems no sooner does a person climb a high mountain or win a golf tournament than that person turns himself or herself into a brand—a marketable commodity. Our aesthetic sensibility pays a price.

We find it difficult to put our finger on the connections here. They are so familiar as to be invisible. To be sure, the Puritan doctrine of election is hardly held by anyone today. The terrible irrationality and denial of human equality in saying that God arbitrarily elects some to blessedness and others—the majority—to damnation became at some point indigestible. Yet the doctrine of divine election didn't actually disappear. It went through a transformation. It persists in a religious, social, political, and economic doctrine of our exceptionalism. We Americans continue to think of ourselves as a great exception, endowed with unique prerogatives.

We regard some nations as more equal than others, and ourselves at the summit; Calvinist arbitrariness and its assumption of an inequality that splits the human species apart at its depths still run the show. A willingness to trump the ordinary usages of law by providing special privileges and opportunities for the American way—and by providing privileges for some Americans over other Americans—is in plain view. We who follow the American way act as an elect people still. We may say we do so from a sense of noblesse oblige, but often our actual program is neither noble nor governed by a sense of obligation to others.

Elect though we be, we've gradually been drawn, kicking and screaming—and resisting even now—toward an awareness that we're supposed to be equal within the confines of our own nation—are supposed to treat fellow citizens as equals. When a Martin Luther King reminds us of this, we do give some attention to what he says. Regardless though of whether we achieve that equality at home, we see ourselves as an elect people in relation to the world's population at large. When, in the last year of his life, King presumed to deny we have this special status and demanded that we treat people in every corner of the world as equals, we ignored him; and we still ignore him. We've set aside a special day for ignoring him annually called Martin Luther King Day.

When we sing "God bless America" there's reason to fear we're not so much asking God's blessing as asserting we've already got a special entitlement to it. When we sing Irving Berlin's song at our national sport, it's often a person in military uniform who performs it. The occasion moves us, I fear, by reminding us we are a holy nation. So much so, that when we invade a country to punish its leadership for keeping from us something we want, we praise ourselves as willing to die for the American way; we're thinking of our soldiers and ourselves as protecting America by maintaining for it the special privileges God intended us to have.

Regarding the tenor of our daily lives, a moral reconfiguration has gradually taken place. What began as a quest for "the good that can fulfill the heart's desire" has been diluted into a mere quest for goods. Black Friday heaped on Black Friday. We're so busy increasing our acquisitions, we've little time to reflect upon the preciousness of what we already have. The Thanksgiving meal is encroached upon by the quest for yet more stuff. Consequences for the maintenance of habitat are considerable.

The key, as suggested by Weber, to understanding this lies in grasping that our desperate search for justification has required palpable signs of sanctification—has required Success in three-dimensional form if we are to achieve the sought-for reassurance. And this reassurance is never sufficient. An ironic consequence is that we descendants of Puritans find ourselves indistinguishable from secularists and atheists. We can find in the atheist Ayn Rand a spokesperson for our agenda.

To review: The desire to know if one was "saved" was irresistible. It seemed one could perhaps know one was among the elect if God confirmed one's lifestyle with the blessings of success. When Puritans gave up (once the non-Puritan Stuarts had regained the English throne) on reforming the Church of England, the Puritan Mission came to be geographically redirected; the Mission turned from east to west. An errand to establish

Eden in New England as a temporary sanctuary re-emerged as a long term project to "win" the West. Manifest prosperity, achieved under Christian auspices, would be the token of victory; and the individual's saving participation in that victory would be marked by acquisition of personal wealth.

This version of our development (embroidering on themes of Weber, Perry Miller, and William Appleman Williams) allows otherwise puzzling things to come into focus. The resolute opposition to taxes of people who label themselves Christian seems easier to understand in the light of such a version. Taxes are compulsory sharing. But such sharing tends to dim the radiance of triumph—the full physical prominence—that should distinguish those who've most successfully served the Mission. Governmental intrusion has, in effect, the character of stealing luster from the specially blest. Such intrusion has a taint of sacrilege. If the poor are to be relieved—and Jesus says they are—let them be relieved not by grey and godless acts of government, but by those generous personal gestures, those thousand points of light and acts of individual kindness, that will reflect back upon the giver, and beyond him or her, enhance God's glory. This sense of how the righteous are to be known among us has relevance for our care of nature and good order; for a fairly predictable corollary of the contraction of government's role is that the preservation of habitat and civic infrastructure should be more a matter of private dedication and donation than a matter administered by law. Conspicuous giving goes some way toward certifying publicly the membership of the rich at the apex of the elect. Unfortunately, and to the loss of all of us, this certification becomes more important than actually taking care of things.

The analysis being drawn here from Weber seems confirmed also by light it sheds on the Spanish-American War—and the many wars, mostly undeclared, which have followed. That, with the exception of a disenchanted Mark Twain or a skeptical Will James or a metamorphized Andrew Carnegie, practically no one with an important voice could find an alternative to the Spanish-American War and its aftermath is instructive. It accords neatly with the notion we'd become by then a people in thrall to a machine-like ethos of acquisition—no longer appreciating or taking care of the things nature had plentifully provided. Misgivings Twain had expressed in *The Gilded Age* in the 1870s—where he and co-author Charles Dudley Warner chronicle an accelerating decay of humans amid an increasingly mindless worship of Progress—were strongly confirmed in Twain's lifetime. It's instructive that the inhumanity he had sensed at the center of things in the 1870s was so manifest in the slaughter of defenseless Philippine Moros thirty years later as to render this most articulate of Americans almost speechless with anger.

When the Spanish-American War was over, McKinley lived long enough before assassination to say it had been a mistake. Late in his own presidency, Theodore Roosevelt publicly acknowledged regret for the acquisition of the Philippines—the part of the war in which he'd had the most influence. Even John Hay, who'd called the war "a splendid little war," didn't seem to find much in its aftermath to lift his spirits. He worked harder than ever once the war was officially ended (among other things, penning those notes about China); but before the "pacification" of Filipinos was complete, he died abruptly, still in harness as secretary of state, in 1905—done in apparently by his exhaustive service to the expanding Republic.

These earnest men seem the incarnation of Max Weber's "obedient servants" who bear "a chilling weight"—the greater their possessions, the heavier and more life-draining their sense of responsibility for securing and enlarging them. Roosevelt correctly predicted that the acquisition of the Philippines would eventually lead to a "catastrophic" war with Japan. It was beyond him however to apologize for the war he envisioned. Further, the contemporary deaths of thousands of Filipinos—while regarded as "necessary" to the exercise of the American Mission— left these earnest men, not bathed in some glow of victory but numbed with a sense of perplexity and futility. (This is much like what later leaders and the foot-soldiers under their command would find in Vietnam and in Iraq, and what we've now come to experience in Afghanistan, and are beginning to experience in Syria.)

Further, this version of our past supplies a context to understand how it is that even as the Gulf of Mexico was serving up a murky brew of oil and dead waterfowl and contaminated fish, a preoccupation of many of us (even among those living along the oil-drenched shoreline of the Gulf), and of our media pundits, and apparently of our president was that we not let ourselves get discouraged or carried away by the disaster, but that we resolutely and heroically continue our deep-ocean drilling for oil. American optimism demanded we do no less.

The revision of The American Story presented here makes it easier to understand our preoccupations. If our utilization of natural resources is not a means to some other end, but is itself an end to which we're willing to subordinate just about everything else, then a lot of things fall into place. BP makes sense. Wal-Mart makes sense. Monsanto makes sense. This unqualified and uncritical willingness to "move ahead" lends force to the hypothesis that it's rooted in an inherited sense of mission—a conviction this is what we were born to do. We seem to have lost all instinct for appreciating and nurturing the harmonies of nature, the beautiful synergies by which the natural order protects itself. Currently, as it were to corroborate this notion, we're "fracking" oil shale deep in the bowels of the earth while seeming to turn a blind eye to evidence that we're triggering earthquakes and leeching toxic substances into drinking water in ways not good for children or other forms of life. Here too our attitude seems counterintuitive enough to make one suspect that spontaneous responses are being overridden by an inherited program—as if the very cells of our brain have been reconfigured to accept dictates from a kind of ideological template.

This view of how aesthetic sensibility has been suppressed in us helps also toward explaining the almost inexplicable conduct of financiers who so game our economic system that they seem likely finally to destroy its credit and render it inoperable. If the accrual of monetary profit is the measure of Success, then each increment of money is an increase of points, promoting one to a higher score. And there's no such thing as having too high a score; it's a contradiction in terms. One therefore reaches toward as high a score as possible. One will do this even if "winning the game" by such means, results in ending the game one has won. The behavior is irrational only if the money game is, as Aristotle insists should be the case, a mere means to something else. The risk in the go-for-broke behavior is that Aristotle is right. If he is, then playing the game out to its point of failure does not seem a good idea after all. The connection with aesthetic sensibility is that it is only if we have suppressed aesthetic sensibility that we can absolutize the pursuit of money in the way we have.[8]

That it seems so unnatural to us even to talk of the danger of "too high a score" confirms we're engaged in compulsive behavior. Aesthetically blind, our natural instincts smothered, we seem committed to a mission that imposes on us the kind of ultimate claim that only God could place on our ancestors. This is the evidence that we are a puritanized people. We seem, in fact, to be engaged in a modified version of no other than their mission — secularized perhaps, but holding us in the iron and unyielding throes of obsession with precisely that blindness which is obsession's touchstone.

Returning from there back to the bearing that blindness seems to have on national education, here too this "Weberian" version of our history may shed light. There is, I postulate, a longstanding tradition of American anti-intellectualism, one about which Hofstadter wrote insightfully throughout his career (albeit with troubling inconsistency in his treatment of Puritanism), and about which Susan Jacoby and Naomi Klein have written more recently. This anti-intellectualism can be seen as a predictable requirement if we are to hold ourselves to, and be constrained by, the American Mission. As John Winthrop seemed to realize, criticism must be suspended if the mission is to proceed.

Education, of its nature, fosters critical thinking; it cannot occur without it. As Hegel pointed out, one can't really think critically about things without engaging in dialectic. I mentioned already, if I say, "John's a good man," you can't really weigh my statement — that is, process it critically — unless you're willing to conduct a thought experiment in which you ask yourself: "How would things look on the supposition John is *not* a good man?" You must then ask how well that imagined world fits the world that actually confronts you. In other words, a thesis about a good John must be checked out by examining a hypothetical antithesis

---

8. Some will respond that the complete collapse of the money game is unimaginable, and therefore not worth worrying about. The premise of their response seems to be: "What can't be imagined, can't happen." The premise does not seem sound.

about how the world would look with a non-good John. (John may of course come through this process just fine. When you think about a world with a non-good John you may conclude it is nothing like the world you actually know.)

But to do this sort of thing with the proposition "America is the greatest nation on earth" is to enter into temptation. To check out this proposition by entertaining its opposite is to flirt with heresy. Its to give aid and comfort to our enemies (currently an imprisonable offense). Keepers of the national conscience (George Will or Charles Krauthammer, Karl Rove or Barack Obama) will call "foul" if you do such a thing. Education however moves, as we can see in the example of Socrates (with Hegel concurring), towards just such testing of value judgments. While our politicians praise education, few personally chance the burdens and jeopardy a critical thinker can expect in our American context. Not daring to venture into critical thinking themselves, is it any wonder our leaders prove less-than-reliable providers and guardians of the education of others?

We find a critical thinker an embarrassment to the American project. When, say, a Noam Chomsky comes along, many among us are quick to dismiss him out of hand as a man who "hates his own country." We do this lest we get drawn into an enterprise of reflection and criticism that's both unfamiliar and dangerous—an enterprise often viewed, in fact, as "un-American." One who believes as I do that "an uncriticised past is prelude to repetition" can trace our rejective response to critical thinkers back to the paradigm provided by the Puritan exiling of Roger Williams and Anne Hutchinson, and to the Puritan execution of Quakers. It should be no surprise that one who suppresses his affinity for nature suppresses too his affinity for humans.

Particularly, then, the critical version of our history set forth here provides a context for understanding the Christian right.

The Christian right insists it's Christian. Yet it is deeply committed to money-making; it's opposed to taxes; it's in favor of most wars our politicians propose; it prefers a well-established and aggressive foreign policy to one that's accommodating; it seems to regard most efforts at critical thinking as troublemaking; it opposes Darwinian views that would see man as a part of nature; and with regard to nature itself, it seems generally complacent and careless, dismissing most scientific concern for the protection of species and habitat as elitist—that is, as ill-founded, un-American, and motivated by hidden agendas.

Little of this, at face value, seems even remotely to echo Jesus as he's presented in the gospels. Jesus looks to the lilies of the field and to the sparrows as emblems of God's love. He sees God's love mirrored in the care of a father for a wayward son and a shepherd for a lost sheep. He says it will be difficult for a rich man to enter heaven (and not because the rich man has stolen, but because the rich man is rich). He calls on those able to share to do so—to be protectors of the young, and to provide relief to the sick, and to the widow, the orphan, and the outcast. Jesus is presented as the Prince of Peace, and warns against living by the sword; he is shown demonstrating forgiveness. In his dealings with others, he aggressively transgresses boundaries of ethnicity, gender, and status, going out of his way to repudiate and violate well established games of segregation and subordination. He does not exemplify nor advocate an uncritical acceptance of authorities (even those who quote scripture), but speaks of truth as that which can set his disciples free. His parables encourage conscientious care for God's gifts, including a care for one's personal talents. By his actions he manifests himself as one who thinks and acts independently. He was crucified for resolute political incorrectness.

If we ask where in history we find something that corresponds to the behavior of the American Christian right of today, there seem severe obstacles to finding a counterpart in Jesus as portrayed in the gospels. If however, rather than look to Jesus, we look to the seventeenth and eighteenth centuries, a notable correspondence to the Christian right can be located in the Puritans of that time. They too interpreted acquisition of money as a signal of God's favor. They too resented taxes and regarded those who collected them as generally unauthorized. They believed in aggressive warfare against neighboring "savages," and celebrated their victories over these neighbors (even such "victories" as were simple massacres) as acts manifesting God's glory. Believing those who dissented from their doctrines should be exiled or executed, they believed that much of what counted for secular learning in their day was godless and should be denied or neglected or excluded. As for nature, they regarded it as a wilderness—a realm in which Satan had a free hand, a place to be regarded with "weaned affections"—above all, a place needing to be mastered, tamed, put into harness.

Pundits have written how political strategists, particularly in the Reagan/Bush era (1981–2016, and counting), "shrewdly brought the Christian right into politics." What the pundits seem to overlook is the steady Puritan presence all along. Puritan ideology has been the controlling ideology of our politics from the start. What the Christian right represent is the branch of the tradition that's modified but not abandoned the explicit theological moorings of the original Puritans. This is in contrast to those in the secularized off-shoot. Let Jefferson represent these. His defense of profit-making by way of breeding "slaves"—people he delusionally thought he owned—was largely unbeholden to theological reflection.

In summing up, it is hard to get a firm grasp on what's going on today. Let me suggest there are three phases to consider. First there is the devaluation of nature that's achieved within a Cartesian context and that's carried forward with Puritan vigor. Nature has no interiority. Too indifferent and busy to study it, we eviscerate it. We deny to it internal form and dignity. We see it as altogether subject to our designs. We see it purely as plastic object.

Then there's our identification of "enemies" (whatever human or non-human we find blocking our path) with that "plastic nature" which we've devalued. These enemies too become mere grist for our mill, no more than fresh opportunities for the exercise of our freedom. These enemies can be "savages," or African-Americans, or Mexicans, or Filipino Moros, or "gooks," or contemporary Muslims. They can be deer that threaten our suburban foliage.

Thirdly, a final phase of this devastating perspective is a move toward its more perfect realization within the boundaries of the United States. As we've seen lately, the logic of our foreign policies is being increasingly applied among ourselves. The dismissive ways which we used to reserve for "foreigners" (alien parts of an alien world) are now coming home to roost. Those with economic and political power incline increasingly to treat the rest of us as mere empty matter also, awaiting more total integration into their designs. They are increasingly successful. Their control can be benign (*Brave New World*) or menacing (*1984*)—or a mix of both. The contrast developing so starkly today between them and the rest of us is no embarrassment to them; it's a contrast by which they achieve a desperately sought validation. Without it, these elect would not know who they are.

Stepping outside the perspective of the demented rich, a couple aspects of what's going on are daunting. (1) The natural world is neither inert nor inviolable. As its free and conscious offspring, we can so violate the conditions by which it has managed to bring us forth that we turn it into a place that can no longer support us. We are moving with quickening pace toward achieving this. The rich and powerful, who—very much with our complicity—increasingly control our behavior, have insight neither into the compulsions that drive them nor the very real constraints of nature under which they operate. At a quickening pace, they treat "nature" as an externality—something of no proper concern to them except as a business opportunity. (2) The second daunting aspect is that even when the rich and powerful would prefer to maintain their elect status through benign rather than menacing forms of control, they lack insight into what others need. With loss of aesthetic sensibility have gone wisdom and the ability to empathize. As the rich prove increasingly inept at benign control, they're likely sooner or later (from the start, in the case of minorities) to resort to efforts at control by intimidation—employing tools well honed and tested beyond our borders. For decades the CIA has spied on people of other countries and subverted their attempts at self-determination; now, increasingly, the NSA is spying on Americans, and our government is persecuting and seeking to prosecute those who have revealed this. While this second daunting aspect may be the first to focus our full attention, it's the first aspect—the inability to see ourselves as part of nature—that portends the more drastic and irreparable harm.

5 | How the Signs of Incoherence Cohere in Pointing Toward Dissolution

If I seem to be assembling what I've presented as grounds for dismissing the Christian right—or, for that matter, America—my intentions are read in a way that falls short of them. To twist the phrasing of Mark Antony: my purpose is not to bury America, but to unbury it. If I seem to be constantly repeating myself, it's because I am. It's because it is only by circulating around our topics over and over that these things, which seem so familiar they've become almost invisible, can be brought to light.

We've buried America too much. Let's begin by further examination of connections between the ascendancy of the rich and our reliance on force.

When I've talked with students in history classes about the cruel treatment of Indians by our white predecessors, I've been dismayed at how quickly they've tried to bury the topic. "I didn't do it!" they'll say with predictable regularity. Those of a more social cast of mind will say: "We—the people of our generation—didn't do it" or "We—the subgroup to which I belong—didn't do it." They say the same of other past cruelties I bring up. What I don't think they understand is they and I are not only identifiable beneficiaries of injustice in the cases of which I speak, but that most of us—at a deeper level—are wounded and bent as a result of them. We are among the victims of our injustices. We seem doomed to replicate the injustice that we've celebrated and not repented.

And we replicate our replications. We've done injustice to Indians. To kidnapped Africans. To the children of deprived Indians and the children of kidnapped Africans. To Mexicans. To Filipinos and Vietnamese. To Iranians. To Chileans. To Panamanians and other Central Americans. To Iraqis. To Afghans. And this is the short list.

We say Vietnam is the first war we ever lost. The statement seems less than accurate. Repeatedly, we've emerged from war battered, desensitized, and bitter. This was true of many veterans of the Mexican War. It was vividly true in the case of the Civil War. It was true again of our bloody effort to subdue the Filipinos. Later, the pain wasn't novel but simply more obvious in many who returned from Vietnam. We're seeing it again today in those who come back from the Middle East. We see it daily in the suicides of our soldiers.

Our character is coarsened by things we've done. Our conscience is bothered, and we cannot return to the persons we were. Were our society in general to recognize the extent to which we've inherited a pathology, we might reduce its hold on us. What impedes recognition is our improbable conviction that our way of doing things has always "worked." In these matters, we speak of those who shrug and "bite the bullet" as the courageous ones; but we seem not brave enough to tell ourselves the truth. We seem not to recognize that "the good ole days" are a convenient legend. We shunt our veterans to the side lest they tell us what they've learned. Too many of the good ole days are bad ole days of unrecognized and unrepented recklessness—days of doing unto others that which in our wildest dreams we would not have them do unto us.

Our days have hollowed us out. The thousands of suicides give testimony. By episodes we've been drained of vision and aesthetic feeling—rendered sterile in spirit if not in body. After 9/11, there were young men who volunteered and went to Iraq to avenge that day. Some of them killed men and women and children. Some of them suffered a loss of limbs. When they returned, we thanked them for their service; but neither they nor we could articulate in what that service consisted. There is no logical path from the desecration of the Towers to the invasion of Iraq.

I've recounted a story in which an Anglican priest was directed to apologize for his unauthorized attempt to make Jesus more central to Christmas than Santa Claus. Though Santa Claus is nice, it's been more demoralizing than we care to notice to substitute Santa Claus for Jesus. We've come to believe in extensions of commerce at any cost. I've mentioned our Black Fridays in which adults wrestle with each other over Christmas presents. One reason we're insensitive to curtailments on our liberty is because the companies with which we forge relations—relations seemingly intended by the companies to be more permanent than marriages—dazzle us with such variety and convenience. While we have here a new corporate mercantilism, addictive and manipulative and more extensive than anything Adam Smith sought to liberate us from, we seem disinclined to recognize it as such.

In the administration of John Quincy Adams, there had seemed a chance that the federal government could become a careful steward of westward real estate; and that it would sell land, not to speculators, but directly to the very people intending farms and homes. This was a part of the "American System" of Adams' secretary of state, Henry Clay. According to the plan, a rich revenue would accrue to the federal government. Each land-sale would be moderately priced, but the total accrued by the government would be considerable. There would be no middlemen. Adams, the last Federalist, seems to have intended that the money from such sales would then be spent on infrastructure—roads, water ways, bridges, schools, hospitals, concert halls, museums—so that an orderly infra-structure and a vertical cultural development would be sponsored among the American people with monies garnered from its horizontal expansion westward. It was a thoughtful vision.

To the people of his time, though, Adams seemed elitist. His program may have had the scent of socialism though that term was not used at the time to discredit it. That it was paternalistic was clear. It would have been a kind of New Deal for the 1820s, a century and more before FDR's. At the end of one term, unable to rally the people, Adams was replaced by Jackson. Jackson initiated what some have hailed as a grand democratic revolution, but what others see as a mere scramble to participate in ill-regulated land grabs in western real estate—with speculators collecting the high prices that actual settlers needed bank loans to afford.

Henry Clay, the pre-eminent Whig ("Whig" meant "anti-Jacksonian"), tried to keep his and Adams' vision alive; but it never caught on. The idea of government as an active promoter of the common good seemed to many then, as to almost all Republicans today, un-American. Government's function was to ward off foreign enemies and protect white people; beyond that, it should leave people alone to do what they wanted. What the white majority wanted was to compete among themselves for the very overt and palpable signs of success: land, wealth, servants and slaves, conspicuous consumption—and to be able on public holidays to say we're the greatest people on earth. Rugged Americans required no vertical development.

Perhaps Adams had earned this defeat. After all, it was he who had authored the Monroe Doctrine. It can be argued it was the crass spirit of expansion—for which his Doctrine was perverted to act as cheer leader and enabler—that doomed his pursuit of quality. Quality was for effete young men of northeastern schools. Horizontal development triumphed. (If the phrase has connotations of "rape," that's OK as a metaphor for what happened.) Regarding specifically the westward lands, the popular will seems to have been: "Let the free market decide who will sell what to whom—and at what price." This was a get-rich-quick scheme for speculators, and it was the loan-burdened farmers who got the short end of the deal.

At the end of the same century, we had in the 1890s another opportunity to structure our society differently. The depression of 1893 sounded a clear warning of something amiss in the American design. We'd plunged head-first into exponential development of an increasing production of goods at the lowest production-cost achievable. Like the Sorcerer's Apprentice, we were in danger of being swamped in what we'd conjured forth. Economic and political leaders feared we were about to drown in surplus product. In fact the fear was general. The relentless economic model to which we'd hitched our future required that the laborer and farmer be paid as little as possible. It seemed that soon there'd be no one around who could afford to buy the cornucopia we were ginning forth, and the whole economic system might come crashing down.

At this point we could have re-evaluated what Adams and Clay had proposed. We could have taken seriously what the preamble to the Constitution meant in stipulating we had a national goal "to promote the general welfare." We could have redirected our energies to: (1) making equality-of-humans tangible in our society through a more equitable sharing of the rewards of prosperity; and (2) taking quality-of-life as the gage of American success. Had we been willing to share across the board the profits of our productivity, we could presumably have maintained a robust market here at home for products then glutting our market. Giving flesh to our bushels of words about political equality (something Adams, after his presidency, worked tirelessly in Congress to extend to black Americans), we could in the midst of shared prosperity have attempted a quality-of-life unparalleled in previous history. A vision along these lines fueled the eloquent but insufficiently radical critique of William Jennings Bryan.

A vision of change is not as far-fetched as it may seem. We had eventually, through a civil war and three amendments, addressed emancipation of African-Americans. As a follow-up, a general white-and-black economic emancipation does not seem to have been beyond the realm of the possible. In the populist stirrings of the 1890s, there was popular momentum to achieve this more equitable distribution of rewards, and thereby raise the nation's quality of life. We've all learned from the film *Inherit the Wind* that Bryan lost the respect of the public in his struggle against Darwinism. Far more important, but few seemed to notice, is that in the course of his career Bryan lost the struggle to save America from "Social Darwinism"—an ideology which Darwin himself rejected but for which Puritanism ran interference by sanctifying as divinely decreed the privileges of the powerful. We regarded as an eleventh commandment and sacrosanct: "And thou shalt pay the laborer as little as possible for his or her labor."

Our decision to go along with this was not done by divine decree but by us. We had at the time a choice. In the age of robber barons, we could resolutely have worked to put a more generous share of America's unparalleled wealth in the hands of farmers and our multitudes of laborers, whether white or people of color. But a majority of the white voters (and white male voters were the electorate) envied the robber barons and wanted to be like them.

The alternative—the decision we made—was to work toward "enlarging the pie." Let us, we said, expand our markets. Let the Chinese soak up the surplus product of our fields and factories. Expansion abroad was viewed as the less painful approach. It was a step that moved to the cadences of our traditional westward march.

No matter that we sought expansion on a scale that would require war with Spain, and would, down the road, bring us into collision with Japan. This expansion was presented as "win/win." The robber barons could keep hold on their top-heavy share of the nation's wealth, but there would be enough new wealth to effect incremental improvements in the lives of everyone. Expansion would leave the rich rich—no doubt richer in fact—but it would pacify the unrest of the farmer and the laborer by keeping them gainfully employed; it would allow our great commitment to America's mission to continue its westward course.

That such expansion would require at least two world wars was not entered on the accounting sheet, although policy-makers of the 1890s had some sense of what they were getting into. War was an externality. War was, as Theodore Roosevelt explained, a natural part of the human condition; and a good war now and again was a necessity for maintaining the muscle tone of a nation emerging into manhood. The American people seemed to agree.

Had we attempted a reassignment of shares in wealth instead, while it would no doubt have required consumer boycotts, labor unions, and strikes to achieve the rearrangement, it would not have required some radical abandonment of private property. What it really required was a willingness to pay farmers something more commensurate with the value of their service to the rest of us, and a readiness to do the same for the miner and the industrial laborer.

We're actually quite familiar with the line of thinking involved. In a barter arrangement with a neighbor, one attempts to give the neighbor the value of what one receives; one attempts to match value to value. This is done in the interest of honoring and nurturing a sense of community. One wants the neighbor to be a friend as well as a short-term opportunity. Beyond neighborhoods, in our larger society, fairness could have been presented as a sound investment in maintaining a wholesome domestic market for the indefinite future. As noted, that way, the farmer and laborer would have had purchasing power, would have been able to exercise "effective demand"—not merely aspiring to a comfortable share of the goods they were producing, but holding in hand the money to achieve it.

The logic for such an innovation was as valid for black workers as it was for white. (Booker T. Washington understood this well. So do advertisers today, who conscientiously feature representative images of black affluence in their commercials.) Worth noting too is that such an innovation was compatible with "hard currency," whereas the "soft currency" proposed by Bryan seemed ready to dodge the issue of inequity while inflating the currency.

The principle of "a fair wage" isn't as elusive as some would claim. When, as a young inventor-entrepreneur—before success and greed had gotten to him—his accountants came to Henry Ford and told him he could hire labor at a lower rate than he was paying, Ford rebuffed them saying: "I want the people who make Fords to be able to buy Fords." His logic was as wise as it was obvious. (Unfortunately, as time went on this the vision faded for Ford, as did the warmth of his relations with his workers, and even with his family.)

Contrary to almost all business schools in America today, there's no need that private business run on Scrooge-like principles. Instead of the entrepreneur asking: "How little can I pay my workers and still maintain a labor force?" there's no reason he or she can't ask: "How much can I afford to pay my workers and still maintain, with them, an ongoing enterprise?" W. Edwards Deming frequently insisted this second question is more likely than the first to foster the kind of consistent excellence in goods and services which provides competitive advantage in any market-place genuinely responsive to consumers. Adam Smith had made the same argument. Even today in "family businesses"—business owned and staffed by family members—this ethos of equity seems the prevailing standard. In rejecting Deming and Smith in favor of bottom-line profit maximization, we've persisted on a path leading to a market subjected to pervasive manipulation, fraud, and exploitation. It's a market where misrepresentation, cutting of corners, and outright lying are regarded as acts of virtue. It's difficult to imagine anything more counterproductive to the human happiness of all concerned.

As mentioned here frequently, what was too little taken into account in the "larger-pie" scenario which we opted for in 1898 were the costs of war and other "externalities." In addition to some routine and easily rationalized exploitation of workers and hoodwinking of consumers in the interest of larger profits, there had to be a shoving, pushing, and cool trampling-under of peoples and nations throughout the world if we were to have our larger pie. And there had to be a willingness to sacrifice the blood of the best and brightest among our young if our enterprise was to prevail. These costs have been altogether real; in the accounting process however, they've been pushed to the margins—written off as collateral damage. This continues.

(If our soldiers are so unlucky and "improvident" as to get wounded, our actual inclination is to say let this be a matter of concern for their families and for private charities. Let our maimed veterans bootstrap their way out of whatever emotional and physical mess they find themselves in. We treat our wounded veterans not unlike the way we've tried to treat subdued Indians who have survived our agendas; we try to put them off some-place where we don't have to think about them. We—our president and Congress and society—have more serious things to do than tend to their wounds till the day of our veterans' deaths. True, every few years this matter of neglect intrudes onto our radar screen, and we make promises of reform. The promises are important. They salve our consciences.)

Further, recall that the example America gave at the end of the 1890s, in pushing unreflectingly forward with a project of expansion, was fresh stimulus for those in other countries to do the same. They too wanted special advantages in the guise of an "Open Door"—but Japanese style, or Russian style, or German style—copying us as we were copying the British. Mahan's book, a handbook for the arms race, was a worldwide best seller.

These "externalities" are, as I say, part of the real cost of such commodities as we can obtain only with their help. Let me repeat that. These "externalities" are a part of the real cost of such com-modities as we can obtain only with their help. We seem to have trouble taking that in. They're the enabling circumstances with-out which we can't achieve the kind of lifestyle of the elect we do. They're a part of the real cost of our not-too-mysterious economic miracle. Not only do we pay the cost of gasoline at the gas pump; we pay for it too in funding our incalculably expensive wars and awkward political arrangements in the Middle East. And while the cost of our car and its fuel and its insurance and registra-tion fees and its maintenance are a part of the cost of our driv-ing, it's true another significant cost of our driving is an increase in forest fires occasioned by climate change. Yet this last is so totally an externality that if you introduce it into an inventory of the costs of driving, the other parties to the accounting pro-cess are likely to be entirely at a loss and say they have no idea what you're talking about. (The mindset of a student I had a few years ago was expressed more or less as follows: "When I came to this course I knew the difference between driving a car and starting a forest fire. If you're trying to teach me the two are the same, I'm really not interested in taking this course." He spoke sincerely, and would have dropped the course had he not needed the credits.)

With externalities, by definition the tendency is to say: "Those aren't our problem." American economists, as we saw in the case of Milton Friedman, are fond of listing all the things that "aren't our problem." But of course when problems aren't owned by any-one, they grow. When they do, it's our habit of mind to regard them as something dropping from the sky or coming from the hand of God. Consider some of the many evils that currently tend to demoralize us. Consider, for instance, the jostling about, shoving, and destruction of other peoples that's going on around us, and the international turf wars, and the promotion of nuclear proliferation, and the thefts and the fraudulent evictions carried out by banks, and the inequities we see in law enforcement, and the increase in street crime, and the increasing violence in our schools, and the decay of our infrastructure, and the extinctions of species along with the pollution and degradation of habitat that that accompany the quickening tempo of climate change — with regard to this whole list, we wish fervently not to acknowl-edge these are evils that enter the world on two feet. In many cases on our two feet.[1]

In those cases where we do acknowledge that evils come on two feet, we want them to be somebody else's feet. We look for the splinters in the other guy's eye and ignore the chunk of lum-ber lodged in our own. We blame the troubles of our lives on the savagery of Indians, the ineptitude of slaves, the communism of Russians, or the terrorism of Muslims. When a president proudly

---

1. Some have said Reinhold Niebuhr taught at the time of the Second World War that aggregates of people — societies — behave "of necessity" on principles "uncomplicated by morality." If he did teach that, that may be why he was such a popular theologian at the time. Over and over, we reap the bitter harvest of such convenient thinking; and the pattern shows few signs of ending.

announces, "I will never apologize for the American people," he speaks resolutely in our tradition, and we applaud him. (Later, we elect his son.)

Let us proceed carefully. One can't deny that Indians, slaves, Russians, and Muslims have all, on occasion, caused us suffering—sometimes terrible suffering. What might help would be to attend more to how what's happened seems often to have a retaliatory character. It would help were we ready to search closer to home for origins of things that trouble us. But this need to look to ourselves continues to be something one mentions at one's hazard. An immediate and almost inevitable response is: "Oh— so you're saying we're the bad guy? You want to see America suffer!"

What's lost in the anger of such a response is the chance to take charge of a disturbed situation. To the extent we own (own up to) whatever initiative has been ours in generating troubles that beset us, we can take in hand a process to reduce trouble. We can work toward some resolution of grievances. We can appropriate what seems Hegel's distinction between an undialectical counter-thesis (i.e., "So's your old man!") and a creative response that seeks to incorporate the other's grievance ("I recognize some of my behavior has insulted and angered you.").

What makes it so hard for us to come to this is our Puritan heritage. We are the City on a Hill, the Great American Exception; in the language of our forebears, we're the Elect. It's nearly unimaginable to us that significant contributions to the world's evil should have entered on our two feet.

Here then, in this review, we try to take stock of some of the interlocking aspects of the position we've adopted. We believe in acquisition. In our devotion to it, we've been willing to treat outsiders with brutality and—while we did so—we've been willing to suppress sources of grace and health at home. Things that promote a sense of value in our lives and a sense of the preciousness of others' lives—and of lives outside our species—get lost in the shuffle. We economize on education; we question the need for national and state parklands; the preservation of "wastelands" we regard as waste indeed; "nature" we think of as "on its own." We wonder whether we haven't gone overboard in our willingness to fund remedies for the lives of the desperate—including our wounded veterans. We question the National Endowment for the Arts and similar enterprises, saying: "Let those who care for such things finance them from their own pockets." With happy blindness we say: "Let there be a thousand points of light!"

We feel we don't have much money. For the power we so cherish as a nation requires, as Admiral Mahan made clear, that we seek out foreign markets and have foreign bases from which to supply and monitor those markets. Our efforts to achieve these, when pushed without concern for the aspirations of others, call forth both imitation of our behavior by others and resistance to such behavior by others—in short, bring us into ever-increasing tension with non-Americans and into bloody and lethal conflict with them. A culture of violence ensues, and the wars that mark that culture appear to us as a sort of unavoidable destiny. Granted the premises on which we act, they are.

These wars must be funded. Restrictions of funds for maintaining infrastructure and improving the quality of life at home must pay for crusades abroad. Moreover, the less educated the voting public is, the less likely it is to resist this sorry trade-off. The consequent lack of an educated workforce need not disturb us. As Americans become less educated, they're less likely to demand high wages; and we can take up any slack in our workforce by employing hardworking, well educated people in other countries to work on our behalf in their homelands—or when desirable, to come work here in the United States, taking on tasks Americans seem either unwilling or unqualified to perform.

As Americans become less productive, and as the wars needed to maintain America as a superpower become more expensive, further "austerities" can be demanded. The people most closely associated with wars and with defense and with the control of precious planetary resources will become richer still—and they will flourish as convincing signs that America is still the land of opportunity. The rest of us will need to work longer hours for less pay. The young among us will be more easily recruitable for military service. Further, we who lead the free world in the imprisonment of our citizens, can progress further on that front too.

When it comes to exercising care for our habitat, if the trends sketched broadly above continue along present lines, environmentalism will come to have generally that character of a passing fad—a do-gooder hobby—that's been a charge against it from the start. It will be nothing any serious-minded person can give thought to amid mounting crises and increasing economic austerity. It won't matter that the signs of environmental distress grow clearer; that very clarity will help solidify the case that protection of the environment is outside our reach.

If you are still with me, let me make belated acknowledgement this dreary scenario is in reality of course subject to an infinite variety of possible modifications and interruptions. We say: "The past is prelude." But the past need not be prelude for those who understand and appropriate it. What I attempt to suggest here is how closely conjoined the factors of incoherence are. The desire for unmeasured accumulation occurs, for instance, where there's lack of insight and education. This desire to quicken the pace of accumulation diverts funds from what education there is and dilutes the wisdom in our schools that might check the pace of greed. Unchecked, the pace leads to war; and war both further depresses investment in education and—let me say it again—flourishes best where education is lacking. Accumulation—acquisition of goods—is addictive; and war quickens that addictive and competitive impulse. Accumulation is the opiate of our people. The cost to habitat and to kindness and civility in our relations is pervasive. The coarsening of character can be expected to increase. Street crime can be expected to increase. Violence in schools can be expected to increase. Forest fires can be expected to increase. Only when dysfunction has become so dramatically manifest that there's a general loss of confidence in traditional economics and politics is there likely to be a ground swell for radical change—and it's difficult to say what form that will take and what possibilities at that future moment will still be on hand for us to organize around.

Had we opted for a more equitable sharing of wealth in the 1890s, our position in the world today would no doubt have less the character of a superpower than it has. Instead of that, we might be the nation with the most accomplished middle class in human history. By reason of extending purchasing power more generally throughout our society, we could be the best-housed people on the planet (with no foreclosures or homelessness); we might have the finest, most accessible health care found anywhere; we might be the best-educated people the world has seen. A realized fairness that affirms all of us in our diversity might mean we had become the most harmonious people God has yet to see. We might be renowned as a people who had found the leisure to talk at length with our kids and celebrate in their company the most spectacular skill-sets of sports, and the heights of the fine-arts, producing among ourselves performances and masterpieces to rival ancient Greece and Renaissance Italy. (While parents are wonderfully engaged these days in efforts to provide activities for their children, it's sad to reflect that the "family dinner table" seems to exist mostly in old sitcoms, and that the "older teenager"—someone seventeen, eighteen, nineteen—who lives under one roof with both parents is now a vanishing breed. The ability to create and maintain enduring lifestyles of cooperation in one's home seems to be slipping away from us. Regarding our spouse as one more commodity, a great many of us seem interested in trading up. In place of commitments, many of us plan our marriages with careful designs for what should happen when the marriage ends.)

Living peacefully with other nations and enjoying at home the benefits conferred by education and natural abundance, had we chosen differently in 1898, our urgency about personal acquisition might be much tamped down. We might be at once a center for scientific research and a haven where a multitude of ideologies and religions could establish places of inquiry and worship. Tom Paine's deism notwithstanding, we might be that refuge for truth tellers and searchers after righteousness which he'd hoped we would become. (The dreary secularism of our present day is, I suspect, less interested in freedom of religion than in freedom from its disturbing urge toward transcending secularism.)

Instead of choosing a rich and diverse society, we chose in 1898, consistent with our past, to continue the project begun by the Puritans of the 1600's. A corrosive underside of this project is that it requires our respect for outsiders to be a provisional matter. We don't enter relations with foreigners on a plane of mutual respect. We don't regard them at the start as worthy of our respect. How can we? We know they are not Puritans. Rather we'll respect them when they "learn to behave." They must learn to behave as we do and must learn how to facilitate our purposes. As a startling line from Oscar Hammerstein says sarcastically in the middle of *South Pacific*, they've "got to be carefully taught."

We who revolted against mercantilism turn out to believe in mercantilism after all. We believe it is our destiny to manipulate and exploit. In this, we receive no endorsement from Adam Smith. Some cite us here for racial prejudice; for it seems we need to become racists in order to move forward our program with a good conscience. More fundamentally though, our malignancy toward others may seem to be derivative; our behavior seems it may be rooted simply in uncritically seeing our way of doing things as the norm. We are the norm. While we claim to separate church and state, our religious past has everything to do with our complacency in this matter.

An additional point that historian William Appleman Williams was at some pains to make (in discussing Cuba, for example) is that this program of ours hasn't quite the consistency we might think it has. More recent commentary along the same lines has been offered by Howard Zinn, Noam Chomsky, Naomi Klein, Chalmers Johnson, Chris Hedges, and John Perkins. What Williams and these others point out is that even when outsiders have gone the extra mile to accommodate American expectations and demands, there's no guarantee they'll then be treated with respect. There seems among us a deep need to assert superiority such that, even when others conform to our sense of how things should be, we still feel impelled to undermine and exploit them. We have a curious habit of turning on those foreign leaders whom we befriend. And so the depths of malignancy remain hard to fathom, and my inclination is to refer them back to that space where strange things begin to happen when religion sunders its bonds with rationality.

And while I'd say our exploitations originated in a spirit of religious nationalism, this no longer guarantees they're done today on behalf of the nation. As noted, the logic and internal functions of The Game have become so enthralling that its master players, the CEOs of multinational corporations, no longer feel constrained by national loyalties. As Joseph Sottile has pointed out, it would be wrong to call corporate rule in America today a form of fascism; it's not that patriotic. Many American heads of corporations today no longer promote achievement of an American mission, but seem to have left even that degree of social allegiance behind, relocating their companies' headquarters abroad and hiding their companies' profits offshore to avoid American taxes, and relocating factories abroad so as to avoid what there still is here of environmental law and labor law. They entomb themselves in pursuit of a kind of winning that has little reference to anything—even one might say much reference to yachts and vacation homes and family life: "Who has time for such things?"—outside the Game itself. They are our walking dead.

As I write, there's much ranting against the Koch brothers. This is not mainly against Bill—who is sometimes in the forefront of those doing the criticizing. The anger is directed more especially against Charles and David. The hostility must surprise the two brothers. For in spite of what I've just said about executives forsaking patriotism, few people believe so strongly in the American Dream as these two do. They believe in strengthening the strong rather than the weak. They believe in busting the unions. For what do unions do except shore up the weak at the expense of the strong? They believe the land belongs to those who use it—a principle on which we fought and won the Mexican War and then went on to win the West. They want to diminish or abolish taxes. For what do most taxes do but take wealth from its originators and rightful possessors, the wealthy, and distribute it among losers? They believe a man should be able to do what he wants on his own property and in his own corporation, and no government bureaucrat should be able to tell him differently. Otherwise, do we not make fools of ourselves when we call this the land of the free and the home of the brave? As for pollution, what's the fuss about? All pollution does is sicken and disable those too poor to live in decent neighborhoods; in fact it serves to alleviate the downward pull that undesirables exercise on the competent and successful. And to what purpose do we fund schools crowded with the offspring of our undesirables? Do we not often say we want to return to the good old days? Don't we often say as a kind of mantra that we want to restore the American Dream? Who then is more engaged in preserving American tradition and advancing that dream than David and Charles? Think back to the golden days when Jefferson was at Monticello. Those were days when the rich ruled, minorities knew their place, and the only good Indian was a dead one.[2]

---

2. To maintain, though, some degree of responsibility in my rhetoric here, I have to admit that Charles and David would much rather see a live Indian with oil rights than one of Sheridan's dead ones.

Two great Enlightenment thinkers struggled specifically with how to avoid the emergence of economic power such as the Koch brothers hold. One was British, the other American. Adam Smith judged the mercantilist hold of the British government over the details of trade to be a source of abuse; and he advocated a replacement of such micromanaging by the free interaction of a vast number of individuals seeking a profit. He did not fully ponder nor foresee how the entry of corporations into this give-and-take could lead to a corporate mercantilism that reconfigured government as a powerful ally in a corporate quest for ever-increasing economic and political control. Smith intended to lead humans away from oligarchy, and didn't anticipate how his words would be twisted to make it far stronger than ever.

The foremost American economic thinker struggling with how to discipline economic power was Alexander Hamilton, a younger contemporary of Smith, sharing in Scotch ancestry. His plan was to bind the business community and its companies to a strong central government with such enticements that business in America would readily enlist to serve our government as its agent to promote the common good. His goal—the general happiness—was not significantly different from Smith's. The difference between the two was in the choice of means. Hamilton saw a strong central government as the solution rather than the problem. He has often been called a pessimist. To me it seems he might more rightly be faulted as an optimist; he saw government as a countervailing power that could protect the public from the greed and recklessness of American tendencies toward profit and acquisition. (He did not foresee the extent to which Black Friday could encroach on Thanksgiving.)

Both Smith's and Hamilton's programs have foundered on the shoals of corporate power. Corporate power was still a mere faintly visible star on the horizon in the time Smith was collecting data. That corporate power could prove to be a problem was not all that surprising to his American contemporary, born a quarter of a century later. What neither managed to provide against is the now-proven skill of corporations—like agile wrestlers—to shift the center-of-gravity and take control of the government that was supposedly controlling them. In *Citizens United v. Federal Election Commission*, the Supreme Court simply gives voice to what's become a transparent fact in America:

the purpose of elections today is to give corporate power the opportunity to install politicians who will see to it that government works for corporations while it engages in only nominal efforts to regulate corporate interests and activity.[3] In this matter, regard for instance the recent careers of Timothy Geithner, Eric Holder, and Ken Salazar, all appointed by Obama. In this new order, people are awarded with federal offices essentially on the basis of an unspoken understanding they will come to Washington and—at their worst—do nothing to impede corporate interests, and—at their best—do much to promote those interests. Democrats, as names above suggest, can often be more useful in this regard than Republicans, with Obama arguably proving to be one of the most useful ever. (If some regard him as a failure, they may be judging from the mistaken premise that he came to Washington to curb war and the excessive power of corporations.)

In view of this, today there's a growing question whether any form of capitalism can long put up with traditions of democracy, even if democracy was originally a premise for the emergence of capitalism. It seems the two, which fit so well together in our slogans, have proven incompatible outside them. (To state the matter with greater refinement, capitalism has shown dazzling success at manipulating the judgment and aspirations of the people in our democracy, so that traditions and institutions which the people reliably support are often deeply subversive of their well-being. Whether this is to be seen as a triumph over democracy or simply as the predictable exercise of democracy in a Puritan nation is perhaps no more than a choice about nomenclature.)

As the determination to accumulate wealth, and to secure wealth which has been accumulated, continues, a need for ever more sophisticated and effective weaponry grows. As reliance on force and as our actual resort to violence become more routine and unobjectionable, there's an increasing need for extraordinary resources and a need to recruit more people into the design, manufacture, and use of weaponry—and to recruit diplomats, informed by superior intelligence, who are ever more adroit

---

3. For a critique of the way *Citizens United* accords to corporations the status of human beings, see Justice Steven's dissent (in which Justices Ginsberg, Breyer, and Sotomayor concur).

at deterring others from doing the same. We hope thereby to increase our power to intimidate potential rivals. As we succeed, however, the number and dedication of hostile rivals increases too. While Machiavelli shrewdly advised that it's good if your enemy fears you, Hobbes was perhaps shrewder yet in suggesting what is nearly the opposite—that an enemy who genuinely and sincerely fears you is arguably the most dangerous thing on earth.

No doubt the point above has become déjà vu all over again by now, but what I'm engaging in here is one more effort to make real to our imagination the vicious, intertwining cycles of our times. I've belabored already the consequences for education. To foster critical thinking in such an environment as ours today would clearly be a subversive act. If one wishes to get ahead in our current mainstream media, one must demonstrate that one has accommodated to this. (Gary Webb clearly did not accommodate soon enough, and had to go. Robert Scheer acted like we still had a free press, and was fired from the *L.A. Times* as the price of his mistake. Dan Rather proved insufficiently subordinate and respectful to the powers that be [too much Edward R. Murrow circulating in his brainwaves], and CBS felt the need to cut him loose. Etc.)

Of course, the media need not kill or fire every noncompliant messenger who might spread news of what's going on; it's less messy to neutralize such messengers by other means. The benumbing function of the mainstream media is facilitated when the educational establishment has so dumbed down the body politic that it no longer exercises critical attention to realities-at-play. A public subdued by a pervading academic relativism, but plied with a ready supply of here-and-now distractions and gratifications, can find in our two-party system's circus a comforting sense that there remains a wide scope for free choice in America, and that the people are still in charge.

What is striking is the increase in momentum downward in all of this. The synergy of it all! The war-making tendencies feed off the accumulative tendencies; the accumulative tendencies feed off the war-making tendencies. Both depress education. Amid the negative synergy, injury to habitat is consistently written off as unintended—therefore unimportant—collateral damage. Only an under-educated public would tolerate such recklessness.

(While wounds we inflict on habitat often still aren't acknowledged, surely they're felt. Perhaps it's the rumblings in our house of life that quicken our unease and send us scurrying forth from home before the plum pudding is served. Is it not a uniquely American optimism that hopes Black Friday can save us all?)

Regarding war, as Hobbes warned (and Einstein seconded): if we max out our tendencies on this front, most all will die. Regarding our accumulative tendencies, there's clearly a readiness, witting or unwitting, on the part of key players in the global economy to push our system to its point-of-failure. It's as if NASCAR drivers were intent to achieve a climax in their flirtation with mayhem and wouldn't feel they'd tested the limits of their sport till the whole track and stadium were consumed in fire. As we pleasure ourselves with our toys of nuclear-delivery systems and credit-default swaps, we neglect the natural order that spawned and supports us. That order, in turn, is simmering with maternal exasperation and shows a growing inclination to evict the lot of us as obnoxious children.

Perhaps something of Freud's late-in-life perspective on the human predicament is proving true. Perhaps our special aesthetic enthrallment with ever-greater acquisition and consumption is becoming too much for us. Perhaps as we push forward our eros, an eros configured and stoked by our Puritan heritage, we have at some subterranean level decided to call a halt to all proceedings. Churchill once remarked on the sweet lure of the commuter train as it rushes towards one who stands waiting on the platform. A simple step forward and all problems are solved. Perhaps the death wish is becoming a shared principle of community life, and we—like lemmings—now worship Thanatos.

With all the factors mentioned—education, financial affairs, foreign policy, ecological relations—falling in a quickening spiral toward incoherence, our summary can perhaps more properly end, not with a final dismal speculation, but with two questions. Can we Americans recognize the anti-climatic and banal finale into which a Puritan heritage—often no longer tied explicitly to God or nation—is leading? And can we, who are children also of the Enlightenment, finally choose against our failed Puritanism and submit instead to the principles of equality and justice we have so often professed?

Facilitators of Incoherence: Convenient Skepticisms

Perhaps this book should have ended with the last questions on the previous page. Much of the material up to now may seem to some to be trite and self-evident. Such in fact much of it seems to me. I wonder then how it is that this material escapes the consciousness of so many Americans today. Here, in this section, I try to examine the epistemology (or lack thereof) that makes this possible.

In the opening chapter I compared education to mother's milk. A mother doesn't wait till her child has earned a right to be fed; she draws her child close and nurses her or him. Education is something like that. To treat it as a privilege or a reward is to suspend our wholesome instinct in the matter. We override intuitive wisdom with a convenient rationalization. Convenient that is to the powers that be. Among other functions, education—resembling mother's milk—stimulates the immune system of the mind. As a part of my unease about contemporary culture, I fear one reason education has become as problematic as it has is because the powers that be don't want a general public well immunized against nonsense. When prophetic voices among us disclose the mythic character of our economics and our foreign policy, efforts are made to marginalize and silence them. Government treatment of Julian Assange, Chelsea Manning, and Edward Snowdon is instructive here. Think of the outrage of the Nixon Administration when Ellsberg, Zinn, and Chomsky brought *The Pentagon Papers* into the media mainstream. In many cases, our government prefers that we work within a foggy blur.

"What you don't know can't hurt you." We've all heard this; no one can really think it's true. The bus hurtling toward you as you jaywalk across a busy street engrossed in your cell phone can certainly hurt you. Flip the stupid phrase, and you arrive at something close to the most basic premise of common sense: What you do know may be of help to you. Confirmations are more numerous than there are grains of sand.

What's insidious about skepticism is that it smothers the quest for knowledge before it can get fairly started. Skepticism is our soup du jour. It's become the artfully contrived mother's milk of our times. It expresses itself as irony and cynicism. It raises an eyebrow. It keeps reality at bay.

Skepticism shouldn't be confused with critical thinking. Skepticism and critical thinking are like identical twins in a comical farce—two characters whom others continually mistake for each other, but who have altogether opposing agendas. Critical thinking leads to science and wisdom; skepticism leads to word games and sophistry, ending in disengagement. Both skepticism and critical thinking may express themselves with the question: "How do you know?" Yet the intentions in asking are quite different. Skepticism intends to shut down the quest for understanding; critical thinking embarks upon it.

The reason I speak of the skepticisms that follow as "convenient" is because they provide an easy way out. They're not convenient in the sense that they allow us to arrive at what we want; their convenience is limited to permitting us to stop asking what we want.

Why is skepticism attractive? Well, the actual task of our time is uniquely daunting. People my age are glad they're old. The kind of challenge facing us—once the ecological dimension is factored in—is without parallel. For a whole society to reconfigure its internal sense of who it is and where it's going is a monumentally greater task than for a cruiser to swerve from an iceberg toward which it's headed. It's a much more demanding task than to send a man to the moon. To relinquish the specific sense of mission that began with the Puritans and that manifests itself lately as still alive and well—in our wrathful behavior toward Iraq after 9/11, for instance, and in our supine response to financial extortion in 2009—would impose a burden of reconstruction on the American people that almost everyone in America would rather avoid—politicians, media pundits, clergy, teachers, and, to tell the truth flat out, typical Americans everywhere. To examine our life and recognize the extent to which our coping strategies have only made matters worse—really, there's nothing more painful. It's "a long day's journey into night." Instead of doing that, we choose to be gamblers doubling down. If we'd just be more forceful in our foreign policy, we tell ourselves—if we can just arm enough drones and kill enough terrorists to convince our enemies that violence never works, we tell ourselves—then all will be well. As for our finances, in the wake of the bankster meltdown, we say let's unfetter the apostles of greed once and for all, and then surely they will serve us devotedly. That's only logical, isn't it? I mean, who knows more about the ills of our financial system than our financiers?

Ominous thinking. How, though, does all this connect to skepticism? If the indictment I've made has truth, it seems our problem is one of rampaging, uncritical complacency and trust. Skepticism would seem in order. Is it not the remedy?

The opportunity for skepticism and its lure today among the eyebrow raising intelligent is the manifest credulity of the herd of true believers we've mentioned at such length by now—the great numbers who never question their familiar opinions but simply forge ahead. Such true believers are in the grip of obsession, and the intelligent, including the thoughtful young, can see this. Worse yet, the obsessed people in charge of our society are clearly in the ranks of the credulous true believers. A very common response of intellectuals then to the manifest absurdity of current foreign policy and current financial policy is a shrug in the physical order and a shift into skepticism in the mental order. "Look where convictions lead people! The last thing this world needs is another true believer!"

Have I described the situation accurately? The response of the sophisticated is to look at the triumph of folly, and rather than be motivated by it to look for answers to say instead: "Do you see what a mess people make of things when they think they have answers?" (This question was in fact a favorite maneuver of David Hume.)

That response—a retreat into civilized and urbane despair—is too easy.

To elaborate: among many it's fashionable today to greet almost any statement of conviction with an ironic smile. To do so has become a mark of political correctness among many of our young at universities today, and the behavior is modeled and reinforced by many of their professors. The consequence of this tendency is paradoxically conservative. If we've found that all ideology leads to egotism and bloodshed, then it becomes fashionable to have none. Students these days study ideologies as taxonomists study butterflies. The butterflies are all dead. Such detachment in turn leaves those who blindly possess (are "possessed" by) an uncriticized ideology firmly in control of all things outside the classroom. The thoughtful people have surrendered to those among us who are least sane. The Milton Friedmans and the Pol Pots rule.

The compensation for such an inglorious surrender is that it absolves one from Herculean/Augean labor of sorting well-grounded convictions from ill-grounded ones (or, as the Greeks' metaphor would bluntly suggest, from getting the bullshit out of the stable). Meanwhile, it allows a docile society to soldier on without let or acknowledged misgiving in our mission. Ours not to reason why, into the valley of death ride the three or four hundred million Americans; and the world at large twists in the after-draft.

In this section we will investigate skepticism about history, skepticism about beauty, skepticism about morality, and skepticism about anything being known absolutely. All are common today; and all contribute toward conservation and perpetuation of the interlocking cycles of disintegration described in earlier chapters. One of the problems the reader is likely to face is a nagging misgiving that none of this is really relevant. That misgiving, I claim, makes it more relevant than ever. We Americans have not much inclination to ponder how epistemological stagnation and paralysis block our path to meaningful action. Bear with me then.

6 | Skepticism about History

Once I was tutoring a young African-American who was about fifteen years old. He announced to me that he and his buddy had figured out that history was a worthless study. I asked how they'd come to that. He said they'd realized history was about the past but that they were interested in the future. I sat there, staring at him. After a while he became uneasy and said: "Well, what do you think?" "About what?" I asked. "About what I just said," he replied. "Oh, that," I said; "You *did* say that. But I've decided to focus on the future rather than the past."

The incoherence of his program was what I'd hoped to demonstrate. In a way, though, he was ahead of many of his peers — for no doubt much that he'd been taught as history was worse than worthless, and he at least was conscious of his act as he struck history from his list of concerns. For many of his generation, history was never on their list. For some perhaps there was no list.

One worries about the digitalization of experience. Is the grand four-dimensional gestalt of things disintegrating into twitterings? As my students emerge from the classroom, I can watch as fifty percent or more reach robotically for cell phones — if they haven't held fast to them through the session — in a conditioned reflex to return to comfort. Some stand stationary in the pathway as they tweet away their breaking news ("on way 2 library, c u there"). They seem oblivious to the four-dimensionally-present others trying to shuffle past them. Journals and diaries are important ways to memorialize events of one's life; but something more radical seems in progress here: a kind of em-bubbling of oneself in a world of one's own making. (Have we here an attempt to make Hume's "Egocentric Predicament" a reality? Does each of us want to become star of his or her universe in cyberspace—and demote what's outside that space to the status of a hypothesis? Does the guy who goes and shoots up a crowd of anonymous others believe more or less he's simply the main character in a video game of his invention?)

In the em-bubbled world where the student moves freely, allusions to the past tend to fall flat. The ability to grip large sequences of the past and hold in memory the figures and facts of them seems (with the exception of baseball commentators) to be in decline. Perhaps, to phrase the matter differently, there's a plasticity and multiplicity in the processing of the past which amounts to the same thing. Some years ago I was discussing the birth of free-market economics and I mentioned Adam Smith. One of the more alert students remarked, "I think he's gone off the air." (There had in fact been a media personality operating with that name.) Suppose I mention MacArthur leading an invasion to regain the Philippines. A puzzled student may object: "But I thought it was the Japanese who invaded the Philippines." (It was, of course, but...)

A story has a plot that connects the incidents. In a slightly different sense, history too has a plot, or at least a pattern. To uncover it is at once the formal task of historians and the informal task of everybody. We ask what were the undergirding trends, conditions, transformations, motivations that provided context and opportunity for such and such to happen. Both to follow a story and to follow history requires a certain difficult exercise of keeping in focus a succession of incidents. One must be able to sustain "long" thoughts. This capacity seems in trouble today. The bleeps and splurges of our digitalized culture seem to work against it.

So half the problem with the past may be that competence to engage it is fading. Let me suggest a second half may be skepticism about the past being recoverable in the best of conditions. This latter I call "skepticism about history."

Why does it matter?

In the struggle to create psychotherapy, Freud acts on a conviction that recovery of the past is a worthwhile goal—in the case of many of his patients a necessity. Perhaps his premise is that the only people who can function effectively in the present are ones equipped with a reasonably accurate sense of their personal past.

At the least, playing the matter from the other end, Freud seems to believe that when one can't function effectively in the present, the remedy often begins with an active effort to re-engage the past. What we don't know can hurt us, and does so all the time. It can, in fact, tie us in knots. The return of the repressed can occur in confused and disorienting ways. The alternative is to summon the repressed forth in a deliberate and painstaking effort at self-understanding.

We have, I've been arguing, a dynamic past—a shared past—regarding our experience as a society. It operates on us and in us but is not necessarily reflected in conscious memory. In fact, pseudo memory may conveniently mask a deeper, more dynamic and darker memory for a society as a whole just as it can for an individual. When that's the case, we're talking about a past: (1) that's operating in us, (2) that's guiding decisions, (3) that's deeply installed in the shared affectivity of us all in our public celebrations, in our expectations, and throughout our interactions with one another (including what we will allow as "common sense" when we carry on discussions), but that (4) is never made a focus of attention in itself. It's the kind of thing that can influence us to choose item A without hesitation, while we recoil from item B. It can explain why we walk through a particular door without hesitation while we do not even consider walking through some other door. To deliberately turn from delving into the actual past if one is a member of a deprived minority seems obviously counterproductive (which is why I made an issue of it with my African-American student); but if one turns from delving into injustices of which one's group was the perpetrator, this too is profoundly counterproductive (which is why I have so belabored the injustices perpetrated by the white majority of America's past).

While then we are capable of being aware of our past, often we're not aware. It's when we're not aware, that its control over us is likely to be strongest.

When my teenage student said he'd written off the past, I thought it likely his freedom would be diminished if he managed to persevere in his disregard. Prompted by Heidegger, I'd say in fact my student was quite wrong about history. Deliberately paradoxical, Heidegger claims history is really always about the future. If you think of history not as something Napoleon did, but as something historians do, you can take in Heidegger's point. "History," as he uses the term, does not occur simply when deeds are done; history occurs when someone creates a record purporting to be a record of such deeds.

The record can be accurate or distorted. It can even be quite fictitious. If it's presented as fiction, the historian isn't precisely a historian, but a maker of legends—one whom the ancient Greeks would have called a poet. When however it's a genuine effort to give a factual account, it can still be distorted and fictitious. Further, a counterfeit of an effort at historical accuracy may be offered in a deliberate effort to deceive. Here a "poet" is at work, but a malicious one.

Whatever of these is the case, what's noteworthy is that the writer is attempting to present to the listener or reader a future to be pursued. We are reminded often enough: "All history is told from a point of view." That however doesn't go the distance. History is always told for a point of view—is told to install a point of view in the recipient of the account. We do know this. When we listen to a long account that begins to seem tedious, we interrupt: "What's the point?" There always is one. The teller of the tale may be saying: "Look out! Don't do what this poor fellow did." Or again, may be saying: "See! In this woman's actions we find how things of this sort should be handled." Accounts commonly admonish in both ways.

The criterion of selection for the historian is the kind of world the historian would like his listeners or readers to ambition. The historian doesn't recount some action simply because it happened, but because the material seems relevant to future action—either clarifying a goal or giving a warning. This doesn't make the historian a poet in the Greek sense. An honest historian doesn't make things up; but he or she does select in accord with a purpose—"raises" the data by directing it toward a moral.

While it would be wrong then to say history is mere propaganda, it's true that all history not perverted by a desire to deceive is guided by an intention to edify. The historian is a moralist.

Patrick Henry spoke of experience as the one lamp by which his feet were guided. George Santayana said those who do not study history doom themselves to repeat it. Paradoxically, it's precisely this power of history to act the aggressive school marm—this tendency to take hold of us, to instruct us, to summon us to do this and avoid that—that can make us want to run from it. When we don't learn from our mistakes, it's largely because we figure the process would prove painful. When we dismiss without reflection moments of insight and clarity, it's because insight and clarity can spoil a whole day.[1]

One way then to deal with history is just to dismiss it out of hand—much as a slothful person may discard evidence of his or her life's triviality, much as an alcoholic or other drug addict may discard evidence of his or her illness. This seems in line with what may have been my student's strategy; perhaps he didn't want the painful nudge that memory of the past can give. In such cases, if the evasion is more or less outright, made in the clear light of decision, it may be less harmful. What's outright can be questioned.[2]

Another approach, more subtle and therefore often preferred, is to say: "In looking to history, there's no way to know if you're getting it right. One historian sees things one way, and the next historian sees things quite differently." Such a charge brings us quite explicitly to what I'm talking about when I talk of "skepticism about history." I call it "convenient" because it provides a way to skip out on history and look principled in doing so. One can exempt oneself from the burden of trying to learn and understand the past on the principled ground that one knows better than to think such a thing possible.

This is the radical skepticism we must examine. Let's look into the case for it.

At a radical level, one can question the efficacy of memory. It's an easy target because, as a function of consciousness, memory

---

1. It doesn't seem too strong to say that in such situations, we often choose for ourselves what may be the tragic plight of some schizophrenics: we choose a state of consciousness in which the past is neutralized and provides no lessons as to what we should do next; we choose to be in a state where the status quo seems inevitable.

2. A professional colleague of mine once said: "You pay attention to history and current events? I've got better things to do." I responded: "Does it not occur to you that you thereby retard your progress toward becoming an adult?" She was stunned—which is what I'd intended. The forthrightness of my colleague opened the door to my stark criticism and to a possibility of change.

entails the mysterious elusiveness of consciousness. One can state one's mistrust saying: "Memory plays tricks on us."

A more grounded approach, I'd say, challenges this challenge and replies: "Is it not rather that we play tricks on memory?" To take a common example: consider an event in one's early childhood that has constantly been retold at family gatherings. Psychologists claim it's frequently the case that the child protagonist in such events does not remember the events themselves, but remembers only the retelling of them in the family circle. Good enough! The child remembers something. What she perhaps doesn't remember is that her first well-focused attention to these events was as material in stories told by relatives. This is natural enough, for her attention is on the content of the story and not upon how she first became aware of it. It does not seem accurate to say memory tricks her here; closer to the mark is to say there is an omission of memory or an omission of attention.

If I may give a trivial case of such an instance, I once caught myself remembering "that time I was fishing for marlin in the Caribbean." Problem is, I've never been in the Caribbean, much less fished for marlin there. The memory was so clear, I was startled by this realization. Then it came to me: "That's Hemingway putting me in the Caribbean by his uncanny capture of detail and mood." My memory is not at fault. The content I'm holding in memory is something I truly experienced. What I'm not initially reflecting on is that this is a memory of literary experience.

For this reason I say we play tricks on memory. Memory works, but we don't always scrutinize it as it works. I'd even say "memory never makes a mistake." While we make mistakes about memory, these mistakes can more accurately be assigned to what we omit to remember—can be referred back to contextual matters we did not bother to note. Lacking a remembered context for an incident held securely in memory, we then improvise later. In fact: all the time and almost inevitably, we improvise context in order to imbed facts. This is why two eyewitnesses can, without lying, give incompatible accounts. What's of key importance here is that it's possible to sort these matters out. (One can observe this scrutinizing process in action on TV by watching Judge Judy at work; she's a tireless master at stripping away and discarding conveniently improvised context from remembered fact.)

Bertrand Russell once presented the most absolute attack on memory he could think of. He said your memory of the past provides no purchase whatever on the past you remember; this is because for all you know, you and your memory of the past were all created just a moment ago. (This is a more radical version of the more familiar argument that, for all we know, the Grand Canyon was created more or less in its present configuration less than five thousand years ago.) We will touch briefly on absolute skepticism in a chapter later on, but not so comprehensively as to destroy this argument for those who find it compelling.

A less radical way of undermining history concedes to each of us a reliable memory (if we will be careful to scrutinize the claims we make), but then goes on to put in question all accounts received from others. People lie. David Hume was so impressed by this that his tendency was toward telling his reader never to believe things on the testimony of others; at most, take what another says as an invitation to go see for yourself. If you are told "there's a three-legged chicken in that field over there," that should not, Hume is inclined to say, function legitimately as anything more than an invitation to cross the field and see for yourself.

Rigidly adhered to, such a policy would overwhelm with uncertainties the context in which one conducts the affairs of daily life. Its effect on the study of history would be very nearly to end it. Did Napoleon exist? Hume's advice to go take a look doesn't take you the distance. Very soon you begin invoking testimony. (That Hume was a practicing historian, and judged to be a good one, shows how quickly he could put aside what he argued philosophically when he wanted to do something else.)

There is, to be sure, lots of data that people do lie. Particularly they lie these days. I've suggested our government and media routinely lie to the American people (especially to motivate continuing participation in the violent world mission this essay claims we've come to think is ours).

This lying comes with a backup strategy. When one objects to the lying, or wishes to investigate something beyond limits our government regards legitimate, one is likely to be labeled a "conspiracy theorist." This, it seems, is a very bad thing. Threat of the label doesn't, I think, exactly convince the typical American that the smooth and sanitized stories presented by the government and media regarding official motives and acts are true; rather it simply discourages one person and then another from further inquiry, so that eventually most people give up the chase. Their discussions with others turn elsewhere. With regard at least to some particular thing (say the death of Kennedy or the circumstances leading to 9/11), they despair in effect of learning from the past; they cease paying attention to it.

This is a more genuinely unfortunate thing than being a conspiracy theorist. Of the death of Kennedy for instance, we know something: we know our government has not told us what happened. Those who studied it know that the assignment given the Warren Commission was to so massage the account of Kennedy's death as to do minimal damage to The American Story. They know the report of the commission was riddled with implausibilities and contradictions. They know, for instance, that the many testimonies and indications that there was firing from in front of Kennedy have not been refuted but have simply been discarded. But think positively. To know that the account we have been given is not true, is to know a great deal. The cover-up is in plain sight even if the details it covers up are not.

In what is a far more complicated case, something similar can be said regarding conditions surrounding 9/11. Those who study it know for instance they've been given four mutually incompatible versions of what NORAD was up to that day—not just regarding incidentals, but regarding mission, orders, and actual deployment. To know we haven't been told the truth is to know a great deal. While we are far from knowing exactly what happened, we do know that what we've been told happened is not—in matters of some importance—what did happen.

If we shrug complacently, and go about our business, not only does this shrug allow us to continue our support for America's crusade against an expanding list of people without examining our premises and motivations, it also means that many related issues, rich in consequence, urgent for our future, also go unexamined. Reluctant to recognize the complex and continuing mental maneuvers and social constructions that have landed us in a box, we slacken in our efforts to think outside it.

Let me, by way of illustration, take up briefly two issues, closely related, where history could shed much light were it not that we have become demoralized about turning to history. Let's take the issue of population growth first. Since we don't readily see a solution for it, our tendency is to act as if there is no problem. Yet our human population size (with our deep commitment, for instance, to eating meat in greater quantities than formerly) is clearly implicated in the whole crisis of habitat. All kinds of systems are overtaxed and in danger of toppling by reason of reciprocal interaction of our numbers and our ungoverned appetites: arable land, fishing, transportation, housing, and water, to name some obvious examples, are all jeopardized. The regurgitations of our waste clog our habitat and jeopardize these systems further.

Some biologists and sociologists hypothesize that the lethal skirmishes of human against human breaking out in so many parts of the world currently may not be due simply to racial, class, and religious antipathies, but may be due to those antipathies as they are heightened by anticipations of scarcity. Our common apprehensions seem, E.O. Wilson hypothesizes (in reflections on what happened in Rwanda), to be ginned up of late by the misgiving that there isn't—or soon won't be—enough for everyone. Our data-intake processing quietly suggests to us, "There may not be enough X [water; food; living space] for my grandchildren and the grandchildren of those others. Let us then strike before their numbers increase." Hobbes would understand perfectly.

In this matter of pressure from population, we are given less leadership than we need. Pastors, rabbis, priests, and politicians have generally been worse than unhelpful. Often enough, they've encouraged their own group to outbreed the competition. Regarding American politicians, surely you've never heard even one candidate promise, "And if elected, I will do all I can to encourage smaller families." Their campaign managers wouldn't allow it. Sooner, would say the managers, attack baseball or apple pie than go after motherhood.

History has something to say about this problem. It provides instances where societies have collapsed when their numbers outran their resources. Our own American experience provides the example of how the increase of each new generation of aspiring white settlers led to such competition over habitat as to motivate the whites to entertain projects of genocide against native Americans. On a planetary scale, history marks time with a kind of steadily quickening drumbeat for those with ears to hear. Often we ignore that beat because the unwelcome message is that the rich need to curb their consumption while the poor need to limit the number of their children.

History also suggests a way of escape. If one is disposed to consult history, what emerges as a salient feature of population growth is that it's often greatest where one might least expect—namely in regions characterized by desperation. This may seem counterintuitive. Without benefit of historical study, one might conjecture that when people are well-to-do, they'd have lots of offspring; and that when they're poor, they wouldn't. The opposite is the more general case. It requires attention to history to take in this trend, and its lesson.

One learns it's useless to denounce the phenomenon and regard the people of poor countries as irresponsible. Neither should we regard the poor in our own country as irresponsible. The poor are in fact responsible in the sense that they're responding. They're responding with a natural reflex to the experience of misery; they're responding by reproducing. When situations are calamitous, people breed. This has been nature's way of maintaining our species. Our evolutionary history has built it into us. A man close to despair may say: "The one thing I can still hope may give my life significance is to have offspring who survive me." Another, less despairing, may say: "I must have children who will care for me when I'm old." A still less distressed person, hopeful but still anxious, may say, "My enterprises will thrive if I have many children. And without them, who will take care of my enterprises when I'm gone?"

Perhaps though this is to be too ready to imply such things are dealt with at a conscious level. The blunt truth is: when things go bad, we breed. (If the pill disappointed some planners because it did not reduce the growth of population to the extent they'd hoped, it's because the planners hadn't factored in the extent to which conception itself, not just sex, can become more intensely desired in times of stress.) The solution is as simple as it is difficult for us affluent people to accept: if we would stop rigging the world markets to our advantage, and stop consuming more than is good for us, the poor of the world would have greater opportunities to achieve local prosperity and would curb the rate at which they reproduce.

My point in discussing this here is that, so far from seeking to master the not-too-difficult dynamics of overpopulation, we prefer to act as if there is no problem. Though history could tell us much about the problem, we prefer not to acknowledge the problem. One might think, for all the attention paid it, it doesn't exist. We seem to have trouble reaching any kind of consensus even on immigration—a problem deeply influenced by underlying problems of population growth and habitat degradation. We avoid the subject in part because we sense—correctly—that a solution will require a radical change in perspective and behavior. Demoralized, we ignore historical trend lines and what they predict. When challenged on this, we disingenuously counter: "What has history to tell us about the unique problems of the present?" If though we will put the problem of population in the context of an historical overview, the solution is, I claim, implicit in the problem. Over-consumption, unfettered development, and the desperation of the poor are the causes of the problem. Addressing these, we can move toward a solution.

History, as we anticipate though, is a tough task-master here. It offers an unwelcome answer. Desperate people breed; to reduce breeding, alleviate desperation. To do this, the affluent must place restraints on their lifestyles and their expectations of ever-greater prosperity in an effort to render the lives of the destitute less desperate. That is, the affluent must do this if they wish to continue to live some kind of shared life on this planet with those who are less fortunate. (The alternative for the affluent is to change, consciously or unconsciously, toward finding "final solutions." As attempted refugeeism becomes more common, the two alternatives—one humane and the other inhumane—are going to test us Americans profoundly.)

As I speak of "shared life," I don't mean free food—which can, as Garrett Hardin argued, put local farmers out of business. What seems indicated rather is a sharing of opportunities—a willingness on the part of us, the substantially more affluent, to restrain ourselves in foreclosing the opportunities of others. We must reverse our expansion in the interest of allowing room and availability of resources for a multitude of diverse and independent initiatives on the part of others. But this means letting go our notion that the world is a wilderness which we have been assigned to tame and exploit. (It means—dare I say it?— wiggling free of the death grip in which capitalism holds us.) On the other hand, if we adhere yet tighter to traditional ways, there will be exhaustion of resources and such changes of climate that desperate people in many parts of the world will become environmental refugees, squabbling in hardly imaginable ways over scarcity.

What history suggests further is that if we can't bring ourselves to a concern for others, we will continue pursuing hegemony and waging wars of attrition against potential rivals. We'll continue to call these rivals "terrorists," and in time many who are not already such will become terrorists in their response to us. We'll intensify confrontations with these others in the interest of moving things toward "final solutions" in a pursuit of air-tight national security. Consequences of sharing and consequences of not sharing seem the options history illuminates for us if we're willing to look to it for guidance. The beleaguered and desperate state in which the Israeli people live may be an example that predicts what may become the beleaguered and desperate situation of the United States.

Perhaps that's enough for now on history and overpopulation. A closely related instance where historical insight can help is, as suggested earlier, regarding the issue of climate change. We see the weather every day. Climate change is another matter. Yet in the melting of the ice caps and the plight of polar bears and penguins and Eskimos, and in the increasing tempo one can monitor in lives of firemen and firewomen, and in the droughts that increasingly plague California, and in the increasing storms that disrupt life further east, a thing as theoretical as climate change can become palpable. In fact it has become quite palpable. Hurricanes, rising seas, fire storms, and the loss of familiar patterns of rainfall are palpable. Increasingly therefore climate-change deniers are pushed toward a more nuanced defense: "OK, climate change is occurring, but there's no reason to think it's from anything we're doing."

Some deniers go further; they say, "You want history; we'll give you history. Climates change all the time! They've been changing all through time." Yet as we scrutinize history, a plotting of climate change against the increase in the atmosphere of carbon dioxide discovers a robust correlation. The Greenhouse Effect was a hypothesis proposed in the 1820s—when the Industrial Revolution was still in its first half-century. The hypothesis predicted that if we continued pouring CO_2, and like gases, into the atmosphere, there would be a gradual rise in earth's average temperature with the kind of climate-change phenomena we're now observing. We've continued our experiment with CO_2 at exponentially increasing rates—rates which accelerate as I write. The confirmations of predicted correlation between CO_2 and climate change that are coming in are very strong. Robust correlation is the lifeblood of science. There is, then, human causality in the present case; but to grasp the robust correlation of trends that tells us so requires that one not only talk of history but be attentive to it.

Our peculiar American resistance to science surely has relations back to our Puritan past, a time when the only truths worth attending were thought to be those relating rather immediately to the salvation of one's soul. The planet was reduced to little more than a scoreboard from which one could hope to coax signs of election. Further, anything historical which seemed to conflict with our superficial, uncritical, and highly westernized and anglicized reading of the Bible was rejected.

This tendency became further rigidified in America's religious struggle against Darwinian biology. The modern-day Puritans among us—supported by the inner Puritan in many more of us—have never abandoned their rear-guard defenses against biological history. Because it's common among us to deny that we are parts of nature, it's inconceivable to many Americans that we're now agents altering the habitat out of which we have sprung. A denial of the scientifically emerging timeline of human origins paves the way for a denial of current scientific reports about our human predicament at this moment. Without an attention to history, we neither know where we've come from nor where we're going. History then is vital to our future.

To return then to the issue of history and validity, is there a way to do history effectively? Yes. But not if we insist that history's lessons all be comforting, and not if we insist on holding history at arm's length, enthralled by an arbitrary and uncritical reading of the Bible that assures us we are God's elect. Memory can inform us, and can correct the errors we ascribe to it, if we want it to. Regarding the testimony of others—and much of history is a less-than-neatly-coherent tapestry woven from the testimony of others—there are means for sorting honest testimony from dishonest testimony, and reliable testimony from unreliable testimony. (One hopes all who accept jury duty are convinced of this.)

From the medieval Schoolmen—who probably owe it to Aristotle—we get: *Nemo gratis mendax*, no one is gratuitously a liar. This seems both reasonable, and confirmed by experience. The impulse of humans is to communicate their sense of things. Hidden agendas notwithstanding, in general we want others to know what we think. We are social, and want to share our view of reality. For this we have coffee breaks, dinner parties, libraries, and theaters. Parents wish, by and large, to empower their children by telling them the truth. It would be a monster indeed who would choose to inundate his child with misinformation.

But this last sets up, paradoxically, an opportunity for exploitation by others. Parents who have raised their children well, conscientiously empowering them with information and thoughtful guidance, may have a hard time putting these same children on alert against the hidden agendas and deceptions of other more opportunistic adults. It's especially difficult to fortify children against the common nonsense of the times. For the well raised child's experience has been that adults provide wholesome testimony.

How do we guard our children and ourselves against those who would take advantage of our inclination to trust? Well, violation of trust by acts of fraud and manipulation requires special motives. In seeking to protect ourselves and those in our care, we look then for those hidden agendas and vested interests that stand to be served by deceit. And we try to engage our children in this exercise of detection from their early years. (Not only is it OK to attempt to raise one's child as a discerning critic of out-in-the-open conspiracies, it's a derelict parent who does not do so.)

This is because, for all I've said about honesty as the default mode of human behavior, hidden agendas are now everywhere in play. Milton Friedman's doctrine (once its empty gesture of respect for ethics is peeled away) that a corporation boss's obligation is to do everything possible to increase stock dividends and values, is a likely culprit here. Standard practice has dictated, at least till very recently, that if a food company's advertising personnel can increase sales by misrepresenting the quality of its food, it's not only their right but their duty to do so. If a car manufacturer finds it's cheaper to pay civil damages for deaths caused by a defect in its cars than it is to fix the defect, then that's the way to go—so long as it can hide the game it's playing. If the Koch brothers can let their oil pipes rot, and bribe regulators not to call them on it, and if they can pay such fines when accidents occur as are negligible when calculated against profits, then clearly it's God's will they do just that. If the Veterans Administration can win bonuses for its personnel by misrepresenting the efficiency of its services, surely sound business practice requires no less. An extreme example—so extreme one finds it hard to credit—is the much-litigated accusation that some drug companies, including Bayer/Cutter, though they had reason to believe some blood they had on hand for transfusions (developed through an outdated technique) could easily be tainted with HIV, decided nonetheless to continue marketing it to Asia. As a commodity, it had a market value. The governing logic, the plaintiffs alleged on behalf of the victims, seemed to be one could not just pour it down the drain. Talk of caveat emptor. The ethos in such examples as these seems to say to the public at large: "It's your job not to trust us; if you ignore your duty, you deserve what you get."

In the business of war-making, we've seen it's entirely in conformity with our sense of national mission for our government to sponsor wars. Yet for our government to do so openly runs contrary to an image of ourselves that we hold dear. Honesty here would violate a cherished fiction. Knowing this is the case, knowing our officials must give accounts configured to fit The American Story, it's reasonable and prudent for every American citizen to regard official statements relating to any and all motives for war with anticipatory suspicion. The track record of our government, brought to light by historical reflection, is of great service if we will attend to it.

Polk informs us that our acquisition of California was somehow a natural consequence of aggressive action by Mexicans. McKinley would have us believe our bloody annexation of the Philippines was somehow necessitated by the misconduct of Spain. Wilson tells us our desire to make the world safe for democracy required our entry into the First World War. Johnson tells us the popularity of Ho Chi Minh in Vietnam threatened American security. (We were warned in quasi-official advisories it was better to fight with the Vietnamese in Hanoi than on the streets of San Francisco.) Suspicions emerging from this record should prompt us to heroic scrutiny of governmental purposes when it comes to new proposals for war. (Norman Solomon and John Perkins can be helpful here—as of course can the publishers of the *Pentagon Papers*: Daniel Ellsberg, Howard Zinn, and Noam Chomsky.)

Regarding destruction of habitat, the moral that history teaches is similarly cautionary. We know that our corporations are, by and large, headed by people in the grip of an ethos of ever-expanding utilization. The ethos that infatuates them requires that with each passing day they find more resources and use them at a quicker pace than they did the day before. Therefore, when they tell us the environment is doing fine, or that only fools are concerned about long-term consequences, we should look to their agenda and their track-record of habitat protection. (Mark Hertsgaard has written eloquently about this; so too has Naomi Klein.)

What we learn is that attention to testimony can itself protect one against the traps that testimony can set. In the climate-change debate, for instance, when one hears geologists in the employ of oil companies say that global warming was invented by an elite band of climatologists on the lookout for research grants, one should not ignore the piece of fossil fuel in the eyes of these well paid spokespersons for big oil. Were money really the controlling goal of climate scientists warning of climate change, we know they could quickly become more wealthy than they are by switching sides. In some cases, it's plausible to think entrepreneurs would pay them just to stop talking. (James Hansen, formerly NASA's chief meteorologist, could probably be living in comfortable retirement in a New York penthouse, if he would just start saying kind words about the oil industry.) Historical awareness of how the money game is played should enable us to know whose testimony is the more trustworthy.

"History" then is self-correcting. If someone's testimony is internally incoherent, that's reason for discarding it. In a more complicated case, there can be remarkable internal coherence in statements of one testifying falsely. When, however, such a person says things incompatible with other things the listener knows well, that too arms the listener against being taken in. Good detectives everywhere know that incoherences of either type in testimony provide criteria for suspicion and rejection (and that incoherence points toward what is being concealed). So do honest judges. (Judge Judy is quicker on an incoherence than a cat is on a mouse.)

Lest I seem to mangle and fray the thread of my argument, let me single it out clearly. Skeptics regarding history will point to the disagreements one finds among historians. "Where there is so much controversy," they will say, "who can know the truth?" Yet the problem they cite is, in fact, the solution. The field of disagreements, entered honestly and with good will, is the field of answers. History will not save us by itself, but the desire to save ourselves without history is basically a desire to save ourselves without processing the painful lessons of our past. It's a desire similar to the cocaine addict's desire to find security and a full life in the sheltering clouds of cocaine.

7 | Skepticism about Beauty

If I have a student who loves to write music and perform it, that student is not a logical positivist. If I have a student who loves to walk trails into the mountains, one who lies under the stars with his or her significant other while they gaze in amazement at the splendor of the night sky till sleep comes on, such a student is not a logical positivist. But, without knowing the term itself, most of my other students are logical positivists. Growing up in our technological society, they have somehow imbibed the notion that what we "really know" is restricted to what can be tested in a lab or certified by a collection of physical data.

Among other unfortunate consequences of this gratuitous belief is that they do not believe there's anything objective about beauty. And though I say I do not believe their theoretical conviction is the product of critical thinking, they do have some experience to make it plausible. For instance, they have favorite musical groups and favorite songs, and have found by experience that these preferences are often hard to communicate to others. Regarding tastes in general, they've found it impossible sometimes to recruit others, and have felt it painful at times when others have tried to recruit them.

They've concluded beauty is simply in the eye of the beholder; and from this, in turn, comes a process in which, notwithstanding their awareness they have preferences, there develops a kind of trivializing—a de-substantializing and dismissive attitude toward aesthetic experience. This demotion of aesthetic experience is worth worrying about because the demotion tends to filter from our culture what could be important clues to the unwholesomeness of our present course; we lose what could be intimations of privation and of unmet needs for connections, connections that is with nature, other people, and the Origin of the order we behold. The experience of nature that was commonplace for Thoreau and Whitman and John Muir has somehow not registered with them. To the extent they experience beauty, it is somewhat in the mode of the man who replaces one trophy wife with another, or like the experience of the dentist who recently went to Africa to kill a rare and beautiful lion so he could display its head upon a wall. We fail to appreciate, that in their eloquent protests and affirmations, Wordsworth, Coleridge, Shelley, Keats, and Byron by no means thought they were indulging in airy nothings; they saw themselves engaged in rear-guard action to save civilization from the numbing effects of the world's industrial and technological revolution. There was a similar agenda among the French Impressionists—even among those who painted steamships and railroads. There was Paul Cezanne with his simple mystical houses, Gauguin with his languid and sultry Tahitians, Van Gogh with his sunflowers. They wanted to place us back in the moment, and to feel the things we were being tutored by the times to neglect.

I've suggested a recent a brand of philosophy offers endorsement for the conclusion about beauty which so many of my students take for granted (or, as James Joyce might pun: take for granite). Logical positivism—while out of fashion currently among philosophers—is alive and well in everyday thinking, and in American schools of education. According to logical positivists, you've only got a genuine statement in hand when you've got something that can be judged true or false by a physical criterion.

Suppose I say: "It's raining outside." I've made a statement, the positivist will say. Why? Because if you or someone steps outside, they'll find either that things are getting wet from water falling from the sky, or they're not. Since there's a way to determine whether it's raining or not, the sequence of words: "It's raining outside" has meaning and is a statement.

While we've been accustomed to divide things said into "true" or "false," the logical positivist begins by dividing things said into "statements" and "pseudo-statements."

We can get into the reasoning here by looking again at how we talk about music. Suppose I say: "Beethoven was born before Mozart." This, the logical positivist says, is a statement.

The reason it qualifies as a statement is because there are certificates, diaries, dates of works published or performed, letters, etc., that can function as criteria for the truth or falsehood of what I've said. It happens that Mozart turns up as born first; but this doesn't disqualify what I said from being a statement; the evidence establishes simply that my statement was false.

Again, suppose I say: "Beethoven lived longer than Mozart." This too is a statement. It happens to be a true statement; but what constitutes it as a statement is not its truth but that there are physical criteria (diaries, etc.) for judging it.

Having made two statements about Beethoven and Mozart, one false and the other true, suppose, then, I go on to say, "Mozart was a greater musician than Beethoven." Is this a statement? "Of course not," answers a good positivist, for there's no physical criterion by which to judge it. How, the positivist will demand, do I measure "greater musician"? I may want to save it; so I rephrase, "Mozart's music contains more beauty than Beethoven's." Have I saved it? Again, the positivist will say: "Of course not; there's no physical criterion by which to measure beauty." Counting of notes won't do the trick; neither will number of compositions. Neither will arrangement of notes; at most one can say one composer arranged notes one way, the other arranged notes a different way. The lack of a satisfactory criterion may lead a truly aggressive positivist to say may in fact: "The very term 'beauty' is nonsense and gibberish!"

While you might think this matter of leaving such things at the level of "to each their own" is very liberating, it comes at a high price. You might notice, for instance, how well this is conformed to Descartes in his reflections on physical nature. There's no color, sound, scent, or taste in things. How could there be? Does sugar in the sugar bowl find itself sweet? Rather all these qualities are projected by us. (Kant, in his *Critique of Pure Reason*, takes this further, saying we never know things-in-themselves at all; we know only what we have generated in our response to them.)

Beauty seems, in the wake of such considerations, to retreat into pure subjectivity. What I find beautiful, is beautiful for me. There's no occasion for argument with others, and no occasion for instruction. If others share my tastes, fine; if they don't, equally fine. "Concerning tastes, there's no occasion for dispute" an ancient adage tells us.

Perhaps you can anticipate why I say a trivialization of aesthetic experience sets in. This approach leaves the joy I take in one of Van Gogh's paintings on the same footing as the pleasure I take in a strawberry sundae. You may never eat strawberry sundaes, always preferring those with hot fudge. Here there's no right or wrong; to each their own. For me, says the positivist, to try to draw you into my appreciation of Van Gogh is as arbitrary and silly as for me to try to recruit you to my preference for strawberries.

This is where we are. It's not a good place. It forfeits claiming a role for art in the intellectual and moral development of us humans. When Aristotle takes up the plays of Sophocles, he doesn't regard them as a pastime. He sees Sophocles' works as powerful engines for the cleansing and enlightenment of the soul—works that can lift us from the self-preoccupations of our normal world into a liberating awareness of the common human predicament. Our sense of shared mortality with all humans comes to the fore. A capacity for empathy with those who suffer is quickened. A sense of our personal moral frailty and past sins can summon us to feel our guilt and seek forgiveness—as was the case with Oedipus when he realized he was a patricide.

Along with friendships with good people, Aristotle—that most practical of men—sees engagement with great art as a shortcut to virtue.

It's true we can seek development of our character by a diligent cultivation of this or that virtue; we can calculate, and attempt to practice a mean between two opposing vices. Aristotle devotes a book of his ethics to expounding this approach. Ben Franklin writes, too, about this approach. But this is heavy lifting—not comparable to the electrifying influence of a friendship with a good person or exposure to great art.

I speak of skepticism about beauty as "convenient" just because it avoids the transformation an encounter with beauty can demand of us. We shun it. We shun it as we sometimes shun the company of people better than ourselves. There's a summons in beauty. There are works of art which we hesitate to revisit because they shake us to our depths. Watching *King Lear* is an ordeal. Some might say: "Yeah! It's boring." No doubt they speak from experience. For an attentive playgoer, however, *Lear* can be excruciating and revelatory. In the storm scene, the sense of one's own folly can induce a terrible vertigo. Likewise, there are films (*Sophie's Choice* comes to mind) one hesitates to see a second time. One doesn't forget how wrenching they were the first time. Film buffs can produce a list of such works. We're ambivalent toward such works, approaching them warily, just as one does well to be wary approaching the third rail of an electric railroad. For while films can cast a spell that allows escape from the weight of things, they can also waken us from a spell, and bring us to a state where fundamental realities hit us with blinding clarity.

Music, too, can have such effects. And a painting or sculpture can ambush one and induce a change of life.

The reluctance we may feel to be tutored by great art testifies to its power. On the other hand, if we weigh art on the scale on which we weigh a strawberry sundae, we insulate ourselves against such power. We shelter ourselves from it in a way that leaves us lodged in comfortable habits and tedious complaints.[1]

On the day Pavarotti died, my car radio began playing his performances of arias by Puccini. My eyes blurred; I felt unstrung by beauty. What responsible man drives in such a state? While it no doubt contributed to my sense of preciousness, I don't think it was especially Pavarotti's death that blurred my vision; I was blindsided by perfection.

Much of a liberal arts education is an effort to lead students, males no less than females, to the masterpieces of great poets, playwrights, novelists, painters, sculptors, musicians, and performing artists. This last category, performing artists, opens out horizons of excellence of unlimited variety. One can be sustained in spirit for a week, buoyed by the grace of a perfectly executed double play in the World Series — an instance among thousands for anyone paying attention.

---

1. My self-congratulatory — delusional? — hunch when students so rapidly reach for their cell phones after a class of mine is that it's because the class experience has opened such vistas for critical thinking and reform of life that they need to hasten back to familiar ground — ground about whose dullness they routinely complain.

The differences-in-taste argument should not lead to the skepticism about beauty it often does. Differences in taste are due to differences in cultivation. One sees the beauty one has prepared oneself to see; and each kind of beauty has its own apprenticeship. An experience of baseball can be as bewildering to the newcomer as it is exhilarating to all the other people in the stands. (A successful sacrifice fly can look like a failure to a newcomer.) One can't expect to get jazz on a first encounter. Some do. Perhaps Mozart, at the age of five, would. Most of us have to put ourselves under discipline (as Mozart at the age of five serenely was). And as suggested, even when art begins to speak to us, most of us have to hold ourselves in discipline so as not to run from it.

Important things are at stake. When we trivialize art, and say there's nothing "objective" about it, we trivialize our own aesthetic sensibility and leave our souls untended. We close down an encounter with being that only our affectivity can provide. Keats said, "Beauty is truth." He said well. Art is objective in the way that some art is more revelatory than other. Great art can disclose the sublimity of the familiar; it helps us hear the whisperings—catch the glimmer—of the mystery of existence. If it can't reveal God's nature, it can at least bring us to a state where a denial of sacredness is no longer possible.

In the earlier chapter on nature, I noted how hostile the ethic of Puritanism is to the experience of natural beauty. We have fortified our state of deprivation by telling ourselves beauty isn't really out there. So long as we believe and feel this, we will have little incentive to restrain ourselves regarding those redundant and mindless intrusions into nature that now threaten us all. Just as the dentist who beheaded Cecil the lion tried to defend himself by claiming it was all perfectly legal, so we attempt to defend ourselves on similar grounds regarding our unrepented rape of mother nature. What can be more fatal to our sense of beauty than an ethos that invites us to see it only as something to own?

Here, let's conclude this reflection on beauty. Our reflection lays groundwork for the next chapter. Those who know and respect beauty are on their way to knowing that morality too is somehow objective. Not to know this about morality is to be reduced to a life that offers no genuine opportunity for insight or heroism. In a depleted world where "justice" is an empty word, what room is there for commitment or loyalty? What meaning can such a world deliver? If we demote beauty and ignore moral-ity, is it any wonder that marriages are fragile and that relation-ships in general are difficult to sustain? To echo Thoreau, in such a world, one resigns oneself to a life of quiet desperation. Worse yet, one turns to war. This is the devalued world, the familiar wasteland, in which currently so many of us — good descendants of good Puritans — move restlessly about.

8 | Skepticism about Morality

Here, too, in challenging times, skepticism is "convenient." Think of all the things you don't have to worry about if there's no right or wrong. But convenience comes at a price: drama and meaning pretty much evaporate. In a moral vacuum, things lose all density. Chronic depression can be a matter of hormones; but it can also be a matter of ethics—that is, of a lack of ethics. Even if someone attempts to restore a sense of actuality by becoming a "law unto oneself"—a serial killer, say, engaging in horrendous deeds—such a one achieves only, as Hannah Arendt suggests, variations of banality. Each absurd deed clamors to be topped by a new one. A moral desert is a boring place.

The argument for a total subjectivity of morality (which amounts to a denial there is morality) begins pretty much in the same place the argument for the non-objectivity of beauty does. Not only do we see people disagreeing on questions of moral behavior, we see people of notable intelligence and integrity disagreeing on such questions. And bringing a third party in to referee doesn't seem to help, but just adds another participant to the fray.

Law can't really solve the problem either. Not if the problem is one of how to escape sheer relativity. Laws of one place are contrary to those of another. Different times in the same place deliver different laws. The laws of Germany under Nazism provide an instructive example. When these laws were first promulgated, they were very clear, and most people in Germany obeyed them. Yet nobody, including elderly Germans who once obeyed them, thinks today such laws were just or moral. The skeptic will use this to deny there's any objectivity to morals.

The classic argument against objective morality belongs to Hume. He imagines a murder scene, and asks what conclusions an observer might be able to draw from it. Such an observer might be able, he concedes, to conclude from physical evidence to objective facts about the murder. An astute detective might be able to determine the time of the murder, the weapon used, and even reach likely surmises as to the motive of the murderer (whether robbery, say, or revenge, or personal amusement). Hume then asks, could that same detective also conclude as to whether or not the murder should have happened. He answers with a follow-up question: "On what basis is such a conclusion possible?" Where is the data that takes one beyond what the facts are to what the facts "should or should not have been"? How, he asks, does one travel from "what is" to what "ought to be"? Our senses, operating at their best, he says, give us facts; they report on the physical world. But facts are always about actuality. We have no senses for what should not have happened.

It's true that in his *Enquiry Concerning Moral Principles* Hume provides an account of human affectivity and emotion that roughly parallels that of his friend, Adam Smith. Hume's account is however non-prescriptive. He doesn't say people *should* have certain feelings of empathy, or that they are *wrong* if they don't, or that they are wrong when they don't obey such feelings as they have. To say as much would be to return to a conventional morality, which Hume refuses to do. He doesn't retract here what he'd proffered as a serious reflection in *A Treatise of Human Nature* earlier—namely that the word "should" is devoid of content. (When people prove lacking in empathy, the best Hume can do is say that fortunately they seem in the minority.)

In *A Treatise of Human Nature* Hume provided a foundation for the logical positivism we discussed when we were treating of beauty. In this system, every valid use of language requires "sensible correlates" for the terms used. Let's return to review the detective at the murder scene. The term blood has a sensible correlate; we've all seen it—red, sticky stuff. Blood can discover to us the cause of a death. From the way it has poured forth or splattered, we can know in some cases that the cause of death was murder. Blood can register the approximate time of death, and help determine therefore the time at which the murderer acted. It can, in the way it was shed, discover to us in some cases the weapon(s) used—and may even tell us something about motive. Murder committed in anger may have a bloody look different from the bloody look of murder committed with premeditation. How though can blood—or anything else at the murder scene—discover to us the moral character of the act? What is the evidence on which a moral judgment can rest? What is the objective "correlate" for the term "evil deed"? What does an evil deed look like? What state of blood reveals it?

Logical positivism systematizes what Hume offers. We can make genuine statements only when the claim they contain can be put to the test of what can be seen, heard, touched, tasted, or smelled. When we speak of things that can neither be confirmed nor denied by sensible experience, we talk nonsense. All claims for a rational aesthetics, for morality, for metaphysics, or for religious teaching fall into this category—all are sheer nonsense. (Hume suggests at the end of *An Enquiry Concerning Human Understanding* that we should burn the books which engage in such claims. In other words, he seems to claim it is morally better not to make claims for morality than to make them.)

The inconsistency of logical positivism notwithstanding, this is strong stuff, and many a young person finds it liberating. It seems to say: "You can do no wrong." Like Dostoyevsky's Rashkolnikov, one can feel excused from the burden of moral reflection. Exempted from deliberations about right and wrong, one can simply do what feels convenient at the moment. One is absolved from sin by the revelation there's no such thing. One is a law unto oneself.

Some perhaps come to recognize the cost of such convenience only when they, or someone they care about, becomes a victim. Then one feels wronged or feels another has been wronged. One feels injustice has been done.

Aye, but there's the rub. There can be injustice only if there's such a thing as justice. Unless there's justice, what can be done to make that feeling of victimhood more than a mere ungrounded sentiment? A toothache certainly can feel bad. We want it to go away; but we don't generally assign to it a moral character. Except in a joking mood, we don't call our toothache evil. To give the feeling of victimhood substance, and to be able to call upon the community to do something about it, requires that one import something like "justice" into the discussion. Only then does "evil" acquire a definition: it is a violation of justice.

Unwelcome acts can then be renamed as acts that violate justice. Otherwise, one's grievance remains weightless. "Get over it!" might be the advice. "What is, is," the stoic may remind. As victims know, such advice is thin comfort and new outrage. Something important is being overlooked.

If, though, abandoning a victim to victimhood is intolerable, what is the objective correlate of "justice"? What is there "out there" in the realm of reality to which the term points? (It's exactly here Hume conducts his search for a sensible correlate; but since justice is nothing like a pine tree or a turtle or a Cadillac, Hume draws a blank.)

Plato wrote his masterwork the *Republic* in an attempt to give an answer. His answer: the idea that justice is when everything is in its proper place seems too abstract and bloodless to do the job. And to define "the just" by introducing the category "proper" seems a begging of the question.

Kant presented the "Categorical Imperative," not so much as a speculative answer, but as a practical way to test whether justice is, in fact, being exercised. You're acting justly if you can will that your example be a principle on which all can act: "If you can will that people in general act as you do, your action is just." In effect, Kant does then offer Hume and other skeptics a criterion of sorts. Rooted in experience, it's a criterion that shares some ground not only with Hume but also with Hemingway's partly facetious but much-cited proposal "An act is moral if, long after you've done it, it still feels good." Kant makes no effort to prove you should act morally; he states rather that you already know that.

A promising place to start thinking about this matter of whether there's anything objective in morality is to begin thinking about whether "human rights" exist. Kant guides attention in that direction when he says one way to formulate the Categorical Imperative is: "So treat humanity, whether in yourself or another, as always to treat it as an end and never as a mere means." In other words, we exercise morality when we act with regard for human rights.

Louis Pojman, a philosophy teacher formerly at West Point, recounts his way of directing his young cadets toward the issue of rights. After "losing," in class discussion, to his students on his position that "morality is objective," Pojman assigns a paper on the issue in which most of his students put in writing what they've already said in class—namely that morality is purely subjective (or is perhaps just a meaningless word). Pojman then grades the papers, not on their content, but in accord with some arbitrary system (say, giving A's to those students sitting closest to the front of the room in the previous class, and lower grades to those sitting further back). After assigning these grades, in the next class, he returns the papers, explaining—while keeping a straight face—the system by which he graded them. Uproar! Pandemonium! "You can't do this!" "This isn't fair!" At that point, Pojman springs his trap: "How can you say what I do is unfair when most of you have just argued both in class and on your papers there's no such thing as justice or injustice? Are you telling me now you don't believe a word of what I find in most of your papers?"

Locke and Jefferson could think of no way to prove human rights from sense experience. Locke, with his doctrine of the mind as a blank slate, is at a loss here because if the mind begins as a blank slate, there are no truths that are "self-evident." "Self-evident truths" is a phrase that seems to imply the mind comes equipped with some truths without regard to any empirical test. Locke was so sure though that human rights do exist, that he took the bit in his mouth and declared that human rights are self-evident. In drafting the Declaration of Independence, Jefferson-and-company famously followed Locke, declaring "We hold these truths to be self-evident; that all men...are endowed by their Creator with certain unalienable rights...."

Here I may seem ready to allow the affirmers of rights a too easy victory. But the objection of the logical positivists that all statements must be subject to a test by sensible data is itself arbitrary. The positivists have simply decided that all genuine experience is of sense objects only. This is an act of faith. This proposition which they posit cannot itself be established by some experience of sense objects. This is what makes them positivists. They simply *posit* materialism. What they posit is far from self-evident. All the passions, desires, ambitions, and motivations of humankind (belonging to some realm other than sense objects) seem to stand in contradiction to what they posit. For the positivists do not say merely that it's unreliable to depend on things that can't be tested by their method. Their doctrine requires that we're "not talking about anything" when we speak of anything their method can't validate. Such things don't exist. Or if they do, we have no experience of them—and have therefore no right to talk of them. (Notice the notion of "a right" is implicit in the positivist case and gets slipped unobtrusively back into the discussion, but used negatively and entering as it were by the back door. Hume does the same thing. This explains the low standing of logical positivists among philosophers—even as schools of education and of business continue to worship at their feet.)

Think how the negations and curtailments of the logical positivists work for love. Suppose a logical positivist says: "I will not believe that love exists until you provide some hard, cold evidence for it." Think of the burden the positivist is trying to impose on the person who believes love is an actuality. Unless love registers some dimensions in the space/time continuum or registers some weight in the gravitational matrix, must one who believes in love cease doing so? If one wishes to be thought a sober-minded adult, must one deny the reality of love?

One can of course try to meet positivists on their own ground by turning to, discovering, manifestations of love. But is one ready to say love is simply a box of chocolates handed to another on Valentine's Day? Is love just a red flush on the face or a high temperature that registers on a thermometer? Do a red flush and a high temperature characterize a mother as she rises from bed at night to tend a sick child? (Perhaps one can cite cases when they do; but surely the more significant sign is that she gets out of bed. And even that, surely, does not suffice to take the measure of love.)

It's in the realm of interiority, not easily accessible to instruments of the laboratory (though brain scans are adding new data), that the experience of value occurs. And one's experience of value—of one's own value and the value of others and the value of things—provides a ground for the "objectivity" we're seeking. (What the brain scans provide are precise and intriguing biological changes that correlate neatly with such experience—just as we have always known that blushing and paleness do.) It does not matter that the experience itself remains a matter of interiority. If by "objective" we mean "empirically present," then the experience of value is as "objectively given" for a person of wholesome sensibility as, say, the experience of seeing a mountain is for a person of undimmed eyesight. Confirmability by another is a secondary issue. (Only by adding all kinds of qualifications—bells and whistles, if you will—to this notion of "confirmability by another" can such confirmability even begin to have the status some logical positivists—some biological behaviorists—demand for it as a test of what is real.)

Yet in a kind of accommodation to objections, it must be granted in the case of morality that this sensibility—this sensitivity to value—is not simply "there," but develops in a person through a process. Moral sensibility is in this respect very much like aesthetic sensibility. Where Hume falls short of Kant is in overlooking our common human experience of being "called." What accounts for significant human differences in the matter of moral sensitivity is that development of it is a process conducted in freedom; how we respond to the mysterious "call" makes the difference. Further, because a freely-entered process depends on perseverance by the agent, our response can be aborted at any time, including when it's just getting started. Just as a person being introduced to the study of jazz may declare in the midst of their first lesson: "Say! You know: there's nothing here!" so, in a similar manner, one is free at any time to abort one's moral education.

In the *Nicomachean Ethics* Aristotle elaborates at length on the learning process involved here. At the center of his exposition is an analysis that goes something like this. Suppose I think of some helpful act I could perform on behalf of another. I realize the act is within my competence and I realize this act could provide a significant benefit in the other person's life. So it's an act I'm free to do and know would do some good. If I follow through and carry out the act—if I conform my action to the judgment inspiring me (and, say, like the bishop in *Les Miserables,* give the candlesticks to Jean Valjean)—I get new insight into reality. For there's an opportunity for me to go from the particular to the general, from the individual to society as a whole, and to go from a single act of generosity and kindness to a whole career—recognizing fresh paths to enhancing the happiness of humankind. As I do this, I come to know myself better. Not because some teacher has told me so, but because I experience it within myself, I come to recognize myself as a being who achieves happiness in living according to my judgment (or "my reason" or "my conscience"). In beginning by helping another, I get deeper understanding not only of how this particular person behaves and thrives, but of how people in general do. And as I continue in this path, this growth in understanding continues. Beyond that—if you will allow—I grow in confidence regarding the dialectic by which wisdom is achieved, and get fresh insight into being. The numinous halo of being—something Aristotle surprises students by addressing at the end of his *Ethics*—discloses itself more emphatically to me; and joy is the consequence. Such joy is the karmic consequence of acting morally. (It may require some time in pondering the *Nicomachean Ethics* to see this, but this really is a fair take on Aristotle's description of moral process.)

To be sure, I may find my act didn't have the specific consequences I'd hoped for—may not have had the results I'd intended. This can be painful; it may even be disastrous. Here too though insight is stimulated. The gritty facticity and less-than-predictable oddity and stubbornness of things is brought home to me in such moments; I recognize myself, in Heidegger's words, in "a world not of my own making."

Fortunately though—to go back and view this dialectic of action and judgment in its larger perspective—often enough it turns out my act does have consequences along the lines I'd hoped. To repeat what I've said above, this happier instance, like the negative instance, provides grounds for enhanced judgment. Enhanced judgment, as noted, discloses to me in turn new ways to apply what I've learned. So fidelity to the promptings of judgment leads to judgment sharpened and enlivened. I become more discerning and alert. (Think for instance of what happens in a successful marriage when mutual respect prevails over all the inevitable frictions and frustrations intimacy entails.) With new understandings of reality come fresh opportunities for creative and satisfying activity. As Aristotle declares in book 10, in the life of such a one, the world reveals itself increasingly as meaningful and radiant with value. One contemplates. One begins to see the world from a divine perspective. (He cautions that, although the capacity to do so may seem small and fragile, we should nurture it, for it is absolutely the most important potentiality in us.)

If all this sounds too much like a tale from Mary Poppins, it's because words cannot capture what must be lived. Heidegger speaks of a virtuous circle: what we find precious, we care for; and what we care for, we find precious.

Take a directly opposite case. Granted when the thought of a virtuous activity first occurs, if I decide not to do it, it may be a case of "no foul, no penalty." I prefer to expend my energies in a different activity which I regard as equally worthy or more worthy. Often enough though, when I've said "no" to something which my judgment has proposed as good, I'll experience a kind of internal dissonance and a need to rearrange myself. When I don't do something I regard as reasonable, I typically feel a need to re-establish lost integrity. I will attempt this through denial.

The maneuver goes like this. Since no positive action of mine followed upon my judgment (that is, since I didn't go where my reason invited), I'll try to reconfigure my judgment to fit my inaction. I'll rationalize. I will for instance decide that this person I was considering helping is not in fact worthy of help. Or, further upstream, I may decide that if there is any "helping" to be done by me, it should be restricted to helping myself. "Charity begins at home." "God helps him who helps himself." "Strengthen the strong." "God loves me, so I should too." In other words I'll invent sophisticated reasons to close myself off and foreshorten opportunities for moral growth. (I'll read *Atlas Shrugged*.)

It's because of this I worry about those who say "There's nothing objective to morality." Not only have they adopted a theory likely to become a hurdle for any project of moral growth, but it's quite possible—in an existential way—they've already said "no" to such growth in many particular instances. Action contrary to conscience, or inobedient to it, tends toward lethal consequences for conscience. They may be habituating themselves to strategies that cannot make them happy. They may be starting to go rancid. (The murder of the Indians was most inconvenient both for the Puritans who did it, and for their unrepenting offspring. It is not too surprising that so many of us today find ourselves echoing Macbeth after he murders Duncan: "Tomorrow and tomorrow and tomorrow creeps in this petty pace from day to day....")

To habituate oneself in this direction is to supplant reason with rationalization; it's to install an enervating selfishness in the place of a far more wholesome prizing of self that finds confirmation in opening out in love to others. We sometimes feel pity for *medecins sans frontières*—doctors and nurses who starkly exemplify an indiscriminate love for others—but we shouldn't. If we would be happy, we should end our admiration and envy for the likes of the Koch brothers, and replace that envy with a wholesome envy of *medecins sans frontières*.

This brief review of morality may seem a parenthesis in our effort to diagnose America, but isn't. If we wish America to have a future, we need to cast off our convenient skepticism about morality and address the issue of selfishness. We need to take our affirmation of human rights out of the clouds and bring it down to earth. A mere change of our office-holders (as I'll argue at length later) can't save us. Even were we somehow able to deny power to all the corporate leaders now dismantling our habitat, we would not be saved—for we would seek their replacement with other persons as misguided as they. For the sake of harmony with nature, for the sake of health and prosperity among ourselves, for the sake of peace with other peoples and countries, we must address and question our personal habits of selfishness as part of combating the shared culture of selfishness we've inherited. The alternative to calling ourselves to account as we surrender our illusion that we're somehow the Elect is to continue in our aberrant and absurd narcissism and to continue our immense agency toward producing an increasingly desolate world.[1]

---

1. This is no easy matter to deal with. I'd suggest a long pause—taking a break from the dental chair—before proceeding to the next chapter.

9 | Skepticism about Anything Being Known with Certitude (Absolute Skepticism)

If nothing is known with certitude, a logical corollary is that everything is uncertain. The person who says it the first way may sound like a moderate. "I don't deny that we know things; I'm just saying we're never sure." That's the person you want on the jury when you're being tried in a capital case. He or she finds nothing true beyond a reasonable doubt. Without quite realizing it, he or she is in a flirtation with absolute skepticism.

If nothing is certain, all the other skepticisms can come wrapped in this one. History is just someone's opinion — or perhaps a tissue of fairy tales like stories about Santa Claus. The same can be said of science. The fact a lot of people proclaim themselves experts and say something in concert doesn't make it true; think of all the times scientists have admitted they've been wrong. As for beauty, it's something people pretend to discover. People praise Shakespeare and Mozart because they've been taught to. Or maybe it's just a matter of neurological firings; some things "turn one on." (And if that's all "beauty" is, why not take a shortcut, and get the same from drugs?) As for morality, surely it's a con. It's a way by which some try to manipulate others; those who preach it most, observe it least. The same can be said for religion.

These attitudes often pass for wholesome cynicism — for necessary defenses against being taken in.

There may be cases in which that's all they are. But absolute skepticism (in contrast to mere gestures of hesitation and doubt) endorses all that's negative in such propositions, and works to cut off retreat back toward any unqualified affirmation. Where a moderate agnostic may say: "I don't know," an absolute skeptic says: "Nobody knows."

Once one arrives at such, one has no more lessons to learn or duties to fulfill. That's as convenient as things get. A state of rest is achieved. The purchase price of such sublime disengagement is the despair of achieving any coherence. One takes this nettle in hand. One bites the bullet. There's no northern star by which to steer one's troubled bark through choppy waters.

For coherence in one's thinking requires that there be somewhere or somehow an absolute in the system, and one other than absolute denial. Without such, there's no fulcrum for Archimedes' lever; everything's left up in the air. For all that some deconstructionists may say to the contrary, if all things are regarded as subject to interpretation, there's no "given" material for interpretation to address. Nor is there any standing principle for interpretation to utilize. Interpretation needs starting points. Anchored in those, or at least governed by them (or at least by one of them), it can move along. The alternative is a mental block of infinite proportions. If we cannot be sure of what the number "3" is, and of what its difference is from "4," all counting has been compromised. Equations cannot be trusted. The attractions and utility of mathematics have been greatly diminished. (And school's out early.)

Consider how, if everything is changing, there's no fixed backdrop against which even change can be measured. Much less can there be a purpose in accord with which it might make sense to help along one change at the expense of another. To seek a "balance of nature" or speak of maintaining a "sustainable lifestyle" is sheer nonsense amid such randomness. One must reconcile oneself to Macbeth's "tale told by an idiot, full of sound and fury, signifying nothing." (Interestingly, for all his acknowledgement of flux, Heraclitus was not so destitute—he had his "Logos" as a source of meaning; and Hegel for all his celebration of contradiction, had his "emergence of Absolute Spirit.")

In his discussion of speculative reason, Kant asks what a "fact" is. To take Kant's discussion off the page and bring it home, let me direct it toward an act of snapping my fingers. Suppose as I'm working at the keyboard, I stop and snap my fingers twice. (I just did.) Will that action (O'Neill just now has snapped fingers twice) constitute a "fact"? According to Kant such an act will.

He then asks what an assertion of that sort means. Suppose we posit an eventual loss of all memory of this deed (in the face of all my efforts to memorialize it) and suppose we posit the very collapse of the universe in which this act occurred. "Will that event remain a fact?" is Kant's question. He answers that most of us intuitively feel it will. The universe may come and go, but a fact is not thereby undone.

This leads Kant to say he sees in our intuitive response that we humans spontaneously regard the world of our experience, and all the details of all the acts that occur in it, as taking place in full view of an absolute spectator, a divine witness. Here Kant seems to anticipate Hegel. In speaking—in *The Critique of Pure Reason*—of God as a "regulatory principle of speculative reason" Kant claims that in asserting the eternal endurance of facts, one regards a mere snapping of fingers (my example, not his) as taking place against a backdrop of Absolute Consciousness; we regard it as caught up and eternally conserved in a divine mind. Kant makes no effort to use this to prove the existence of God. He thinks all attempts to prove God's existence involve an illegitimate maneuver—involve a begging of the question. He says however that it seems evident we cannot think at all without *thinking* God.

Kant is very modern in a way. He finds there are all kinds of things we humans must think, but finds too there's no way to know these things are true. We cannot get outside the phenomenal order—something like Plato's cave—in which we discover ourselves to dwell, and escape into what Kant calls the "noumenal"—the world of things-in-themselves. This is a world about which we can think (and that's why Kant labels it "noumenal" or thinkable), but it remains inaccessible to us, at least in our present state. Kant thereby ends up closer to Hume than he may have intended. Along with Hume, Kant anticipates logical positivism by confining our experience to the phenomenal world—which for Kant means: the world as we constitute it (reliant on a priori categories with which consciousness comes fitted) in response to our sensations.

Should one accept these fashionable modern restrictions on knowledge? Can we only think things, but never know them? Is a conscientious organizing of our thinking, as we respond to a phenomenal world we generate in consciousness, the most we can achieve in our intellectual life? Or is this an extravagant contraction? Is there a subset in the circle of things we think? Among the things we think, is there a subset containing things we *know*?

Surely this latter is the case. There are things of which we are certain. We know things. (And among the things we know is that memory is something more than shuffling through a bunch of images that may or may not put us in touch with the past. By memory we inhabit the past. This may seem miraculous, but—contrary to what Bertrand Russell says—we know it is the case.)

The suspicion we don't know things does not, I suspect, come to us directly from Hume, or Kant, or any other philosopher. (In his *Treatise on Human Nature* Hume diligently employs reason to persuade us reason doesn't work. Somehow most of us find this unpersuasive.) Rather our suspicions about knowing come generally from two common, and ongoing, experiences. One is the familiar experience, mentioned already, of finding that very intelligent people disagree. The other is finding that we ourselves are often mistaken—mistaken even regarding issues about which we care deeply and to which we've given full attention.

There's no getting around these kinds of things; one can however put them into a perspective where they function as invitations to a richer intellectual life rather than as excuses from having one.

With regard to the first—the disagreements among brilliant and people—let me offer, as a case for study (among the literally millions of case studies one could conduct), the fractious relations that developed between Freud and his two most famous disciples.[1] Both Carl Jung and Alfred Adler eventually had trouble with Freud's pan-sexualism. Where Freud saw libido or sex drive as the fundamental motive force of the human being, Adler said rather that it was the will to power. Jung too seemed to find that rooting everything in libido was too confining, and he proposed that the realm that roots our affectivity and motivation might more usefully be labeled the "collective unconsciousness."

---

1. My account here can no doubt be improved; specialists in the history of psychoanalysis may shiver, but my hunch is that even as they refine my very simple presentation, the point of my argument will stand.

Three brilliant men disagree. But is there in this kind of thing any serious excuse for doubting that truth can be known? All three men collaborate in trying to unveil the mysteries of consciousness and motivation. Jung, with his profound awareness of a "shadow side" of the human psyche, can easily be read as an elaboration of Freud rather than a rejection. There is within us, Jung says, a largely unexplored ground of human concerns—things, contents we do not choose, but which "choose us"—out of which we act but about which, by preference perhaps, we remain largely ignorant. Particularly when we sense a negative or shameful character in these contents, instead of "owning" them, we may in cases project these vaguely felt but unacknowledged contents—the very stuff of sin no less than of life—onto others. Then we are apt to fight these others, righteously and complacently, and commit time and again sins of violence whose source in us we deny; for we do not acknowledge that the true target of our hatred is inside ourselves. (This isn't all Jung says, of course; but I'm impressed that this is there.) This, says Jung, can become our program; we can deny what consciousness we have in common with our ancestors; we own to no share in their guilt; and so we are free, in perfect "innocence," to recapitulate their crimes.

Doesn't this sound a lot like Freud? (See Freud's *Moses and Monotheism*.) Only it is less "one note" than Freud was. It elaborates on Freud, much as Freud himself (no rigid Freudian) felt free eventually to elaborate by introducing the "death wish" to supplement the "pleasure principle." Even in Freud, libido doesn't get the last word.

As for Adler, he does not exclude Freud's pleasure principle. It seems though he "complicates" Freud's doctrine of sublimation. Whereas Freud would say of a man who spends his life climbing mountains or becoming boss of a huge enterprise that such a man is no doubt "sublimating" his sex drive, Adler is free to suggest that having sex might be a poor second best for a man who really wants to climb mountains or be a corporation executive.[2] Echoing in a way Plato in the *Symposium*, Adler sees Eros as having

---

2. This reconfiguration of Freud is fairly caught by the message on a shirt I saw on a pedal-pushing, hill-climbing San Franciscan cyclist: "This is what I fantasize about when I'm having sex."

from the start a self-affirming horizon-expanding agenda that can, if one will, instantiate itself in sex, but which has never been confined to it.

Shared questions, and shared conviction as to the importance of those shared questions, continue to unite Freud and his disciples long after they part company. Their very rivalry is a bond. One should take no scandal here. These men are jointly caught up in a broadening encounter with reality. One hears in their disagreements their emphatic testimony to the reality and importance of their common subject matter in those very moments when one hears them conscientiously at odds with each other regarding which hypotheses and interpretations and metaphors do most to clarify it. What greater invitation to an intellectual life could one request?

As for the second cause for scandal, namely errors in which one finds oneself engaged, we know that each discovery of error is, genuinely, a discovery, an uncovering—a learning experience which opens the door to further learning. We can recognize mistakes in our thinking because we have a known context in which to identify truth. Successful golfers and pitchers, for instance, can make great use of their errors because they have a context—the rules and goal of the game, and knowledge of the discrete physical arena in which they play—in which to recognize them. In general, good athletes (the most successful of them) tend to be distinguished by calmness.[3] They regard their performance with the Zen-like attentive detachment of the scientific observer. As the ball veers disappointingly from the hole, the kind of golfer I'm talking about doesn't curse and ask, "How could I have been so stupid as to swing like that?" She or he's too busy adding new knowledge to old: "So the turf just here has a near-invisible rise. Tomorrow, I'll allow for it." So too the reflective pitcher says, as he hears the batter connect sweetly for a base hit: "So that's the pitch he can't resist. I'll use that against him his next time up."

---

3. Tiger Woods in his salad days, Buster Posey anytime, Joe Montana and Jerry Rice in the legendary closing minutes of a game, Michael Jordan in the legendary closing minutes of a game, Madison Bumgarner most anytime, Steph Curry anytime, Russell Wilson most anytime, Serena Williams year in and year out, are examples that come to mind.

Rather than support skepticism, acts of ours which go wide of the mark, if analyzed, point to new tactics and abandonment of false assumptions. That we can recognize acts that are wide of the mark suggests that beyond the things we think (and can be wrong about) are things we know (and are not wrong about). Our moments of frustration resolve into moments of insight. Horizons of knowledge open. Amid temporary setback, the attentive human finds an invitation.

If this sounds a bit too like the breezy "by-your-bootstraps psychology" that floods our media, let me hasten to concede that when it comes to understanding contemporary affairs, there are so many interlocking unknowns and hidden agendas that the effort to understand them is indeed daunting, and tends to overpower one. If we've wondered whether official governmental reports involve cover-ups and lies, surely the *Pentagon Papers*, the Nixon tapes, the refusal of Obama to disclose videos of CIA torture, the information and documents made available by WikiLeaks and Chelsea Manning and Edward Snowden, etc., should put the matter to rest.

Complicating things further, as one's eyes open to the duplicity and manipulations of our government and begin looking into the myriad things that remain unknowns in our government's public reports, one is likely, as noted, to be labeled "a conspiracy theorist"—which carries the implication one is not quite sane or at least not quite adult. This has been effective in dampening down the curiosity of us Americans. (Even when governmental cover-ups have been uncovered, we seem at times less displeased with the agents of the cover-ups—the government conspirators—than we are with those who have disillusioned us by uncovering their conspiracies. We are uncomfortable, and turn away, when James Douglass uncovers our government's involvement in the Kennedy assassination, when Robert Parry delves into the sordid details of the Iran-Contra scandal, when Gary Webb discovers the collusion of the CIA in the affairs of gangsters who were poisoning our ghettoes by importing drugs into them, when Edward Snowden discloses the officially-denied spying of the National Security Agency on the American people, etc. In turn, our tendency to reject the messenger is endorsed by presidents and mainstream media when they label the messenger a traitor.)

The retreat of so many of us from the world about us (the only planet those currently alive are likely ever to inhabit), while we take up residence in a personally designed neighborhood in cyberspace, tends to leave under-exercised our capacity for truth-finding regarding this more primary and immediate four-dimensional world—the one where trucks can run over us as we tweet. While there is much to hope for from social media, our escape from immediate physical habitat into psychic habitat can have as its flip side the abandonment of our physical habitat to the care of those who can least be trusted with it. By reason of the many lingering tokens of American prosperity, and the palpable comfort and longevity many of us continue to enjoy, such an escape strikes many as affordable. For this reason, withdrawal into a personalized alternative reality has probably played out more freely among us here in the United States than, say, in India or China. As our electronic embubblement continues, our feeling of responsibility to make sense of the world which feeds and sustains us often tends to shrink. Our desire to understand gets undermined. From a daunting world, we can seek refuge in electronics; but if we retreat there and take up residence, the world surrounding us will—count on it—become more daunting still.

What I've argued in this section on skepticism is that the things many of the most sensitive among us are relegating to the margins are the things that offer coherence. In putting away history, we reduce our sense of identity and forego our opportunity to discern and elude the traps and flaws that others set for us. In trivializing beauty, we consign our affectivity to a process of numbing. When we do the same with morality, we all but lose the ability to live purposefully. When we hitch up our pants, stand straight and stoical, and loudly proclaim: "There are no absolutes!" we despair in general of our understanding and effectively close down effective response to current challenges.

I agree with Kant that we cannot think without thinking God. But I depart from Kant when he says this is the best we can do, the closest we can get to anything absolute. We don't just think an absolute but are in touch with one. Somewhere, somehow, in our exertions within the common reality we all share, we interact with the structure and laws of being; we have ontological insights and certitudes. We know that what is, is actual. We know that events which have taken place will without extinction remain "what has been"—so that the past is eternal. And we know, as Descartes says, that even if we are making a mistake, we must *be*—else we could not be making it. So we know that we exist, that memory is a source of contact with reality, and that the complex and confusing world in which we live, move, and learn—this world into which Heidegger says we have been "thrown"—is not a world we've cooked up on a personal whim, nor is it a world simply devoid of pattern, intelligibility, value, opportunity, and purpose. We know further, that when we retreat from interaction with this world, we culpably chip away at our confidence about everything. We know that if we indulge ourselves in games of skepticism, we leave what's precious and fragile in our world to the un-tender care of the Second Law of Thermodynamics—and things fall apart.

SECTION THREE

False Hopes

I didn't say this would be easy. No sooner do I call us out for decadent games of skepticism, than I turn and warn against ungrounded hopes. Of necessity, this section is tentative. It's not its purpose to condemn all hope as naive or delusional. Lacking hope, we who live are as the walking dead. Yet the denunciation of skepticism I've attempted in the last four chapters, and the rejection of skepticism I've called for do not at all mean one should extend a welcome to just any hope that comes along. Hopes can easily be mere wishful thinking, and when they are, they distract us from the task at hand. (It was of course this insight that moved Marx toward his uncompromising rejection of religion.)

In these next four chapters, I deal with the hopes of people who are, on some level, aware of the jeopardy in which we Americans—and the rest of our species—find ourselves. The hopeful among us attempt, each in their own way, a mindset for coming to terms with the jeopardy we're in. It is toward what's wistful in their mindsets that I invite criticism; the people who hold these mindsets can be admirable. As noted earlier, humans without hope are the walking dead.

10 | "Fundamentalism Will Save Us!"

Today, perhaps no one actually says this. The term "fundamentalism" has attracted too many bad connotations for that. But without using the actual terms, many still posit mentally the substance of the statement above. So bear with me here as we initiate a long, inwardly spiraling effort to reach the core of fundamentalism. The efforts that follow are attempts in casting about for a thoughtful sense of what that term represents.

By reason of economics and communication and travel, the world has shrunk and become palpably One World. Thereby a goal of some idealists of the past has been fulfilled. But this fulfillment is proving less comfortable than its promoters had hoped. A disease in one part of the world more easily threatens now to go global. An economic failure in one country sends ripples everywhere. Political troubles have a way of not staying localized. America's Open Door statements at the end of the nineteenth century meant that in our quest for economic hegemony we'd joust with whatever political arrangements were out there. The colonizing initiatives of European nations, and indications that the Japanese were becoming very restless, added to our readiness to take on the world. In turn, our forward leaning example stoked the incentives of our rivals.

At the brink of the twentieth century, while it may have gratified Alfred Thayer Mahan to see his eloquent tribute to the influence of sea power translated into so many languages, his book became in effect a manual for more intense international competition. The benign revival in 1906 of non-violent athletic rivalry in the world of the Olympics was paralleled by malignant preparations for violent worldwide rivalry a few years later.

While John Hay's notes capped the Spanish-American War and guaranteed we'd be a participant in the First World War, their influence didn't end there. After the Second World War, our persistence in seeking an Open Door everywhere for American commerce led to an effort to contain the Soviet Union as it struggled to incorporate Eastern Europe politically and economically, and thereby close it to us. During these times—the founding days of the United Nations—shared interests, competition, friction, conflicts, and alliances drew the peoples of the world into tighter interactions, positive and negative, than they were in before the war. By reason of the Cold War, one might think we Americans turned our backs on the Russians, but really we became more acutely interested in them than we'd ever been before. It was, of course, mostly negative. Any initiative of the Soviet Union was likely to be felt as threatening our national security; a success of the Soviets, such as the launching of the space satellite Sputnik, was processed as a challenge and taunt to America.

Fortunately, in the years since the Second World War, the frustrations, rivalries, aggressive agendas, and distrust generated have not incinerated the planet. On the other hand, what they have done is intensify, in places all over the world, the human inclination toward xenophobia. Fear breeds fear. In our fearful responses to others, we have added to whatever grounds those others have for fearing us. Machiavelli advised his prince that it was good to be feared. People everywhere seem to have appropriated his lesson. Surely though, as suggested earlier, Thomas Hobbes, said the wiser thing when he counseled his readers that a fearful neighbor is a dangerous and volatile thing.

An upshot of all this is that, even while much activity on the planet is becoming more integrated, there are strong countermovements everywhere from people assuming hostile stances. In more ways than we'd anticipated, the New World Order manifests itself as a new-world disorder. People hunker down. They dig in. They prepare themselves to come out fighting. It's predictable, howsoever counterproductive and reprehensible, that some will attempt ethnic cleansing and genocide, and many will engage in deadly skirmishes. With each effort to settle scores once and for all, fresh seeds for retaliation are sown.

An aspect of this pushback against globalization is the intensification of fundamentalisms. Fundamentalism is a reaction of people who feel religiously and culturally—and often, territorially, politically, and economically—threatened. Such fear intensifies when a people feel an alien culture and religion actually closing in. Further, this spiritual response to encroachment by hostile outsiders can be further heightened by the leveling secular culture of globalization itself. Many traditional people have a fear this secular culture will swamp the planet and become its only culture.[1]

As secularists so often seem not to understand, their emergent secular ethos can be as dogmatic as any religion. It routinely disallows any claims that can't be established from its own premises. Its contemporary un-Marxist version absolutizes economic principle as much as Marx ever did. It's a less humane but an equally as materialistic version of things, compared to what Marx advocated. (I speak here of Marx himself; not of Stalin, Mao, etc.) One hears at times that this globalizing secular ethos is tolerant of religion. One has to wonder. What may look like tolerance is arguably more a form of strategic patience. Religions all over the world have felt the presence of this secular ethos as a threat. They sense its basic opposition to religious commitment. Their sense is that when this secular ethos gains ground, religious commitments weaken.

One might naively expect then that the religions of the world would unite in opposition to their common enemy. The opposite of this is what has happened. The world's religions seem more commonly to have suffered such spirals of desperation that each has tended to seize on just those things most peculiar to itself and, shibboleth-like, have promoted precisely these unique features as the test case and index of genuine religion and godliness.

---

1. As we see from its current adoption in China, capitalism is less entwined with its Protestant origins than it once was; the culture of capitalism seems currently—as it melds in the Far East with an immemorial Asian work ethic—to be completing its evolution into an altogether secular, spirit-free and non-religious worldwide ethos. Perhaps it is time to see resistance to Beijing by the Dali Lama and Tibetan Buddhists—and by the Falun Gong—as less a matter of resisting communism than a matter of resisting the global triumph of capitalist ethos.

The religions of the world seem often to be strengthening the case for secularism by engaging with new vigor in their history of bad behavior toward each other. (In the case of Catholicism, Pope Francis seems heroically struggling to pull his church back from the abyss, but the inertial resistance is considerable.) One way to label the waves of bad behavior is to speak of an increase in fundamentalism.

We may improve our sense of the term by noting recent instances that have called it into play. One might expect Hinduism at least, by reason of its great tolerance for diversity and celebration of variety, would prove immune to fundamentalist tendencies. Of late, however, we find among Hindu politicians some leaders who are resolutely rejective of all things Muslim (and rejective of the example set by Gandhi). Perhaps more surprising yet, we've lately seen in Sri Lanka clashes between Hindus and Buddhists. Does this imply that even among Buddhists there can be fundamentalists? It seems to.

That there are Christian fundamentalists seems hardly to need argument. Fundamentalism operates as a force within American exceptionalism even as the secularization of America threatens fundamentalism. The threat of secularism summons our vital subterranean currents of fundamentalism into the full light of day. "You're either with us or against us" is not just a slogan for Americans in general, but has special authority for fundamentalists. The "Tea Parties" that dot our landscape can be places of retreat and consolidation—places for returning to fundamentals. Frequently, they are places for those who, in defense of what they take to be American Christian tradition, are surprised and scandalized to find themselves in opposition to contemporary forms of American secular society and government. When they find themselves in opposition to America, it's not themselves they want to reform, but America.

They're surprised because our country has long been a familiar and fertile field for Christian fundamentalism. The term "fundamentalist" was coined as a means of self-identification by certain American Christians. Threatened in the early years of the twentieth century by such foreign influences as Darwinism, Marxism, and Freudianism, and more intimately by the "higher criticism" of German biblical scholars, certain Christians in the twentieth century seem to have wrapped themselves in the "fundamentals" of their faith as a shield against contamination. It is easy to recognize how the term "fundamentalism" (the affirmation of what's left when you wipe away the dross and frivolous trimmings) arises as an echo to the term "Puritanism." As critics of Rome, that's just what the Puritans were trying to do.

As for fundamentalism among Jews, I do not think it is anti-Semitic to note that the two-thousand-year tradition of rabbinic humanitarianism seems currently challenged and undermined by the extremes to which Israeli leaders extend themselves in asserting special prerogatives over real estate. When the Puritans claimed such prerogatives, they thought they were simply copying ancient Jews. Today the politicians of Israel return the compliment. Traumatized by the Holocaust, and haunted by fear of its recurrence, Israeli politicians have accustomed themselves to speak of "the existential crisis" in which Israel finds itself. By this phrase they seem to imply that historical precedent and international law are overridden by the non-negotiable need of the Israeli people to be precisely where they are, and that Israelis have a bible-based right to expand from there. It's the assertion here of a non-negotiable and fundamental right that lends plausibility to use of the term "fundamentalism" as a description of what's going on.

Thirdly, to say that the groups of jihadists among the Muslims are fundamentalists seems a legitimately grounded use of that term. These jihadists often assert fundamental, non-negotiable obligations as binding Muslims everywhere to some quite particular version of Islam—obligations so firm and unquestionable that they override obligations to family, neighbor, huge populations of fellow Muslims, religious tradition, and the customs and observances of international law.[2]

By now the reader may wonder what I'm really up to here. (Voltaire once wrote sarcastically to Rousseau, "Thank you for forwarding to me your charming little book against the human

---

2. To repeat myself, it strikes me as ironical that while we Americans decry this fundamentalism with a suggestion we can't imagine such a thing, the truth is it has stark parallels in our own practice; we seem magnificently to have modeled something close to this fundamentalism in our jihad against American Indians. Ask the ghost of Custer.

race.") By bouncing about here and there, pointing fingers in all directions, what I've been up to is reaching for a legitimate and useful—rather than purely opportunistic—sense of the term "fundamentalism." As for a blanket condemnation of the human race, I leave that to Rousseau—who, when he wasn't eloquently praising the human race, spent a lot of time denouncing it.

In the section preceding this one, I argued that humans can hardly function lacking awareness of an absolute. Further, I argued that the sense of this absolute seems to be dimming. I have lamented this. In this chapter, we note that the fundamentalist is typically someone keenly aware, as I am keenly aware, of threats to confidence in the absolute. The fundamentalist is a passionate opponent to relativism. While the fundamentalist often feels he or she is defending an actual turf, a deeper root of fundamentalism seems to be something approaching panic in the face of ideological challenge. Fundamentalism seems a response in defense of the ideological roots that make live worth living.[3]

Further, as argued, there's a complicating duality here. One may in the same breath fear the multiplicity of cultures and fear the emerging uniformity of culture. A sense of vertigo may take hold. Amid the variety and confusion of the modern world, featuring both relativism and conformity, Nietzsche asks: "Can you not feel things are getting colder? Do you not feel the ground crumbling beneath your feet?" and the fundamentalist, if honest and self-knowing, answers: "Yes!"

So while territory may be at stake, it need not be the sole motive, nor the most important, for a sense of foreboding. At the end of the First World War for instance, when there seemed no imminent threat to American territory, Attorney General A. Mitchell Palmer organized massive roundups of people suspected to

---

3. Things can become so bad, that rather than defend against encroachment by hostile forces, it can seem the only thing to do is to migrate. But if one is trying to migrate to countries that have been causing the encroachment, there's a high possibility of resistance to immigration, and even if one succeeds in immigrating, there's a likelihood the hostility will persist in the new location. If the spiritual climate in the new place is as unsympathetic as it has become in the old, migration may have simply relocated the problem.

be America-based Bolsheviks. It seems any socialist or radical critic of The American Story could qualify as a Bolshevik and be marked for jail or deportation. During this time, socialist and presidential candidate Eugene Debs was imprisoned for having spoken during the war against the draft. Though the spirit of American fundamentalism reaches back to the beginnings of settlement in the 1600s, we've noted it was at this time around the First World War that some American Protestants first used the label "fundamentalist" to identify themselves.

Their intent, we noted, in coining the label echoed that of their forefathers in coining the term "Puritan." Both regarding Palmer and regarding his fundamentalist soul-mates, a way to interpret the firming up of fundamentalist impulse is to recognize it as response to the First World War. The horrors of the war seemed to have made a statement about Progress. (Hemingway captures the mood of this huge, looming, amorphous statement in *The Sun Also Rises*.) The First World War taught its survivors that Progress did not after all ensure improvement. At most, what Progress seemed to entail was increase of technological power in the hands of humans. The war had proved this power could be used as effectively to destroy as to build.

In response, in America, there were on the one hand the Jazz Age, the Charleston, speak-easies and bath-tub gin, flag-pole sitting, acrobatic stunts on the wings of airplanes, and the ever-ascending stock-market. On the other hand, there were Sacco and Vanzetti's trial and execution, A. Mitchell Palmer's crusade against Marxists and socialists, the Scopes trial, and the emergence of self-identified fundamentalists.

So the war's demonstration that Progress wasn't the guarantee we'd thought was not just a deep scandal to American expatriates in Europe; it rocked Americans here at home as well. The war's lesson was incompatible with our dearly held notion of Manifest Destiny—the notion to which Wilson had keyed his speeches in guiding us into the war, the notion our mission extended to our rendering the whole world conformed to our notions and safe for our lifestyle. The loss of any guarantee this would happen was altogether too demoralizing to be faced head on. The Charleston and bathtub gin were an effort to step into an alternate reality (not unlike what cyberspace can be). Palmer's suspicions, the fundamentalists, and persecutions of "foreigners" were at once opposite to the spirit of the Jazz Age and similar to it. For these sour and nativist reactions too were a form of bravado, of whistling in the dark. They too were efforts to say the evils of the time had nothing to do with America—to say such evils had incubated on foreign soil, and good Americans would act to keep them from taking root here. (Was this not a very Jeffersonian and Quixotic way to view the world? It had all the earmarks of Puritanism and American exceptionalism.)

We remind ourselves that the key insight for understanding fundamentalism is that it is conceived in fear. Prominence of fear doesn't mean of course there are no grounds for fear; nor does it mean that fearful fundamentalists are timid and harmless. Fear can make fundamentalists dangerous in the extreme. One overwhelmed by fear can figure he or she has nothing to lose; one can go for broke. If you've ever trapped a squirrel in the corner of a basement or attic, you may have insight how this works. Big as you are compared to the squirrel, something tells you to be careful. In a fear-crazed moment, the squirrel may tear your thumb to shreds.

Fear, then, is matter for study. It may seem to some in fact that I should wholeheartedly endorse the fears felt by fundamentalists. For I've said we cannot function without an absolute, and I'm saying here that fundamentalists know this. I seem to be agreeing with them. Why then say fundamentalism can't save us?

Think of a person in the throes of a dreadful disease, and of how quick the person may be to grab onto whatever's offered as a remedy. The fundamentalist is like such a person. The patient's desire for a cure is not what's wrong. Even his or her conviction that there must be "out there" somewhere a remedy for their threatening condition is not notably at fault; for at least in many cases, what has gone wrong can be put right, what's needed for a return to health can be supplied. What leads to counterproductive behavior isn't then a patient's wholesome hope and desire for health; rather it's a patient's impatience. The patient can prove too ready for the first thing—or the most obvious thing—that comes along.

A fundamentalist can be compared to a person adrift in a river who, white-knuckled, holds fast to a handy log. Such a person won't let go easily. Imagine yourself as someone standing on the shore who knows the log is headed toward steep falls and a dizzying plunge. For all your shouting, you might have a hard time persuading the one holding the log to let go.

I offer these analogies not in order to demean fundamentalists. We're trying to get a handle on our topic. Alfred North Whitehead speaks of a "fallacy of misplaced concreteness." I like the phrase though I may not understand it in the way Whitehead intended. I use it to indicate taking a part for the whole, or a symbol for the symbolized, or a name for what is named. One way to view a fundamentalist is to regard him or her as someone involved in such a fallacy. The fundamentalist seems one who holds onto the finite as though it were the infinite, seems to hold onto the passing and insecure as though it were the eternal and fixed, seems to regard the imperfect as though it were perfect, the provisional as though it were the final and absolute.

For all its abstractness, I think that's a good preliminary description of religious fundamentalism. The matter, though, remains murky. This is because it may seem to cast too wide a net; it may seem to set up too wide an indictment. All genuine religion involves a response of the soul to what is infinite and beyond reach. It might seem then that all religion is fundamentalist in character. The effort of religion to grasp, in passing time and finite circumstance, what is eternal and infinite and good beyond all vocalization may seem to condemn religion in general to falsification. We may seem to be saying religion is always an instance of misplaced concreteness, and that every religious person is either a fundamentalist or on the way to becoming one.

Eastern religion has fortified itself against the pull of this temptation better than have the religions that come out of Palestine and the Arabian Peninsula. The Buddha tells us "nirvana" is the goal of spiritual struggle, and when asked to define "nirvana," refuses. Taoism tells us: "Those who know the Tao don't talk about it and those who talk about it don't know it." (This helps one understand why Zen Buddhists spend so much time in silence.) As for Hinduism, it allows us to speak of the ultimate reality principle in so many forms and conceptualizations that it comes to the same thing: namely, there's no conclusive and comprehensive notion and vocabulary available to us — no "one-size-fits-all," no non-negotiable way — to characterize ultimate reality. For a Hindu sage, the ultimate is many — or more plausibly, it is one; it is male or female — or more plausibly, it is both or neither;

it is personal—or, more plausibly, it is beyond everything we can think about persons.

This tentative character of eastern religion is echoed by the great mystics of all the religions. Relentlessly, they insist we are in over our heads. They insist on the inadequacy of everything we say or do in matters of religion. This is true for Jewish, Christian, and Muslim mystics no less than for Hindu, Buddhist, and Taoist mystics. But, as just noted, warnings against taking our formulations about the absolute for the Absolute itself seem to have been better heeded among religious people of the East than among religious people of the West.

The temptation to think we and we alone know the absolute by its First Name is distinctly stronger in the Abrahamic western religions (originating in the Middle East). The sense of intimate, personal dialogue with the Ultimate is sharper here; and while this may be a source of great vitality in Judaism, Christianity, and Islam, it's clearly their great peril. Claiming to know the absolute on a first-name basis, we westerners have a major difficulty with any similar claims by people of traditions outside our own—even, perhaps especially, by people of traditions very close to our own.

Western Europeans crossed the Atlantic and became the new Americans. We, their descendants, expanded westward across the continent, and then yet further westward across the Pacific for an opening of doors in Asia. In every case when we encountered indigenous people with their own religious beliefs, we disparaged those beliefs and tried to replace them with our own. We've reasoned that since we know the right name for God and the right way of relating to "Him," others who make claims for different names and different ways must be in error. A fundamentalism seems to have blinded us to the possibilities of heterogeneity. In making claims for God we've shrunk God to fit our conceptions. We've made God mean, made of God a talisman we hold in our pocket.

What then precisely is it that makes a fundamentalist? Some have said it's "idolatry," and I think that can be helpful. The charge will seem outrageously paradoxical to any actual fundamentalist; but then it seems essential to the character of idolatry that its devotees not regard it as such.

Here too, one must be careful. In the wake of the likes of Henry David Thoreau, John Muir, Thomas Berry, Bill McKibben, and the Sufi poet Rumi, one can argue, for instance, that we've a need to venerate nature far more than we do venerate it. When this veneration is genuine and heartfelt and is accompanied by ritual behavior (e.g., blessing valleys, dancing at harvest time, getting up early to hail the sun's rising, reveling in the purity and beauty of rivers and streams), such veneration can be mistaken for idolatry. As I suggested in the chapter on beauty, we stand in need of a passionate love for the physical world, a love some Christians — John Muir's Presbyterian father comes to mind — would regard as a return to pagan idolatry.

A loving and ardent response to the world's preciousness would be neither idolatry nor fundamentalism. Likewise, when Mexicans and others regard Our Lady of Guadeloupe with fervent devotion, they're not, I think, idolaters or fundamentalists. An achieved Bhakti Hindu (one whose love has gone from love of a person to love of all things and to love of their Source) would say of Our Lady of Guadeloupe that she is — for those who pay her homage — an "ishta." The Bhakti adept would mean Our Lady of Guadeloupe provides a favored or specially suited opportunity, an instantiation, whereby her devotees can enter the presence of the Ultimate. (For those who do not find her such, the Bhakti would say "no foul, no penalty.") Bhakti Hinduism not only doesn't condemn worshipers for finding an ishta in this fashion, but encourages those who haven't found one to do so.

The fundamentalist, on the other hand, does not simply say: "I have found a means by which I relate to the Ultimate." Granted, a person would almost need to grow up "talking Eastern" to say a thing like that. But then, to rephrase for the West, a fundamentalist does not simply say: "I have found a truth," or "I have found something of great importance," or "I have found something that lifts me out of humdrum and mean-minded concerns." In his or her desperation, that doesn't suffice for the fundamentalist. He or she must say: "I now possess the whole truth." And this fundamentalist is inclined to add: "To the extent anyone speaks contrary to what I say, or even says something more than what I say, to that extent that person is in error." A fundamentalist isn't content to have a word; he or she must have the last word.

In this respect, a fundamentalist always acts in contradiction to the original inspiration of the religion to which he or she is attached. This is a difficult point to take in. Up to now our discussion has been rather abstract and general. Let's try now to make it more concrete. Let's do so in the face of all the hazards that specific analysis of religious commitments can entail. The case I argue is that while religious inspiration is affirmative, and value-finding, and positive in its origination, the fundamentalist who would protect that gift does, by reason of being a fundamentalist, twist the inspiration into something that has a negative bearing on other people. In order to test this out, we have to wade into the treacherous waters of citing particular examples.[4]

In Roman Catholicism, the fundamentalist tendency bears upon dogmatic affirmations. Leaders in the Catholic Church regard as sacred and irreformable some statements of theirs which they call "dogmas." These statements have been formulated by humans in language inevitably bearing the limitations of human speech. The language used is often Greek or Latin, and some formulations are close to two thousand years old. The formulations are shaped by and respond to the preoccupations of the formulators. The language employed is often abstract and can be metaphorical. The language is laden with the denotations and the connotations current at the time of formulation, and it has developed in a culture that is itself continually undergoing change.

There is no scandal here. Almost any scholar working with earlier writings is more or less in the same predicament as a scholar who is working with these formulations. It isn't even a problem that the Catholic scholar regards these particular formulations as true. Many a scholar and many a scientist brings a kind of vote of confidence to the propositions under study in his or her discipline. The problem is that the leaders of the Catholic Church have wanted to absolutize statements which are inherently imperfect and provisional. And they have wanted to absolutize their historical interpretations of those statements as well. They have taken themselves so seriously in this matter that they burned Giordano

---

4. The reason religion is hardly mentioned in k-through-twelve public education is to avoid just these dangers. The reason there is so little ecumenical (i.e., inter-religious) discussion these days is to avoid just these dangers. The cost of avoiding them is horrendous. We get Kissinger saying, "If I had known about the rivalry of Shiites and Sunnis, I never would have endorsed the invasion of Iraq."

Bruno at the stake when he wouldn't go along. They used the fire from that burning as a means to intimidate Galileo into silence.

While we can be absolutely sure of some things, we cannot impart that same absoluteness to the propositions in which we express ourselves. When we regard them as true without qualification, and claim they are perfect and irreformable, we are ascribing to these creations of ours characteristics which more cautious believers reserve for God. In other words, we stumble into fundamentalism.

This has real consequences. When, back in the sixties, Pope Paul VI appointed a commission to study Catholic restrictions on birth control, the commission came back saying unanimously that Catholic teaching on birth control needed to be revised. Nonetheless, Paul reaffirmed the traditional prohibitions. Paul's reasoning, even if not explicitly stated, seems to have run along these lines:

> The Church is infallible in matters of faith and morals. But the Church has long taught, in a public and deliberate way, that artificial birth control (i.e., contraception which can be accomplished by interrupted ejaculation, or the use of condoms, or diaphragms, or anti-fertility pills) is immoral. If then one were to revise this teaching on contraception, one would be saying "the Church is fallible after all." Since however the Church is infallible, it follows that contraception is immoral.

(This isn't, to be sure, anything near a direct quote, nor am I trying to lampoon the pope's position; I'm doing what I can to set forth the only conditions I think can explain it.)

This reaffirmation of traditional doctrine seems to have continued a hardship for some Catholics, seems to have driven other Catholics from the Catholic Church, and seems to have decreased the confidence in church teaching of most of the rest—those who neither left the Catholic Church nor accepted its teaching on contraception. (I don't know what European Catholics make of these matters. In America, this third group seems large. Sociological research, always a tricky enterprise where sexuality is involved, seems to indicate American Catholics these days practice contraception to about the same degree as the rest of the American population.)

I see this effort to take past historical teaching and give it universal status as a fundamentalist act.

Similarly, in the Catholic Church's sex-abuse scandal, fundamentalism seems to have played a role in the way bishops and the Vatican reacted. Regarding the Church as the rock against which "the gates of hell shall not prevail," church officials in America, under guidance by the Vatican, closed their eyes to reports that told them of predatory sexual behavior in churches under their supervision. When news of such behavior forced itself on their attention, there was a church-wide pattern of irrational denial and inappropriate response. Strong efforts were made to discredit and intimidate abused children; silence was purchased with bribes; known predators were transferred to distant locations where it was hoped their reputation would not catch up with them. There was widespread concealment and lying.

Church officials seem to have focused their efforts almost exclusively on maintaining the reputation of that "Church" which their theology and seminary training had taught them exists. In place of serving the children of God, they rendered uncritical service to a figment of their theological imagination. To label their behavior as an example of "dogma idolatry" doesn't seem exaggerated. Had churchmen been less enthralled by fictitious claims and faltering dogmas on their own incorruptibility, they might have seen what was going on and have responded in accord with admonitions of Jesus as reported in the gospels.

Take one more example from Catholicism—this one too has a bearing upon sexuality. The long history of dismissive and hurtful treatment of homosexuals by the popes and bishops and local pastors of the Catholic Church seems to be motivated primarily by a desire to maintain consistency, as in the case of contraception, with past church teaching. Contemporary psychological theory offers little or no support for this teaching, and much opposition. In the days of Galileo, the Catholic Church felt itself obliged to maintain, for the sake of its authority as an interpreter of scripture, that the sun daily orbits the earth. In similar fashion, the Catholic hierarchy seems today—gripped by the same fundamentalist regard for its own teaching authority—to feel itself obliged to teach that homosexuals are "objectively disordered."

Why belabor these points? It's not to drum up anti-Catholic feeling. It's because only by citing specific instances is one likely to make the character of fundamentalism clear. Also, I'm at some concern to see we don't limit our recognition of fundamentalism in an opportunistic and arbitrary way, bringing the term into play only when discussing those whom we take to be "foreigners."

Let's proceed. If next we look to Judaism, here the current temptation to fundamentalism, as noted, seems directly concerned with land. Judaism by and large is less centered on orthodoxy (that is, on insisting every Jew holds the same well defined doctrines) than on "orthopraxis" (observance of identity-providing behaviors); it's "down to earth" and is concerned with the practical matters of what's to be done habitually by "us as a people"—and of what's to be done soonest. Doctrines about contraception and homosexuality, though related directly to behavior, are less likely to have the hard dogmatic edge at a synagogue that they have at a council of the Catholic Church. Much is left to rabbinic disputation and rabbinic/lay dialog.[5]

As remarked elsewhere, among Jews there's a notable degree of liberty of spirit—not well understood by Christian fundamentalists—regarding interpretation of scripture. How far this can go is striking. With breath-taking freedom, rabbis led their congregations into new paths after the destruction of the Temple in 70 C.E. For all that the book of Leviticus seems to require to the contrary, the priestly caste seems to have disappeared from active Judaism around that time; and the rabbis who led Judaism in the Diaspora (the dispersing of Jews into many places, which intensified after 70 C.E.) seem to have left animal sacrifice altogether to the past.[6]

No, with possible exceptions among Orthodox Jews, fundamentalism about matters of dogma and scriptural interpretation

---

5. It was, I think, the Jewish violinist Itzhak Perlman who commented playfully, "A Jew chooses his synagogue by its *cantor*, and puts up with its rabbi."

6. A Jewish student of mine responded to my assertion of this lack of interest in continuing the sacrifice of animals by saying that animal sacrifice has never been repudiated, and could be revived at any time. Be that as it may, I'd be amazed to learn on TV or from a newspaper that animal sacrifice was about to be re-instituted at a Jewish place of worship.

doesn't seem at the forefront of Jewish concern. Yet fundamentalism is an abiding temptation for religion, and particularly, as noted, a temptation for the three radically personal monotheistic religions that arose in the Middle East. As has always been a possibility among fundamentalisms, current Jewish fundamentalism is directly connected to an issue of land. (So it was for Puritans; so it may have been for Anglicans and Orangemen in Ireland; so probably it is for Muslims in Sudan and Darfur, and between Muslim and Muslim in Iraq and Syria.) But there is a special predisposition toward such in the case of a people whose exodus and coming together entailed a promised land. Exodus-and-arrival-at-the-Promised-Land is seen as the constitutional moment of the Jewish people. This suggests that if there's going to be a characteristic fundamentalism among Jews, it's likely to be a fundamentalism about land.

For the sake of the "Promised Land," the "Holy Land," some Israelis and some who sympathize with them (including some American Christians) have been willing to discover in Genesis 15 and in Exodus 23 a quite literal land grant or deed of real estate which they regard as "inextinguishable"—without date of expiration. While many Jews would not put it this way, to a remarkable degree—both for some Israelis and for some supporters of the Israeli state who live elsewhere—the very test for endurance of the Jewish covenant with God has come to be that Jews occupy, at whatever cost, this land. It seems some would not hesitate to say: "For Judaism to survive, it is necessary that 'The Promised Land' be occupied by Jews."

To a non-Jew, this can look like a very unfortunate case of a fallacy of misplaced concreteness. And many a devout Jew regards it as just that. While commitments can be admirable, the fundamentalist character of this commitment is brought to light in all the things one must deny in order to maintain it. If one regards the Jewish prophets of biblical times and the rabbis of the last two thousand years as major architects of and witnesses to the doctrine of universal human rights (the historical contribution of the prophets and the Talmudic tradition in promoting human rights seems to me clear and undeniable), it seems rash and extravagant—even with the unspeakable horror of the Holocaust as context—that Jewish biblical teaching on human rights over thousands of years should be overridden by the claim of "an existential crisis."[7]

A fundamentalist character seems manifest here in the willingness to present a "part" for the "whole." I'd say it's not that Israelis must deny what Jews and all decent people affirm, namely that Jews have a right to live securely. Rather it's that Israelis must continue to maintain what some Israeli politicians and their followers lately deny. Much that they affirm today, they need to affirm; but some seem to have discarded too much on its behalf. For it would seem that for a believing Jew, all the children of the world must be blessed in the blessings conferred on Abraham and his progeny. And in light of that, it would seem a reckless contraction of Judaism to let the sheer "comic book" or thrilling "action movie" character of the book of Joshua, and the like, supplant the faith of Abraham as the touchstone of Jewish faith.

Our purpose here, however, isn't to "straighten out Israelis." It's rather to clarify the nature of fundamentalism. By now, I'd hope the character I would assign to fundamentalism is starting to come clear. It's by no means restricted to any one faith among the three great faiths of the West. All three of the Abrahamic religions have strong tendencies to fundamentalism within their traditions.[8]

---

7. Without denying the special and dramatic predicament of the Israeli state, can one not claim in company of existentialists that we are all—Muslim, Jew, Christian, and Hindu—irretrievably and habitually in a state of existential crisis?

8. It's my conviction that each of these rich traditions is strengthened when these temptations are recognized and resisted by those holding the tradition. No else can do it for them. At the same time though, secularists who sneer at religion in general would do great benefit to themselves were they able to exercise similar discretion in their reactions to religion. When Christopher Hitchens or Richard Dawkins or Bill Maher or Matt Taibbi takes on religion to dismiss it, they'd sound less like pubescent high-schoolers sneaking smokes under the football stands if they could avail themselves of what religion is about. Whatever else it is, it's the human response to the miracle of existence. It's as likely to go away as sex is. The task is not to get rid of religion but to distinguish between the response of wonder which is at its core and the accretions of fundamentalism which tend to obscure it.

It may help to speak of fetishes. If we take the term fetish in the negative sense often intended in its use in psychology, it refers to something that absorbs, preoccupies, blocks off attention from the larger scheme of things. The fetish of the Catholic Church might be said then to be its dogmas — or, more generally, its sense of itself as infallible. A fetish of Judaism cherished by some contemporary Jews might be said to be the Holy Land, and the sense that Jews must, by any means necessary, have exclusive occupancy there.

In both cases it's important not to disregard context. In the case of the Catholic Church, a resolutely materialistic and relativistic world, deeply hostile to Catholic values, is no doubt the context out of which the Catholic hierarchy acts on assumptions that are cited here as fundamentalist. After John XXIII and up to the election of Pope Francis, the Catholic Church has been reacting in fear. And its fears are not without grounds. In the case of Israel, it's important to look to the Holocaust. In the long history of inhumanity, the Holocaust continues to shock us by reason of occurring in the circumstances it did, and with such ungodly deliberateness. If this event continues to perplex and startle us "gentiles," think what it must be for Jews. Adding to the trauma of this, there's the present geographical context of Arab states — with one or more of them vociferously hostile to Israel at any given moment. The circumstances for insecurity are about as perfect as they can get. In such a context, is it surprising to hear apologists for Israeli policy resort to fundamentalist premises? Fear is a bad counselor, but a persuasive one.

Perhaps by now we're ready to attempt a deeper assessment of what fundamentalism there is among Muslims. If I've seemed strongly critical of Catholic and Jewish fundamentalisms, it's partly because I've been anxious to balance the scales a bit from the rant which our mainstream media routinely offer in support of our government's destructive interventions in Muslim affairs. Just as we know that not all Catholics embrace the fundamentalism that seduces many among the Catholic hierarchy, and just as we know not all Jews embrace the fundamentalism espoused by some leading right-wing Israeli politicians, so we should now be ready to localize (rather than universalize) the elements of Islamic fundamentalism when we speak of Muslims.

As it's been criticism from Catholics, in whose ranks I spent my youth, which has done most to disclose to me what I take to be fundamentalist characteristics in contemporary Catholicism, and as it's been criticism from wonderfully humane Jews which has done most to disclose to me what I take to be fundamentalist characteristics in contemporary Judaism, so, likewise, a series of encounters I regard as fortuitous and privileged with devout Muslim students has been what has most helped me discern, in their criticism of Muslim practice, what I take to be fundamentalist characteristics in contemporary Islam.

Just as "Catholic teaching" is by no means necessarily bad—but to make a fetish of Catholic teaching is bad; and just as the "Holy Land" is surely not bad in itself—but to make a fetish of the Holy Land is bad; so while the Koran should be viewed positively by Muslim and non-Muslim alike, this view which all can share should not blind us to the possibility that the Koran, if handled as a fetish, can be read and interpreted to excuse the inexcusable.

Context here, as everywhere, is important. When the Koran was given on the Arabian Peninsula early in the seventh century, it was proclaimed as the "Secure Guide" and the "Straight Path" at a time when everything on the peninsula seemed up in the air. Proclaimed as remedy, the Koran, as it confronted human wildness and reckless rationalizations, was not ambivalent. It did not encumber the listener or reader with a multitude of qualifications or extenuating circumstances or alternative choices. Allah spoke through it with all the simplicity and authority of the one and only God telling what was to be done and what was to be avoided. Gray areas went largely unacknowledged. (To be sure, in a separate and perhaps later sura [chapter], what had seemed ambiguous may have been clarified. One may suppose that circumstances of an emergent Muslim lifestyle demanded clarifications. The fact that the Koran is not chronologically organized to make later suras come later in the book tends to make attempts to specify which verses were clarifying which verses a matter of hypothesis. Even in the clarifications, however, the tone is authoritative. Not only must anyone who reads the Koran with full attention recognize this is the case, but one may even argue that this book could not have been effective had it lacked precisely this tone.

The voice of the same Allah continues to resonate today for millions of Muslims throughout the world. The perspective from which the Koran is addressed by devout readers is that all of this is from God; none of this is from Mohammed or from human ingenuity.

In the meantime, some thirteen centuries have passed. There had been, especially in the hundred years following the death of Mohammed, an astounding expansion of Islam to the west and the east. There had been a golden age of Muslim culture that had, among other things, helped lift Christendom from the Dark Ages by reconnecting Europe to the ancient Greeks. But there had also been European crusades against Islam—crusades which manifested Christian much more than Muslim fundamentalism. In later centuries, especially around the time of the First World War when the Ottoman Empire expired, there came in the Middle East a time of political and economic decline coinciding with a quickening tempo of exploitation by Europe, and as the twentieth century progressed, by the United States as well.

During these long centuries, the Koran provided guidance to Muslim life and culture. One can argue whether in the time of near miraculous extension, the Koran was read as a "jihadist" manual. For all that's been said here by way of indictment of Puritan expansion westward, my inclination in the case of Islam is to suggest that Muslim expansion was less "jihadist" than one might think. I say this because the peoples to whom Islam came have, by and large, both endured as peoples and have kept Islam. Islam did not expand without force; but it seems that the force it expended was directed mostly at ruling classes, and that what Islam had to offer, the masses accepted. In obedience to the explicit command of the Koran, it seems religious conversion was not routinely imposed as lands came under Muslim rule. Significant numbers of indigenous peoples must have seen in Muslim rule and the customs that attended it an opportunity for a better life—a step upward; else they would not have so readily adopted and retained Islam.

To some, it may seem with these words I become an apologist for Islam; but to me rather, it seems I'm guilty of damning with faint praise. I tell my cynical students that the aspirations of the human heart are toward some form of permanence in loving relationships and toward a transcendence of human limitation. Islam is a faith. For hundreds of years and for millions of Muslims, Islam has connected with these aspirations and nourished them.

Where force is involved, submission is always a tricky and complex business. That's why the judgment made above necessarily remains subject to challenge. Perhaps further research can help. A calculus of "how many were killed," "who was killed," "at what depth did acceptance take hold," "how enduring has the acceptance proved" must be worked through as part of the evaluation of freedom's role in the submission. Did the conqueror bring liberation or a new form of slavery? Alexander conquered vast territory to the east and south of the Mediterranean almost a millennium before the advent of Islam and is often regarded as a benefactor of humanity. Napoleon in his venture into Russia has a far more dubious reputation. In the case of Hitler and his conquests, there's no ambiguity at all: the man has come to personify evil.

Violence did clearly play a part at the very inception of Islam as the people of Medina warred to protect Islam from destruction by the people of Mecca. Shortly thereafter—and in the long run far more damaging to the harmony of Islam—there were murderous squabbles over who was a rightful successor to Mohammed. These rivalries and the recklessness of these squabbles have put a poison in the veins—I will not say of Islam, but—of Muslims ever since. In addition, I do concede that violence was an ingredient in the rapid expansion of Islam. And later, as mentioned, there were the Christian crusades to "re-conquer the Holy Land." These raised the passions of war in Muslim warriors, and provided just those circumstances for which the Koran authorizes war. Yet I'd say making all these concessions still doesn't justify the stereotype that Islam is a violent religion. If, as our media do, one insists on saying this, it seems to me sheer fairness requires that we then assign the description "violent religion" to all three Abrahamic religions.

My hunch, though, is that for most of its history, the activity sometimes called the "Lesser Jihad" (the practice of war in defense of Islam) really was the less important jihad. The "Greater Jihad" of the Koran was central—and this concerned the conquest of self. It ambitioned what's symbolized by the posture, head to the ground, of the devout Muslim at prayer. It demanded surrender of self to Allah. That, according to the Koran is the holy conquest that leads to peace.

One cannot however deny that for some Muslims today the violent Lesser Jihad figures centrally. This "lesser" is, as noted, the practice of holy war for the preservation of Islam. For some Muslims this practice has come to seem a matter of the utmost urgency. Yet to promote this to the point where one abandons the Greater Jihad is undeniably a perversion of Islam. This is done by numerous groups in the Middle East today—with broad effects elsewhere. The Koran explicitly condemns this.

I know as I write this that it's almost impossible to establish a recognized objectivity for any comments I make. An anti-Muslim may say, "Why does he tiptoe? Surely he must know from the evening news, night after night, there are monsters of Islam afoot—terrorists threatening his very existence as he sits spinning his fantasy." On the other hand, a devout Muslim may say, "How presumptuous he is! He presumes to discourse about shortcomings within a religion with which he has only the faintest acquaintance!"

Likewise a devout Jew is liable to say, "Who is this, a non-Jew, to say what Judaism is, or to say what its greatest values are—and to designate when they are being betrayed?" And a Catholic can object, "How is one to criticize Catholicism who is looking in on Catholicism from the hostile world outside—a world the Church was instituted to correct?"

In the face of all political correctness, there is a response to these objections. It seems fairly common for a member of a religion to be able to find negative fundamentalism in the practice of one who follows a different religion, but yet resist recognizing fundamentalism as a negative influence in his or her own practice. So when it comes to recognizing fundamentalisms, one looking in from the outside—not sharing the blinding but invisible biases of those within—does have a kind of advantage. Further, it seems to pertain to the character of a fundamentalist to deny that anyone outside the group is qualified to judge him or her in any way. Fundamentalism finds, by its very definition, "external" standards to be irrelevant; but this is the very condition for its excesses.

Finally, one should consider whether it's not the case that in every instance of fundamentalism, the disease masquerades as the cure. (There's a legendary Chinese king who was persuaded to take mercury as a remedy for weakness; not surprisingly, the more mercury he took, the weaker he felt; and so his demand for mercury constantly increased. On his deathbed, he's crying out "Mercury! more mercury!" as he dies.)

While it's wrong to demand one's own religion be practiced by others, this doesn't mean one is required to approve everything done by others in the name of religion. Not every religious remedy works. (To reverse this: while the secularist has the right to say that no religious remedy works, nonetheless if the secularist attempts to demand that out-of-hand dismissal from others— bypassing argumentation and resorting to ridicule—the secularist becomes by that behavior the narrow kind of person whom he or she denounces.)

Acknowledging the all-but-insuperable difficulties about objectivity, let's get on with our assessment of fundamentalism in Islam.

Under the great pressures that western religion and culture, and technological development, and new forms of colonialism have brought to Muslim lands in the Middle East, it's to be expected that issues over how to understand Islam are now in a state of crisis. There is of course the crisis of those outside Islam looking in. But I speak here of a crisis within the Muslim world. It's not surprising that for some Muslims, the legitimation of war presented in the Koran should have come to the fore—should in fact have come to be the central focus of their life. Yet I say to lift the Lesser Jihad (the military jihad) from its context and limitations in the Koran and make it the central activity of Islam is—as I define the phrase—a fundamentalist act. It's to take the part for the whole. It's to make a fetish of certain verses. Such an act doesn't draw one to an authentic understanding of Islam or to a life compatible with the Koran.

While then we say it's a great mistake for non-Muslims to think Islam is all about violent Jihad, we must acknowledge it's a mistake that non-Muslims might be less inclined to make if Muslims themselves weren't making it. Jihadism has created, as is evident, immense trouble and division and death among Muslims themselves. And, yes: complicating and enlarging the harm is that this lethal jihadism, especially when exercised against non-Muslims, tends to become the only lens through which many outsiders can now see Islam.

It won't be easy for Muslims to institute unity and community among themselves. Derivatively, it won't be easy for Muslims to present a more generous and accurate version of Islam to the non-Muslim world. (Here though I wish to insist much of the problem we Americans have is from our obdurate willful readiness as westerners to misunderstand or overlook what we have done, particularly since World War Two, to Muslims.) For the sake of Muslim unity, an act of reflection and critical self-analysis that may not have been urgent in Islam's earlier history has become urgent. But to perform such reflection will demand a great deal from Muslims.

For both Muslims and non-Muslims, an act of analysis is needed that will distinguish the core of Islam from its fundamentalist accretions. Tentatively, and realizing I speak as an outsider, let me presume to make some observations—observations I offer in order to suggest fundamentalism is not an essential feature of Islam. I do so, not as one attempting to impose Christianity, or Judaism, or any other religion, but simply as one considering what exigencies must be met if the Middle East is ever again to become a place where people can live together in peace. (If the U.S., Britain, France, Israel, etc., will not restrain themselves politically, I realize of course the hope for harmony among Muslims, and for harmony between Muslims and others, shrinks to a vanishing point—regardless of any thoughtful observations I or others may make. Sadly, the habit of our meddling is now so ingrained it seems predictable that continued meddling by the West will delay peace in the Middle East for decades to come. In fact, the eventual accommodation, if accommodation occurs, may come not in the Middle East but in the West—once Muslims have found the Middle East so totally dismembered that large numbers of them have become, if the West will allow, political refugees in the nations that have intruded on them.) Here are my observations on fundamentalist accretions to Islam:

1)   The "Uncreated Koran," while arguably defensible as a theological notion, tends to be the source of a problem. It's a notion analogous to the notion of Jesus existing before his

birth as the pre-existing Word of God from all eternity. Just as a notion of Jesus as an all-knowing being existing from all eternity can drain the historical Jesus of all historical conditioning, so the notion of an *uncreated* Koran can leach over and seem to drain a tangible Koran one can actually hold of its ties to human history and cultural context. Consider how a human Jesus who knows at each moment of life what's going to happen next is not a human after all. The Christian protest against Scorsese's *The Last Temptation of Christ* was at root a refusal to consider Jesus as a man—to consider specifically that he was a man who could fall in love. What the protestors, with their bias against the human body, didn't seem to understand is that their refusal was a rejection of Christianity; their Jesus wasn't a man after all. Likewise, it seems a mistake to deny that a physical book, the Koran, is a creature of time and place—a document with a history. For in that case the book becomes mythical and eternal. All expressions in it are eternally wrought by God. There is little room for interpretation, much less for revision. I'd say the trouble here is that so long as Muslims allow to this three-dimensional, physical Koran qualities that can't rightly be attributed to *any* created thing, they shouldn't be surprised at outbreaks of extremist behavior from their eccentrics. They shouldn't be surprised at the horrible sectarian squabbles that have rent the harmony of Islam from almost the earliest days up to the present. For if this is a magical book, wrought by God from all eternity, it would seem to provide for no accommodation to differing human experiences and differing cultures. A pluralism of interpretations seems excluded on principle. This can lead a devout Muslim to regard all Muslims who disagree with him as mere pretenders and "infidels." It is no problem that devout Muslims hear in the Koran the very voice of Allah. What's become unaffordable is that some so absolutize their personal experiences of the Koran that their readings and sense of it go uncriticised. To regard the Koran with unqualified worship moves one away from Islam; for one is likely to end up worshipping, not Allah, but the particular way one processes the Koran.

2) Demonstrably the Koran cannot support such weight. As a created entity, the Koran—howsoever more perfect than all other creatures—is not ultimate perfection, is not absolute. It speaks differently to different hearers and readers. It has ambiguities. It does not contain all knowledge in the sense that all other books could be burned without any loss. One cannot on its authority shut up all other voices on the face of the earth. The language in which it is written is a human language, emerging out of a human culture; and it is marked by the pre-occupations and limitations of the time in which it came to be. The warning: "There is no God but Allah" actually summons one to awareness of this. Only Allah is Allah; the voice of Allah may be heard in the Koran; but the Koran in one's hand remains Allah's creature.

3) The most radical change needed is this one—to make a clear distinction between the Koran as the Secure Path and Allah as the goal of that path. Following on this, a change in perspective associated with this seems less fundamental, but still very important. A confining and extravagant way to read the Koran is to say that whatever it does not directly mandate is forbidden. (This is comparable to Thomas Jefferson's impossible "strict-constructionist" reading of the Constitution; even he could not follow it.) Contrary to such a letter-of-the-law approach, there are schools of Muslim theology which advocate a way of reading the Koran that protects it from being reduced to a mere code book of particular injunctions and particular restrictions. Tracing their roots, I dare say, back to Mohammed's successful administration of the city of Medina, these schools say instead that whatever the Koran does not expressly forbid is matter for consideration in accord with known Koranic principles. This second approach can accommodate changing circumstances in which a living Koran can continue to be a guide for how to be a Muslim today. It was consideration along these lines that made possible the marvelous Islamic civilizations of the past in which Muslims and non-Muslims dwelt together in peace—fostering architecture, science, and magnificent scholarship.

4) Another matter for consideration is the doctrine of predestination. The doctrine of predestation is neither unambiguously rejected nor directly taught in the Koran. I've already argued at length that this doctrine has had ruinous effects on the Puritans who gave to America what's been its special character. It seems permissible here to argue, in recognition of the Koran's ubiquitous verses in which human responsibility is affirmed, that the passages in which some find a doctrine of predestination should not be interpreted as denials of human freedom, but rather as affirmations that nothing happens outside Allah's providence. To claim this is to claim a great deal while, at the same time, it refrains from canceling human responsibility. When evil human deeds occur, they occur, according to a providential theology, because Allah has willed the freedom of humans and is capable of providing victims of evil with divinely sponsored ultimate compensation. An interpretation that goes beyond this and affirms that God predestines all that happens is an interpretation at odds with Koranic teaching—prominent virtually in every surah—on the capacity of humans to sin. To let a doctrine of predestination override this teaching can suggest the following dreadful line of thought: "Since whatever I manage to do has been eternally decreed by Allah, I can do whatever I want, knowing that what I do is exactly what Allah has willed." I cannot think of a prescription more likely to corrode all dignity in human affairs and all sense of meaning and responsibility.

5) It's a kind of get-out-of-responsibility-free card. Not only is there a theoretical possibility of chaos here; the card has actually, observably, been played at times. Further (as we saw in the case of Puritanism), if I believe I am among Allah's Elect, I may thereby discover in myself license to despise and destroy those whom I regard as cast off by Allah. (Atrocities perpetrated by Christians have been rationalized on the ground one is only destroying those whom God has from all eternity marked for destruction. The same seems true of similar atrocities by Muslims.) Predestation is an inhumane doctrine, reducing human

existence to an empty charade. It dishonors the strong and steady Koranic teaching that my sins are mine and that Allah is just when Allah condemns them.)

6) Finally, in this effort to use Islam as an example of how to distinguish between the core of a religion and its fundamentalist accretions, let me briefly address the status of women. Some Muslims seem insufficiently responsive to the example of Mohammed regarding women. A Muslim male may claim it's the preciousness of women which requires the far-reaching constraints he and other males place on them. Of a particular woman, a Muslim male may say: "I protect her so because she is the jewel of my life—my most precious possession." One suspects Mohammed never regarded Khadija or Fatima or any other woman as a possession. To regard women that way was one of the great evils of "the wild times" that the Koran denounced. Beyond that, if a male Muslim intends outright exploitation of a woman, he has only to read the Koran to find his practice condemned. A Muslim need not go outside Islam for the grounds for reform. He should behave as Mohammed behaved. (Westerners who satirize Mohammed on this score should be ashamed of their ignorance. The entrenched ignorance of these Westerners is a sign of their ill will. In the Koran the harsh warnings and punishments laid on women for their moral improvement should be read within the hyperbolic context of harsh warnings and punishments laid on men. We find much of the same in what as Christians we name the Old Testament. Read in the context of the place and time in which it came forth, the Koran clearly worked toward an improvement in the status of women rather than toward condoning disparagement; and there are ample reports indicating this was confirmed in the behavior toward women of Mohammed.)

As I've suggested though, reducing the role of fundamentalism in Islam will not come easily. The fetishizing way some Muslims treat the Koran has opened a way for taking parts of it out of context and, in the name of Sharia [Muslim law], twisting such excerpts to support what is un-Koranic and irresponsible. A win-nowing task is the task of the hour. Until the day when Muslims in general, as they read and hear the Koran, make a clear distinc-tion between the Koran and Allah—as Jews and Christians must distinguish between the Bible and God—tension and trouble are likely to continue. Islam is not in its very nature fundamen-talist, but the belief of some Muslims that they have a right to unrestricted violence in Allah's name is. They become as misled as violence-addicted commentators on *Fox News*, the *New York Times*, or the *Washington Post*. What they say runs against explicit verses in the Koran, and is contrary to the spirit of Islam, which is surrender to Allah, "the All-Merciful, the Compassionate." (Yes, you can find apocalyptic celebrations of divine violence in the Koran as you can in the biblical Jewish book of Joshua and the biblical Christian book of Revelation. It is a function of sane people to know how to process these.)

By now, perhaps we've discussed fundamentalism among Cath-olics, Jews, and Muslims at sufficient length to arrive at some fair sense of the term's meaning. The strategy has been to travel a broad circle by which to return to Puritanism and America.

All the strictures charged against the fundamentalisms of Catholics, Jews, and Muslims seem to suggest counter-parts for stricture against Puritan fundamentalism. The mythic self-image of the Catholic Church as a perfect institution functioning in an imperfect world is clearly paralleled by the Puritans' sense of themselves as an Elect people. The land fetish of some contem-porary Jews is wonderfully prepared by the way Puritans took the mythic propaganda of the book of Joshua as a model for a centuries-long campaign of ethnic cleansing against American indians in the Winning of the West. The un-Koranic tendency of some Muslims to worship the Koran is fully matched by an un-Biblical tendency of Puritans to bibliolatry.

As large groups of Americans back away from what we feel is the abyss of secular relativism, it's toward Puritan fundamental-ism that many of us non-secularists retreat. One can appreciate the motivation here. It's to achieve coherence and equilibrium by a return to basics.

This maneuver however seems insufficiently alert to the inse-curities of Puritanism itself and to the longstanding cleavage in American Puritanism between "on-Sunday" lofty gospel professions of love for God and "weekday" down-to-earth American Puritan hard dealing. It's especially a fundamentalist sense of themselves as the Elect that makes a transition from lofty intent to vicious everyday practice possible. A task of this book, especially in the section regarding our reliance on force, has been to etch the character of this back-and-forth transition; an attempt has been to uncover the monumental incoherence it entails.

Complicating our retreat from secularism is the manner in which American practice of a Puritan version of Christianity has itself done much to nurture the secular ethos from which we hope to escape. The bed we disdain to lie in is the bed in which we were conceived. By this I mean we are conflicted about our history. Current members of "Tea Parties" for instance often have a religiously grounded and justified sense that things have gone quite wrong. What seems, however, often to escape notice is how even as they clamor against corruption in government and throughout American life, they have as voters done much to invite corruption by resolutely championing a marketplace ungoverned by reasonable restriction. An unregulated marketplace — one which ends up paying no heed to ethical or religious principle — is at once that which they support in their voting and shopping and that which they denounce in their Sunday rhetoric. There's some insight on one day of the week, for in their Sunday rhetoric and meditations, they have glimpses that the buyers and sellers have desecrated the temple. That we have a tough time holding onto Thanksgiving Day is a symptom of our times.

Setting to one side the sometimes difficult business of deciphering "Tea Party" agendas, it can be argued generally that the literalist reading of the Bible to which Puritan fundamentalists often adhere is not effective in promoting the Bible as a moral guide. It prematurely disqualifies the Bible as a credible and relevant force. If one is concerned to prove that a serpent once literally talked in a literal Garden of Eden, one is going to be so buried in a tangled scrutiny of arguments as to miss the genuine lessons in the Genesis stories, and to miss as well the great voices of Jeremiah and Isaiah and Jesus summoning us to the care of the widow and the orphan. Further, by replacing the Heavenly Father of Jesus with the inscrutable God of Calvin, devout Puritans have driven people into atheism and hastened the arrival of secularism. Confusions abound.

The larger error, then, is to assume that Christianity as practiced by our Puritan forebears ("that ole time religion") can rescue us from the predicaments we experience at present. This is all too much like that Chinese king trying to recover from mercury poisoning by ever larger drafts of mercury. A return to the faith of our fathers cannot save us if, by our fathers, we mean those who—gripped by an arbitrary and inhumane interpretation of the Bible—have fathered our Puritanism and our sense of American exceptionalism.

What I've meant to argue toward—through this lengthy and meandering consideration of fundamentalism—is that it was the Puritans' tragically compromised reading and consequent compromised practice of Christianity that has been central in bringing on the problems we find ourselves in today. While a deeply Christian compassion among Americans would indeed go a long way toward achieving a reconfiguration for the better of the world's prospects, Christian fundamentalism as a descendant of Puritanism simply insists on doubling down on trends already leading to a worldwide free-for-all over money, resources, and power. It's a prescription for universal riot. It fires up all the other fundamentalisms we've noted here—and makes prospects for preserving human civilization throughout the length of the present century worrisome. At the very least, it forecasts increasing disorder in American life. This is true whether we look to family, to international relations, or to provision for our individual health and education, or to provision for our man-made infrastructure, or to preservation of the habitat that's made us possible.

11 | "God Will Save Us from Ourselves!"

(What! More God? In the previous chapter we considered how notions of God can provide sources of hope that lead to violent and aggressive action. Here we consider how notions of God can provide sources of hope that lead to lethal complacency.)

Some of us do try to think long-term. We who do so tend to think by way of processes of extrapolation. We note how we labor compulsively to widen the scope of the dominant trends and habits, mindsets and ambitions of our society, both as these are realized in our individual lives and as they're realized among us as achievements of the group. For instance, we think of the way we fund our government by borrowing, and we wonder how long we can get away with increasing deficits. Reagan famously achieved a kind of "morning in America"—still remembered fondly—by borrowing us into prosperity, and Bill Clinton found ways of continuing the good times by withdrawing restraints on the activities of banks and the stock market—restraints put in place during the Great Depression. Currently the Federal Reserve sustains our banking system by daily infusions of nearly interest-free cash. Again, we think of our unilateralism in foreign policy; we reflect on how we decide which political system to subvert, which foreign leader—duly elected or not—we see fit to replace, which country to invade (when, and for what reason), and on how we will attempt to reconcile the rest of what we call "the free world" to the choice we have made. We note how bitterly we complain when France, or Russia, or Europe in general seems recalcitrant. We note how we recently refrained from "French fries" and ate "freedom fries" instead. We wonder if there are any adults left in America. We note that in some parts of America we are exhausting our groundwater and our aquifers and no one seems to have a plan for what to do about it; rather, some want to use the water left to us to carry out fracking. It occurs to us the extravagance with which we throw our weight around seems to have a connection with our mounting debts and depletion of resources. We seem never to have met a war we didn't like; and where there is no war, we invent one, as we did in Iraq. One bad habit seems to feed the other. We live like a spoiled and brawling playboy, and those among us given to reflection wonder how long the synergy of this brawling and this borrowing against the future can hold up.

We think of our hoarding yet throwaway lifestyle. We wake up in the morning to invitations to guard our house with a state-of-the-art security system, to invitations to try a diet famous for miracles performed on imperfectly shaped celebrities, to invitations to reconfigure our drab backyard by installing a sparkling fresh-cut redwood deck, along with invitations to reconfigure our faces with a series of cosmetological interventions, including—but not limited to—surgeries. We live in perpetual unrest, besieged from dawn to dusk with admonitions as to what is newer, better, bigger, faster, and cheaper—and believe what we hear. Some of us are too restless to sit through a Thanksgiving meal. We replace our car, our cell phone, and our drab backyard. Our landfills bulge with our discards. Rather frequently, we replace our spouses. We use our rivers as toilets down which we flush the waste materials of our extravagant lives. On those occasions when we gaze at idyllic scenes of sailboats off which people fish in San Francisco Bay, we have to hope the happy sailors are too prudent to eat freely of their catch. An uneasy misgiving tells us nature has a way of striking back. In fact, the first half of the evening news is now regularly devoted to showing us how nature is currently doing so.

Politicians play to us on the hunch that many of us feel impoverished. But for millions of us, this is not precisely our plight. Rather we are too locked into a round-the-clock commercialism, and we feel stretched to our limit in our effort to keep up.

We see species on the brink of extinction. There are other species we do not see—they turn up missing. And we wonder what life on earth will be like without these fellow members of the biological web that spawned us.

As the climate warms, and old provisions of nature can no longer be counted on, we wonder too what accommodations will be necessary in some future sharing of declining, no longer reliably provided resources. Will we, backed by our nuclear arsenal and our permanent state of military readiness and activity, simply continue to utilize the share of things to which we've become accustomed? If so, what will this tenacious exercise of privilege cost in our relations with others? How ready will we be to exercise hospitality toward those whose homelands have become inhospitable as a result of the lifestyle we've exemplified?

In uses of water and land, in some places we already experience domestic tension within our borders between those who would retain traditional agricultural uses and maybe protect habitat for wildlife as well, and those who would trade such uses for further development of homes, malls, and factories. The homes may be needed for foreseeable numbers seeking refuge from more blighted areas; and the people who will live in these homes must have places where they can purchase the necessities of life, and they must have places where they can work to earn the purchase price of these necessities. Amid all this, we can easily forget that among these necessities are food and water, and as Malthus foresaw, our demands keep forging ahead as our agricultural and other food resources are thinning. (How come the price of crab is rising, and will oysters still be available as the chemistry of the oceans changes?)

What is the formula for adjudicating the conflicting claims? And what will the world look like if we do not calculate wisely? Can we really leave the calculation to an interplay of greed and the fine-tuning of an invisible hand? Will we Americans continue to have abundant sources of food? Will potable water continue to be generally accessible? Or will increasing demands and disruptions in our food and water systems reduce the quality of life for us as well as for those who live elsewhere? Has our evolutionary history installed in us such a tendency to consume that we are programmed to succeed into failure?

Time to take a deep breath.

I do not say all of us are spending our days on such considerations. Most of us are not. Quite a few of us are too busy tweeting our friends, responding to the latest commercials, worrying about our eyelashes and face wrinkles, and wondering why this or that celebrity has slept with someone other than their spouse.

To a resolute secularist, I have not much to say about all this. Find within your resolute secularism what means you can to cope with it. For the remainder of this chapter, I address believers—people who believe there is some noble and transcendent purpose at stake in our human endeavor.

One should not despise this huge mass of us. As a people of great energy and creativity, it's unlikely that we're genuinely oblivious to the issues just mentioned. If we were, why demand so much from drugs, alcohol, and our storehouses of painkillers? Why elect to dwell in cyberspace?

More likely we simply can't see what to do about these issues. In our workaday lives, we leave such problems to "experts" (special people to be hired and guided by our elected officials)—dreading, even as we do so, that members of that special and rare set from whom we choose our officials are more apt to draw profit from our problems than solve them.

And so the aforementioned pause for refreshment—that deep breath—renders up, does it not, a daunting scene?

Enter God.

What sometimes occurs to us as an alternative to all this dreary casting about is to turn all these matters over to God. This last isn't simply a space-filler for careless people who don't think often about these things; it's a default position as well for some who do. Haven't we been taught to accept the things we cannot change?

"God" as an answer has some plausibility.

I often think the most convincing evidence for God is the habitability of our planet. I know what I speak of isn't really a proof at all, but more in the order of a notion, or perhaps an intuition. Here we are: emerging from nowhere—who knows how?—into a place that has characteristics of having been prepared for us. To be sure, the resolute secularist will protest: "That's a mere truism. It's a tautology. For earth would *have* to be accommodated to us for us to be here!" But I'm not precisely making an argument. The purpose here isn't to make a case so much as to assess a situation. It's as if one walked ashore on an unknown island and found the place hospitable. There was foliage with delightful hues, offering shade; there was birdsong and fresh water. Moreover, there was a library full of volumes well suited to entertain and inform one.

Throw in a candle, lit and shining, on a table spread with food. Coming upon such apparent provision, one would surmise the presence of a host. (I can hear my good friend Spinoza saying softly: surely you don't want to go down this road; surely you'll soon find yourself saying with Bacon, Descartes, and the Puritans that the whole value of nature is its mere utility for us!)

What I present here though is neither precisely an argument nor an agenda. I attempt an analogy for how human beings everywhere and from time immemorial have come to sense a sacred dimension to things, a divinity hovering over us that "shapes our ends, rough-hew them how we will."

Granted the real-world correspondences there are to such provisions as those on our imaginary island, it seems unlikely to us humans that our host would have paid such attention to matters of detail simply so our habitation here would end in dismal failure. It's on these grounds we hear devout people say: "God wouldn't allow us to bring into the world more children than the world can handle" or "God wouldn't let us destroy our environment!" or "God would never put so much power into our hands as to enable us to defeat His plan by nuclear catastrophe." These are powerful messages.

They are "liberating" as well. As argued earlier, we often choose our thoughts for their convenience. The thoughts just cited tell us there's no problem of overpopulation. There's no real problem with the environment. It's only those who look a gift horse in the mouth who worry about climate change or diminishing resources, or some danger of self-annihilation of the human species through our own weaponry. God would never let such things occur.

To our temptations to despair, these messages offer an inviting alternative. Why not adopt them as our answer? Why carry the world on our shoulder? Why not live, instead, in the comforting and reassuring glow they offer? Such messages invite us to sleep comfortably on this Greyhound bus called earth and leave the driving to God. Why say no to morning in America?

In truth, it's very human to take this kind of thing to heart. And not just in America. When devout Hindus say "everything is maya," they are, in a sense, going here. They're saying, "God has not, in reality, let things reach anything like a cul-de-sac. We only think He has. The world we perceive is not the world that is." When Muslims or Puritan Christians opt for predestination, they are doing something similar. A thoroughgoing doctrine of predestination can take the worst horrors human history has contrived and see them as neither more nor less than what God in His eternal wisdom and goodness has decided to make happen. Such horrors are thereby sanctified as products of God's will. The sting of such horrors has been removed.

A dispositive objection (one that gets the job done) to both these approaches—maya and predestination—is that they are in conflict with our deepest intuition of the actuality of the world and of our freedom of action within it. The Hindu sage who speaks of maya denies this world explicitly, telling us that all we experience is mere appearance; he is Plato on steroids. The proclaimer of predestination is less direct. Yet to deny a thing its proper agency (as those who believe in predestination do both regarding things in general, and particularly regarding human beings) seems finally to consign to oblivion the reality of everything but God. Common sense and our experience in general inform us that existence and agency are inextricably bound together. When the proponent of predestination says: "God has all the agency," for such an advocate it follows: "Creatures have no agency at all." In such a conception, we and the world about us are reduced to no more than mere characters and props in a divinely written script; the world collapses into a plaything of Divine imagination. (Contemporary Puritans have trouble with Darwin because of the immense agency he assigns to the physical universe. Good Calvinists want to reserve all that agency for God. Not only has God got the whole world in His hands, but—by the way—there actually is no world.)

The extreme test-case for such a perspective was the Holocaust. In *Letters and Papers from Prison*, the Lutheran theologian Dietrich Bonhoeffer, during the unspeakable anguish of the Third Reich, writes that we must live and act in the world "etsi Deus non daretur"—as if, that is, God did not exist. What had come home to Bonhoeffer was not atheism, but realism about the actuality of our world being a place where evil can take hold. He'd arrived at an irresistible insight into the actuality of evil. He found himself immersed in consciousness of its density and claim to being. While Aquinas and other medieval schoolman spoke of evil as a form of privation, they also anticipated Bonhoeffer by their insistence on what they called "secondary causality." This was the causality inherent in all creatures—the causality we humans exercise. While God causes the world and everything in it, Aquinas insisted that humans have by reason of their participation in being, a causality that is equally real, though altogether rooted in God's sustaining gift of being. That this human causality can go unimaginably awry is the insight that came crashing down on Bonhoeffer.

In the aftermath of the Holocaust, there was a brief surging and prominence of death-of-God theologies. The mood lingers on, though the slogan has retreated. Rather what the Holocaust should have led to was the death of predestination as a credible doctrine and to the demise of God-will-save-us-from-ourselves theologies.

As I suggest, in addition to monstrous events, what should further fortify us against an easy religious complacency is the spontaneous awareness, possessed by each of us, that we exist and each has demonstrable agency as a being who is not infinite. In our human case, although it's a dependent agency dependent on the source of our being, it's a very rich agency, richer it would seem than the everyday agency of rocks, or vegetables, or—it would seem—of the whole order of non-human animals.

If nothing else has sufficed, our daily experience of this rich human agency should lay to rest the notion "God will save us from ourselves." God is not in the business of saving us from ourselves. God who created us with agency is not in the business of cancelling that agency.

Surely, there'd have been no point in creating each of us a "self" had it been our creator's plan to save us from the inconveniences of being a self. In a very radical way—as the existentialists tirelessly insist—we are genuinely "on our own." Yet this isn't quite as atheist existentialists would have it. Contrary to Sartre, it seems it isn't because of God's absence we are on our own, but because God has the unimaginable power to give existence to what God conceives.[1]

---

1. To say this is not to claim we creatures endure in existence without God's sustaining action, but to say that by reason of God's sustaining action, we really do exist and have an agency that is truly not God's but ours. If this strikes one as a great mystery, well, welcome to the club.

For if God really is a creator, creation must, in a sense, be "on its own." A notion therefore that one enhances one's sense of God's reality by declaring God the micro-manager of the universe is bad theology. It diminishes God—for it will not allow that God can create that which can stand against God and oppose God's purposes; it denies nuclear physicist Ian Thompson's assertion that God can create a rock he cannot move. As Thompson says, God did. That rock is us.

Calvin's God doesn't do this. The God of the Bible does. Calvin, one must conclude, is not a reliable reader of the Bible for Calvin cannot take in the opening lesson of the Bible's teaching that God can create what really is not God.

If we're real, if we're intelligent being with the self-determination which intelligence entails, we can't be such that our agency is magically suspended or swept away when it would get us into trouble. Though Leibniz and that kindest of men, Spinoza, would blissfully like to think otherwise, they are clearly wrong. They would reduce us to what we've noted we clearly are not: divinely designed toys for the play of divine imagination. (Whatever is wholesome in the writing of Nietzsche can, I think, be traced to this: his relentless insistence on the actuality and freedom of his own being.)

Because we are real, God cannot save us from ourselves. If God could, it would be in the ironic mode of the American pilot in Vietnam who remarked: "We had to destroy the village to save it." A deliverance of that sort isn't quite the deliverance we desire. Neither, it would seem, is it a deliverance God has ever intended.

While it's a false hope to think "God will save us from ourselves," nonetheless it does not seem in any way false to hope that God will somehow make available to us (indeed has made available to us) sources of direction and guidance amid the predicament and perplexities of human freedom.

Until quite recently, all peoples everywhere have had this hope always—that there is wisdom available to us; that within the miraculous, inexplicable gift of existence, some direction for our response and use of it is included; that there are indicated paths for success in the human project. When we speak of "conscience," and "inspiration," and "intimations," we are addressing this. That different peoples have come up with different formulations doesn't tell against such formulations having a common source in that which holds the whole in being. A good physician suits the prescription to the patient. We wonderfully diverse humans do not lack prescriptions. (More particularly, consider how a recently silenced Catholic theologian Roger Haight has written that you cannot take seriously the vision Jesus provides of God as loving father—and mother—and then go on to believe that God would have rationed the revelation of human dignity and purpose to a mere subset of God's human creatures.) Christians have often thought they, as missionaries to non-Christians, were the first agents of such revelation. But surely, as the Jesuit Roger Haight surmises, God has been there before them.

As suggested in the chapter on fundamentalism, what we must learn is to stop saying: "I've found the only guidepost!" We believers must learn not to be so enamored of our guidepost that we're ready to use it as a stake through the heart of anyone who holds a different one. While God doesn't save us from ourselves, God has provided abundantly, so that no one is without some means whereby to live meaningfully. An urgent part of our task is to learn how to avoid converting the means provided us into a weapon—to avoid making a sword of our guidepost. Better by far if our guidepost comes in the form of a plowshare, or a shovel for planting trees, or a pointer toward development of solar energy, or a formula for worldwide compassion.

To believe as some religious persons among us do that "no work of ours is conducive unto salvation" and to cry "*Sola Gratia!*"—only by God's grace are we saved!—can be a path to thoughts of predestination and desperation. We echo then our Puritan ancestors. To say however "God is gracious" is to speak a saving truth—so long as one realizes God's gracious initiative dies in us if we do not respond. While Luther is right about grace—namely, that we have need of grace (for we lack the means to place ourselves in God's friendship)—Bonhoeffer's truth supplies the necessary corollary: a grace that does not invite and summon us to an act of personal choice is cheap and spurious—no grace God would bother with.

God doesn't save us from ourselves. It is the terror of the God-given human predicament that—with God's help—to save us from ourselves is up to us. (See Kierkegaard. See Pogo. See the Greater Jihad—in which we struggle against ourselves, to surrender ourselves to Allah.)

12 | "The Next Election (or the one after that) Will Save Us!"

When people speak of "the next election," what they seem most often to be looking to is the approaching election of a president. In our system, the president is no mere humble executive officer who sees to it that decrees of Congress are carried out. Importantly, our president is also our head of state; he or she is, at any particular moment, expected to perform as a personification of the American nation.

However modest their achievements may have been, our individual presidents have each become a cottage industry for historians—each has been the focus of a continually growing number of assessments and counter-assessments. The "History of the American Presidency" is, by contrast, a leaner source of books—perhaps because the generalizations in such a history must accommodate vastly different personalities functioning under vastly different conditions over a period of more than two hundred years. Generalizations in social studies are notoriously difficult and subject to challenge; generalizations about what's been happening to something as abstract as "the American Presidency" are especially so.

Nonetheless, let's venture an opening generalization about American presidents. By and large they've been people who have celebrated The American Story. As suggested in the opening chapter on education, that story says we are a people who have cultivated freedom, and who have constituted a shelter for it—a sanctuary where there is liberty and justice for all. Ours is the land of the free and the home the brave. While slow to anger and war, we have been heroic in response when summoned by attacks on the freedom and prosperity of our way of life. Further,

we're a humanitarian people—willing to spend blood and treasure overseas, putting ourselves in harm's way from humanitarian
motivation in arduous missions, necessary but often thankless, to
extend abroad the benefits and blessings of democracy we enjoy
at home.

In the section on force, I've argued at length that this story
is less supported by evidence than we might imagine, and that
indeed a great deal of data contradicts it. It's not my purpose to
argue that case again. Here let's note only that the recitation of
The American Story has been an expected function of our presidents in their capacity as head-of-state. They have tended to be
good Fourth-of-July orators.

(Contrast them with Charles Beard who has argued that our
forefathers in the era of our revolutionary days were largely well-
to-do landowners and businessmen, caught up in a tug-o'-war
between themselves and the governmental elite of England over
who should prosper most from the success of the American colonies. Howard Zinn, while valuing the values asserted in the high
rhetoric of those revolutionary days, says those who spoke that
rhetoric were often less than serious. Zinn is sympathetic to the
story as told by Beard, and in *A People's History of the United States*
Zinn has fleshed out the approach of Beard. But this was Beard's
and Zinn's story; it emphatically has not been The American
Story.)

Not only have our presidents told The American Story, they've
often been presented as exemplifying its promise of freedom and
opportunity. Jackson rose from struggle and mistreatment by the
British to become "a great champion of the common man." In
order to improve his brand, William Henry Harrison was presented as one who emerged from a log cabin in response to a call
to public service that prepared him for the White House. (Actually, Harrison was a member of the southern aristocracy.) Later,
in the case of Lincoln, the story about a journey from a log cabin
to the White House was actually true. In 2008, Barack Obama
used his own story of Kenyan ancestry to present himself as one
exemplifying the upward mobility possible in America.

America is "a city on a hill," and the White House is sacred
space at the center of that city. From there, presidents are
expected to project the radiance of America to the world at large.

How this plays out is instructive. That Jefferson owned slaves was not a problem. That Jefferson called in our merchant fleet off the Atlantic Ocean was a problem. Presidents don't do such things. Temporarily he became very unpopular. When John Quincy Adams, as Monroe's secretary of state, drafted the Monroe Doctrine, there was "an era of good feeling," and both he and Monroe basked in the public's approval. When, as Chief Executive, Adams tried to impose greater order on the way America was developing, his popularity declined, and he was rejected as an elitist. And later, when as a congressman, he declaimed endlessly against slavery in America, many regarded him a crank and an embarrassment; his behavior was un-presidential and out of touch with The American Story. Lincoln, however, as a lawyer for the railroads, was a sound man who could be trusted to know how the West should be developed. As a man who spoke eloquently and acted forcefully to maintain the Union as the indispensable premise of American Destiny, Lincoln was doubly sound. He died in time to escape the ordeal of addressing the consequences of his success; his place of greatness in our memory of presidents is secure. He fit our story.

By contrast, a century and some years later, when Jimmy Carter delivered a speech that seemed, according to our media, to register a sense of national "malaise," he was replaced by a man who spoke of "morning in America."

So, telling The American story and embodying the spirit of that story is an important part of what presidents do. When they do it well, they are popular. When they falter in doing it, they may be rejected as being job-holders who don't understand their job.

Fulfillment of this presidential function has had consequences tending toward a concentration of power in the executive branch. A shift of power away from the Congress and from the courts to the presidency has been enabled by a predilection in our character. We like the spokesperson for our nation to be outspoken and strong. (The popularity, as I write, of Trump's candidacy reflects this, I think. Even those who dislike what he says may like his style.) If our president acts in a way that seems bold and uncurtailed, we tend to celebrate that as representing the spirit of America. Jackson was "a man on horseback." Lincoln could endure against intense opposition and could suspend habeas corpus and could, without constitutional authorization, issue an Emancipation Proclamation because he was seen by many (and in the border states as well as in the North), as a dependable guardian of America's destiny. Teddy and Woodrow and Franklin all knew the uses of the bully pulpit, and this was a source of their popularity.

First Major Current in the History of the American Presidency

Let me suggest, then, that our tendency to turn to presidents for a reassuring sense of who we are provides the context for a major current in the history of the American presidency: namely, a gradual ascendancy of the executive branch over the legislative and judicial. Such growth has been regarded negatively by some who see it as a march towards what Arthur Schlesinger Jr. labeled "the Imperial Presidency." While there may have been a hiatus in the time of Jimmy Carter, and a fierce effort by Republicans to inhibit exercise of presidential power in the administrations of Clinton and Obama, it's evident that the tendency toward concentrating power in the presidency continues in the twenty-first century. The tendency has been artfully re-christened in recent administrations as support for "the unitary executive." Our presidency shows, even in the face of manifest abuses, an apparently irreversible tendency toward ongoing accumulations of power.

Because the American president is the head of state, the American presidency provides our most heightened form of celebrity politics. "America's Got Talent," "American Idol," "the Voice," and "Dancing with the Stars" are distant rivals for public attention compared to our quadrennial contests for the presidency. Nothing else brings in such revenue for the media as this contest does. The media do not pay for this "reality TV"; rather, the contestants pay the media for the opportunity to perform political commercials.

A notable source of celebrity to qualify one as a candidate for this contest is from participation in war. Washington, Jackson,

W.H. Harrison, Franklin Pierce, Zachary Taylor, Grant, Hayes, Garfield, Benjamin Harrison, T. Roosevelt, and Eisenhower had each achieved celebrity as war heroes prior be being considered viable candidates. With the exception of Colonel Benjamin Harrison and "Colonel" Roosevelt, all had been successful generals. Among other candidates whose war records seem to have helped qualify them have been McKinley, Truman, Kennedy, Nixon, Carter, and G.H.W. Bush, as well as unsuccessful candidates John Kerry and John McCain.

War during an administration tends of course to expand the scope of authority for one who's already been elected president. At the outbreak of war, the president taps into unmeasured reserves of power available to our commander-in-chief in time of national peril. The nation as a whole could probably not have survived without this virtually unrestricted allowance of power to Lincoln. Eighty years later, when the frustrating slowness of New Deal recovery was dimming his popularity, Franklin Roosevelt's hold on power was renewed by the darkly threatening clouds from war in Europe, and then by the very real smoke over Pearl Harbor. Roosevelt's "bold executive action" was granted a new lease at the center of affairs. Nixon, during whose presidency the Vietnam War continued, seems to have made attentive use of precedents provided by his predecessors (including to be sure the Republican Lincoln and the Democrat Roosevelt), and it was particularly Nixon's administration that was the object of Schlesinger's complaint in *The Imperial Presidency*.

A part of the congressional response to perceived excess in the executive branch was the War Powers Act, intended to curb the increasingly elastic war-making power of presidents. Noteworthy is how little impact the law has had. Ronald Reagan, immensely popular, was able to flout it with near impunity. Yes, there were complaints, but there were minimal consequences for the careers of those who violated the law. Since then the Cold War has been replaced by the War on Terror, and all the earlier arguments for unfettered presidential power have returned. The advocates have not, of course, argued for an "imperial presidency"; the case they present, and the theory on which they would have presidents act, calls for, as I mentioned, a less ominous-sounding "unitary executive."

The notion of the "unitary executive" has a number of important features. Taken at a fairly technical level, it means that the president is immediately in charge of all executive agencies within the executive branch. This is not the dry civics lesson it may seem. While it may seem a mere truism of Civics 101, in the hands of those promoting it the theory takes a long step toward reducing the executive agencies to the level of advisory committees—groups whose chief function is to suggest to the president what he or she may want to consider in the way things are run. The Justice Department and the attorney general are less the autonomous crime fighters we might expect, and are more an agency for suggesting to the president which crimes the president might decide are worth pursuing. The Food and Drug Administration is decreasingly in charge of regulating food and drugs; it acts at the good pleasure of the president. Its findings can be nullified by the president; its rulings can be revised or suspended by the president. The same can be said of the Securities and Exchange Commission. The same can be said of the Environmental Protection Agency. And so forth.

This of course is far from being altogether new. Strong presidents have always tended to see the executive branch working this way. It would probably be close to the mark, for instance, to imagine that Lyndon Johnson thought of the executive branch as his "ranch," and thought of all who held office in it as his "ranch hands." In fact even very weak presidents (Grant, Harding) have, to their sorrow and our loss, loaded the executive agencies with cronies in the expectation the president would thereby put the stamp of his inclinations and preferences on all the operations of the executive.

But with the concordance of a working majority of current Supreme Court Justices, the logic of the "unitary executive" lately means the reach of the president extends beyond maintaining tight cohesiveness in the executive branch and touches in fact all the activities of Congress. Since the president swears to uphold the Constitution, it's among the president's constitutional responsibilities—so the argument of the second Bush goes—to see that congressional law does not usurp or breach constitutional law. In place of vetoing a bill, the president can in the course of signing it into law explain in a "signing statement" what he or she takes to be its constitutional scope. An irony that has not been missed is that the president, acting as a defender of constitutional law, thus achieves a neat end-run around the Constitution. As legal scholars have been quick to point out, the effect of this practice is to reduce radically the power of Congress and also to encroach dramatically on what has traditionally been regarded as the defining function of the Supreme Court.

When however Congress consents to this innovative version of veto power and the Supreme Court itself goes along with it, the tendency of the public in general is to ask: "Where's the problem?" Among those who inveigh most against "big government," many seem to take in stride the concentration of power that has taken place. Perhaps this is because a clear effect of strengthening the presidency is to facilitate the use of military force. A strong presidency "uncomplicates" the business of engaging the nation in war. Once our commander-in-chief has positioned troops in harm's way, it's a foregone conclusion our nation will rally to their support. Without benefit of Constitutional amendment, the war-deciding role of Congress has laped into desuetude. To use a metaphor from bridge, the Constitution has not been violated (harsh word!), it's been finessed.

There's more. John Yoo, at the University of California at Berkeley, finds in the doctrine of the unitary executive an implied power by which the president, in time of war (such as the current seemingly open-ended war on terrorism), can act as the final arbiter of morality. As with Lincoln during the Civil War, habeas corpus and other due processes of law can be bypassed. In fact, were the president to deem that the security of the nation would thereby be enhanced, there are no limits to what the president might order. It seems the president could order anything. The president could, for example, authorize that fingers of an unwilling witness, on the suspicion that he or she harbored lethal secrets, be incrementally chopped through the bone—like a carrot on a cutting board—till the witness gave satisfaction to his or her interrogators. Yoo, so far as I know, hasn't cited this example; but his doctrine authorizes it. In the nuclear age, where quick response may, Yoo argues, be the crucial factor for survival, the powers of the commander-in-chief are self-legitimating. There is no outside agency that can exercise oversight in their regard;

they have a quasi-divine character. In time of emergency (such as the permanent emergency in which we now live, the American president is the god of planet earth. (The goal of absolute national security can allow no less.)

John Yoo continues to be a tenured lecturer in American law at the University of California at Berkeley. John Roberts, Samuel Alito, Antonin Scalia, and Clarence Thomas—Catholics and comfortable with strong authority—continue to be justices of the Supreme Court; Anthony Kennedy—also Catholic—frequently votes with them. And Barack Obama has not repudiated the extraordinary powers claimed for the presidency during the era of his immediate predecessor.

Such seems a sober account of the growth of presidential power.

Second Major Current in the History of the American Presidency

One might say, well, so far we've proved that presidential elections are more important than ever. With such tremendous powers in the hands of the president of the United States, all we have to do is elect the right person, and our problems will be solved. This is, in fact, what many hoped when they voted for Barack Obama in 2008.

Why it didn't happen requires further consideration—much of it seeming to run contrary to things just set forth. Paradoxical as it's sure to sound, while the powers of the office have expanded to a kind of virtual infinity, the discretionary freedom of action of the person occupying the office seems under growing constraints. To understand this, one should take the matter further upstream. For the constraints regarding who will be considered as a candidate seem to have increased, and it's likely the one who wins the contest and arrives at the presidency will maintain a keen awareness of how he or she got there. This person will not easily forget the assurances given—perhaps not explicitly, yet quite clearly—during the vetting process. He or she is likely to remember not to bite the hand that provided—will you allow?—the pet food, the collar, and the leash.

The matter of who will be in the pool of those from whom the president will be selected is settled in advance, and far from the polling booths where individual citizens cast actual votes. So if anyone thinks this is something the citizen decides through the primaries, they might want to think again. Note the general dismay of the public lately as they listen to the sorry mix of candidates who come forward in the primaries; hear the collective moan as they reflect that one of these is likely soon to be president for the next four years. The people have little control over who is offered to them. By the November election that picks the winner, the voter often sadly feels the only thing left to decide is who among the candidates is likely to do the least harm.

Out of all this comes a second general observation. Just as the process of selecting a president has been found too important to be left to the people, so the politics of how the president will behave in office has been found too important to be left to the president.

We can watch this trend of constraint growing in the years after World War Two. While Franklin Roosevelt provided a service to America's capitalist system (saving it temporarily from its more blatantly counterproductive addictions), he dealt with it in a highly personal and freewheeling manner—one resonant with exuberant disdain. Not only was this noticed, both then and now, but it's been deeply resented, both then and now. Two presidencies later, Eisenhower ended a popular two-term administration with a warning to the American people about a growing military-industrial complex. Among other things, it seems Eisenhower was expressing a sense that constraints on presidential initiative and presidential decision-making were increasing, and that successors would probably have to struggle with increasing pressures from the military and from corporations to control America.

One interpretation of the short and drama-filled administration of John Kennedy is that Kennedy became increasingly aware of efforts within the executive branch to control, undermine, and resist presidential initiatives, and that when he balked at these efforts, he was brought to heel.

Regarding Johnson, let's assume that the Great Society was the apple of his eye. A possible explanation why he escalated in Vietnam a war he seems to have said privately he thought we couldn't win is that continuation of the war was the price he had to pay if he wanted to be architect of the Great Society. In the Far East, our power brokers felt an example needed to be set.

Japan had been duly disciplined; but we had "lost" China. When we'd "won" South Vietnam by setting up the Geneva Accords and then violating them (done under Eisenhower), it seemed to us the unscrupulous Vietnamese were trying to steal Vietnam right back from under our feet; such at least Johnson may have been made to understand. At the time it may have seemed a good idea to remind Asia how high the price could be for thwarting U.S. plans and for proceeding autonomously. When Johnson lost all effectiveness in selling the war, he was exhausted, and felt the need to step down.

Nixon was a reliable steward of the Vietnam War, but he had a brooding and persistent sense that hostile forces were out to get him. This fact is usually set forth as a tale of how Nixon's paranoia led to his downfall. Thinking he had enemies everywhere, he managed eventually to make enemies everywhere. A nuanced variation is reported by Russ Baker in his book on the Bush family. *In Family of Secrets*, Baker depends upon Len Colodny's *Silent Coup* as a source for an alternative explanation. One can draw from these books a picture along the lines that stray from the canonical story. Nixon, taking a select few into his band of brothers, acted with notable independence as president, working at his grand architecture of world peace. He was by no means inclined to keep the intelligence community posted as to what he was doing; nor was he at all inclined to be their puppet. He was disinclined to listen to pedigreed advisors among his fellow Americans, regardless of their party or presumed place in the hierarchy of power. A master manipulator, he did not at all like being manipulated. Important parties in the government and the military found him inconvenient. Using his well-known paranoia, they baited him into a cover-up, and brought him down.

Someone to whom I expounded this passed it on to his teacher, who dismissed it as a "conspiracy theory." I in turn thought this a naïve response. At the very least according to the Deep Throat motif that Woodward provides in his account, there were insiders in the intelligence community (FBI, CIA, etc.) working behind the scenes with Woodward to bring Nixon down. If that doesn't qualify as a conspiracy, I don't know what would. We never ask what the motivation was of these busy people within the executive branch. Is it really all that obvious that it was sheer patriotism?

It can be argued this is wrong. My constructions here are controversial. But the pattern of three "failed" presidencies in a row—Kennedy, Johnson, Nixon—is interesting. Kennedy was shot; Johnson was broken by what was expected of him; Nixon was forced to resign. No doubt later presidents have found the sequence instructive.

Carter clearly was "beyond the pale"—a man who had slipped through the vetting process by mistake. When he wanted to make Ted Sorensen (JFK's eloquent speechwriter) the Director of the CIA, he was firmly shown he could not do so. Later, in the immensely awkward situation of the hostage crisis, there's creditable evidence he was undermined by opponents acting behind the scenes—that is, by people within our own political system exercising leverage in foreign policy over which he, the president, had no control.

Even in the case of Ronald Reagan (usually regarded a strong president), it's interesting at the meeting with Gorbachev at Reykjavik to see Paul Nitze making sure that American staff work was as pedestrian and ungenerous in its estimate of Soviet intentions as possible; and it's interesting to see Richard Perle (who could have made a living playing Richard III) there at Reagan's elbow, staying Reagan's hand when he was ready to sign an agreement that credited Gorbachev with being decent and trustworthy. (To paraphrase Robert Frost: something there is that does not want a peace.) Interesting too is Nancy Reagan's statement after Ronald's death that he seemed less and less his own man during his second term.

For many years now, three full-time students of current affairs, Nader, Zinn, and Chomsky, have—among others—been saying our two-party system is largely a charade. Reading them, one can arrive at a fresh perspective. The power of government does not reside in the person elected president. Granted, our party system is organized into distinct groups, similar to the way some neighborhoods are divided by rival gangs in an inner city. The celebrity politics of the Beltway does genuinely separate Republicans from Democrats. The aversions are real, and the personal ambitions no doubt are divisive and mutually incompatible; what one wins the other loses. For all that, the activity is hardly more than "celebrity politics." It has little to do with real politics, i.e., governance.

Actual governance is concerned with the structuring of priorities, the formation and implementation of policies, the allotment of goods and services and taxes. Our quadrennial contest over the presidency is so much kabuki theater. Or rather it is a matter of determining who will be the designated spokesperson for policies too imbedded to be at issue in any election.

For those of us who accept this view, it's not surprising that celebrities drift into politics. Since politics as we play it has become largely a matter of celebrity, why shouldn't they? This helps explains why the things that interest us about politicians are often the same as things that interest us about other celebrities. When, for instance Arnold Schwarzenegger was solving the problems of California by borrowing on its credit to the brink of bankruptcy, few among us seemed to notice. When, however, we got news of marital infidelity, there was a surge of interest and many said negative things of him for the first time. It's as if we had little stake in his governorship, but had a vital interest in his marriage. Along those lines, we find it comforting to think the worst thing Clinton did as president regarded his personal life. That isn't true, but many of us would like to think it was. Then we can chide him—and turn and forgive him—like a charming but resolute misbehaver one might view on *Big Brother*.

As I say, Nader, Zinn, and Chomsky have tried for years to help us apprehend these matters more clearly; they've been saying what we think of as politics is entertainment—meant to distract and engage us while the consolidation of America into a plutocracy moves forward—or, if you prefer—while the well trained hand of the banker slips into your back pocket and steals your future.

Few things can make Nader and company's case more persuasively than the campaign and administration of Obama. While people had thought they were voting for change, it turns out they elected a gifted performer and a reliable defender of the status quo, a conservative maintainer of the order they had elected him to reform. This was such bad news that even when he was most transparently discarding the promises by which he had won votes, people were writing this off to awkwardness or insufficient skill in dealing with a wily opposition; they did not see it as demonstrating a keen sensitivity to the interests of those whose money and influence had put him in office.

The moral from this review of recent presidencies is that while the powers of the presidency have expanded immensely, the actual discretionary freedom of the person who is president has contracted. Presidential initiatives are exercised on a short leash.

A Concluding Observation

One might think we've reached the end of a train of thought. Some voices on the far left say: "Elections do not matter because we are the captives of the corporatocracy." But that's not quite where I'm heading.

Underlying the best of radical dissent and critique is, I think, a hunch at once more disquieting than that, but also more hopeful. The hunch is that the reason the next election cannot save us is because the sensibility we have developed through four centuries of American tradition disposes us to be the accomplices and enablers of the corporations that exploit people abroad and subvert the quality of life here at home. Let's consult the record here, and see how well the charge of citizen complicity holds up.

In the beginning (and until recently), when the victims were Indians, a majority of "us" were approving. (Michael Huckabee, it seems, still is. He prides himself that he knows which side to root for in 1950s westerns.) Also, when the victims were blacks, for centuries—and with increasing violence after the Civil War— many of us whites stood by while aggressive numbers among us actively engaged in exploitation, segregation, and vigilante hangings of our fellow Americans. For the hundred and fifty years since the Civil War, blacks have been successfully charged with what I call PCWB—Presuming Citizenship While Black— something that continues to be recognized in many quarters to this day as an unpardonable crime. Also, earlier, when the victims were Mexicans of Mexico, a majority of us supported the notion of our manifest destiny, taking comfort in such muggers' slogans as "The land belongs to those who use it!" Later we did not balk when American hegemony was extended over Cubans, and Hawaiians, and Filipinos. After the Second World War, we became informed supporters of a Pax Americana, to be imposed wherever and however we see fit; and we have been able of late, time and again, to shrug off any sense of the painful costs our vision has imposed upon non-Americans — consider for instance how undisturbed we have been over the recent massacre of civilians in Gaza of July 2014 — covering over the mayhem we have endorsed with the mind-numbing phrase "collateral damage."

Through all this history, we've developed almost no critique of "big government" as the enabler of this history — so that even today, when we complain of "big government," it's not about this that we're complaining. In the meantime, we continue to be ever more enamored of the products and conveniences and luxury that big government, by supporting our corporations, makes available to us. We want our lives well decked out with the signs of our election to grace. When push comes to shove, we want big government. Our sense of entitlement seems to have become almost "iron." We're now so habituated and conformed to the rhythms and processes of American affluence (whether we're rich or poor) that any truly genuine complaint of ours against big government tends to be that it hasn't made us affluent enough.

So it's not just corporations that require political candidates to be enthusiastic champions of The American Story; one reason they require it is because we require it.

Listen to us as we demand from our candidates a promise that each generation will live richer than the one before, "because this is what America is all about!" We say this even as mechanisms which have formerly ground down others during the four centuries of our development are now palpably grinding us down as well. Why can't we be saved by the next election? The reason: because it's not simply politicians who are at the root of our problems; it's not the military; it's not finally even the corporations. Pogo got it right: "We have met the enemy and he is us."

There is no soft deliverance here. We have to deserve deliverance if we are to achieve it. When we snuff out lives of others in covert operations of greed, and when we screw our heads into knots to convince ourselves that what looks here at home like a racist act really isn't, we drown all wisdom.

As God cannot save us from ourselves, neither can Barack Obama. Neither can Hillary Clinton nor Sarah Palin nor Michele Bachmann nor Mitt Romney nor Jeb Bush nor Ron Paul nor Rand Paul nor Donald Trump. Bernie Sanders — who, in July of 2014, along with Elizabeth Warren and all members of our Congress, green-lighted a punitive action in Gaza in which four hundred Gazan kids were massacred—is not a plausible candidate for our deliverance either. As the ruinous costs of our way of life become harder to ignore, the issues reduce to two: whether we're willing to change a mindset and lifestyle we've been addicted to for centuries—so we can act on the great truths we claim to believe; and—secondly, whether we're willing to do so while there's still time.

13 | "I've Decided to Be a Survivor!"

Well, good for you!

But one shouldn't respond too sarcastically. There are only so many moves on the board.

We've seen that a fundamentalist insistence on one's particular choice of religion as "the last word" is not likely to solve the problems of America or the world. Along similar lines, we've seen the hope God will save us in spite of ourselves has no foundation either in experience or thoughtful theology. But then when we turn to the political process as a place where we can take up our duties as adults and we discover the process itself seems irremediably broken, for some there seems only one option left. It's the option to give up on society and live for oneself, or for oneself and a few others. It expresses itself sometimes in the declaration: "I've decided to be a survivor!"

If one is going to critique this, it's good to proceed discreetly. For starters, there's a significant difference between "retreat" and "radical separation." It may be "retreat" that is really the goal of the speaker. As one who's taught night classes, I've encountered more than once a woman who broke off her formal education to take up a life as wife and mother, and who—once her children were past their teens—had returned to school. I've heard this woman rhapsodize about those rare days when, somehow, everyone was going to be out of the house for a full twenty-four hours or so, leaving her on her own. This was not some woman engaged in an extramarital affair, nor one who wanted a divorce or who hated her children. But the joy—the sheer unspeakable relief—of having a whole twenty-four hours in which no one would call out to her "Mom!" or "Honey!" was bliss. She just wanted to reconnect with herself, wanted gently to think her own thoughts and live for a few hours in her own rhythm. The bliss of it all!

Such a woman knew the value of making a "retreat." (Typically, she was a wonderful student.)

In the East, the tradition of the Holy Man has a long history. While most Asians are not official Holy Men, even today it would be impossible in many parts of Asia to grow up without having a passing acquaintance with the phenomenon. These Holy Men are people disconnected somehow from the day-to-day affairs of society.

The "disconnection" can have very different textures. In the Asian traditions I value most, emphasis is placed on a social orientation for the disconnection itself. One leaves society, but does so for the sake of society. It's true that Siddhartha fled from wife and child, but he fled toward Buddha-hood. As the Buddha, he founded monasteries for monks and nuns and lived forty years in the service of all who came to him for guidance.

In the branch of Buddhism called Zen, much effort is expended by the novice in achieving "satori." The koans (sound of one hand clapping, etc.) and the rock gardens play a part in this. The Zen-master is emphatic however in insisting the blissful awakening—the breakthrough to bliss called "satori"—is no end in itself. Its value is as a threshold to a life of example and service to others.

So "retreats" can be of great utility—for the housewife; for Gandhi; for Buddhists; for any one of us.

I'd hazard one of the most consequential retreats in American history was that of Thoreau to Walden Pond—for about two years and two months. The withdrawal was by no means complete; he wasn't walled off from the rest of society. To some perhaps his solitude may have seemed a stunt or an episode of self-indulgence. His purpose was to figure out what really mattered. A good pragmatic American can ask: "What could be more conceited and self-centered than such a project?"

Yet to take the measure of its aftermath would be difficult. The essay we call "On Civil Disobedience" no doubt draws much of its vitality from those near eight hundred days in which he was mostly his own companion. What his essay has done in India and America and elsewhere to inspire humane non-violent struggles for freedom during the century and a half since it was published is startling. It could be a much better guide to the human future than Admiral Mahan's *Influence of Sea Power*. That it may yet help head off what some thoughtful people regard a destined nuclear rendezvous with armageddon remains, I think, a hope worth sharing.

Thoreau has fans in many places. Some find in his observation of nature the beginnings of American environmentalism. Some are impressed by his care for words and the construction of sentences. He was searching for a rhetoric that lets things speak for themselves—with minimal imposition from the writer's ideology and assumptions. Like the English Romantic poets and the French Impressionist painters, he wanted to be an open-minded listener and watcher for what nature was presenting. Having listened and seen, he struggled for the most down-to-earth speech he could muster to express what he'd discovered. While a search for this kind of innocence was a very American thing, it belonged to a countercurrent of American culture—for it owed nothing to Puritan distrust of the natural world. The effect of Thoreau's effort on later American diction is hard to gauge. My hunch is that it's been considerable, and that Whitman, Mark Twain, and Hemingway are among those in his debt.

One praises Thoreau in the awareness he's often been dismissed as quaint by fellow Americans, both in his lifetime and up to the present day. (So help me, there are presently intellectuals in our institutions of higher learning who will tell us "Thoreau is passé." What they seem to overlook is that the environment about which he wrote with such care is also on the verge of becoming passé.) For some of us, this only adds to his distinction. He attempted to share with us his savvy anticipations of the harm rampant consumerism could do to us. Long before most of us realized we were enthralled, he expressed misgivings about the way we were identifying the industrial revolution with moral progress. He had reservations too about the way we were identifying a budding American nationalism with moral progress. He took the heretical position one need not be a soldier to be a patriot. You could love America even without going out and killing an Indian, or Mexican, or black person to prove it.

My point in discussing him is that Thoreau's retreat was one with instructive consequences for society. It should keep us from simply condemning all retreats as anti-social.

On the other hand, there are the likes of Ted Kaczynski and Jim Jones, where one has to feel things could not have gone more wrong. Kaczynski's withdrawal seems to have been rooted not only in criticism and near-despair, but to have been corroded by misanthropy. His published manifesto is not lacking in logic and sensibility (some of it echoing Thoreau; some of it anticipating pages in this book), but it's a logic and sensibility insufficiently tethered by humane feeling—not too distant from the mindset of professional advisors to our executive branch who defend torture and death by drone as our path to national security.

The case of charismatic leaders like Jones, who persuade whole groups to withdraw into cadres of "survivors," is more difficult to assess and judge. In Jones we sense something of the fundamentalism criticized in earlier chapters of this book. He and his disciples claimed to possess a wisdom that was unassailable. The claim was attended by a tendency to reject everyone not a member of the group. Still, it would be a mistake to meet this rejection with an equally blanket rejection of Jones and company. I would be very distressed if a child or friend of mine were involved with him; but we won't understand this form of withdrawal unless we factor in its intent that at least something will be rescued from the current dismal scene—a biblical remnant, an undestroyed sample of humanity from which to start afresh.

In fact, here too, lest we slip into an easy demonization of programs such as Jones' program, let us note that, even when they lapse over into killing outsiders, they're not as strange to us as we might pretend. When we undertake adventures in other countries that entail thousands of civilian deaths (our invasion of Iraq for instance) and when we write off these deaths (along with predictable deaths of many of our own soldiers) as collateral damage, our pursuit of national security seems to have landed us in a mindset that rivals the anti-social behavior of survivalists like Jones. That we shield our acts with the umbrella phrase "acts of state" and as requisite for national security, shouldn't blind us to their deep affinities with bizarre behavior and the mental aberrations that separation from the larger community of humankind can give scope to.

In the space between retreats that have positive social consequences on the one hand, and radical separations from society that are misanthropically tainted on the other, there's a vast grey area. Sulks (refusals to resolve grievances) figure into this area as do some forms of despairing altogether non-violent personal optings out. Regarding the latter, I had a brilliant student, an expert at writing scientific reports who worked at one of our national nuclear labs, who—so far as I could tell—eventually came to regard the human future as so daunting that he turned from the contemporary scene to immerse himself in study of his family tree and in pursuit of an understanding of Celtic poetry. I understood him quite well. Another student, whom I regard as the most gifted I've encountered, has frequently threatened to forsake all attention to current affairs and go live at peace with his soul in Amsterdam. (I tell him it won't work; but the impulse to try is understandable.)

Various programs of survivor-hood present themselves for attention. One hears of people who are busily collecting canned goods and bottled beverages. Among them some also are stocking firearms. Others, like the student of Celtic poetry, are burying themselves in hobbies that shelter consciousness from the undeniable manner in which, in Chesterton's phrase, "the sky grows darker yet and the sea rises higher." Some, as noted earlier, seek refuge in drugs and alcohol. Some retreat to gated communities, seeking at least a delaying action there from the encroaching ugliness, unpredictability, and danger of the contemporary world. Others place their hope in financial advisors, and hope the right stock portfolio will enable them to weather whatever storms may come.

These people surely should not be despised. Darwin has taught us that the survival instinct is evolution's great spring.

The dividing line I'd say for judging these tactics for survival is whether they function within the context of a social strategy or are taken up in rejection of such. It may seem a truism to say that if it's the latter—a radical rejection of social context—they won't do much for society. The point we ought not to overlook is that neither will they do much for the survivalist.

Once in an informal seminar (there was neither tuition paid nor attendance kept) I listened as the delightful literary critic and social anthropologist René Girard posed a riddle. He asked us: "What books would you read were you truly stranded alone on a desert island with no expectation of escape?" People around the table made various proposals. Eventually Girard called a halt:

"You're all wrong. You wouldn't read any books at all—for reading's a function of our sociality; once there's no longer a prospect for social interaction, reading stops." Girard, with Gallic exuberance and a smile, was playing with us, and I can't say how sincerely he was invested in his answer; but he was making a point.

The world of "meaningfulness" begins to collapse when there's no sociality. This is why "I've decided to be a survivor!"—if it's intended as a get-out-of-society-free card—fails even before it can get started. There are, of course, subsidiary arguments too. If human folly incinerates the globe, a mere decision to survive is not going to prove efficacious. Likewise, if global warming undoes the food chain, that may be inconvenient even for those living alone on mountain tops. Epidemics could also prove a problem. And any project of emigration to another planet—something I hear my more technologically inclined friends take seriously—would seem problematic too if there's no coherently functioning society here from which to launch. But these are subsidiary considerations. The trump card to most of this thinking is where Girard played it. Our world is pretty much held together by our human relationships. What does it profit a man if he gains the whole world at the cost of these relationships to others? He loses in fact the only world he cares to inhabit.

Assigning to a special parenthesis the case of the Buddha, there's a sadly common case: the young father who, wishing to survive, runs in panic from the family he has started. In his middle years, he may return, hoping to reclaim what he abandoned. Typically, the opportunity isn't there. It's not even from lack of forgiveness. People have simply moved on. In those fortunate cases where he does reintegrate, he still can't recover what he lost. One must allow for special cases, but typically, the man he once was, and the man he might have become, is not what has survived.

Conclusion

This conclusion is going to be work. For it's no mere cheerful summary of points already made. It's intended as an opportunity to reach conclusions—to conclude the diagnosis envisioned in the title. There are three major distinctions that need to be worked through to do this.

The first distinction is a distinction between Enlightenment thinking and the Puritan project. These two are interwoven and conflated in rhetoric and policy throughout the whole of American history, yet they are clearly in opposition to each other. It's not just a matter of two things co-existing in tension, but of two things that are polar opposites. If we've been moving toward one, we've been moving away from the other.

The second distinction is between society and the state. Around the time of the First World War, Randolph Bourne wrote that "war is the health of the state." He did not say it is the health of society. Throughout our history, there has always been a residual wholesomeness in our society; yet, for all Bourne's effort to make a strong distinction here, our society cannot be regarded as simply innocent in the manner it's been recruited by the state for purposes of war. We've been complicit in the process of our seduction. So Bourne's distinction needs further attention.

The third distinction concerns our present condition. On the one hand, there's statistical probability; on the other there's opportunity. It's incumbent on us to consider the difference between these. Statistically, it's likely we'll continue along the destructive path we've been on, endorsing and engaging in activities we refuse to acknowledge as detrimental to our character even as they heighten tensions and disrupt human relations and do irreparable damage to habitat. If our sense of statistical probability is so strong that we believe, as many of us seem to, in a kind of destiny and fate, then it would seem the handwriting's on the wall. One should despair of the common good and seek what enclave of personal happiness or pleasure seems still available. (An opium den comes to mind.)

The statistically improbable but urgently needed alternative is to find in the past an opportunity for self-instruction. Rather than regard that past as the template for our future and let inertial momentum carry us into the future, there's a discomforting (no typo here!) opportunity to believe we are free—and then go on to validate that belief by acting on it. It's of freedom's essence not to let the past weigh on one as a doom. Our freedom is not held in thrall the way rocks in an avalanche are held in thrall by the laws of physics. We know this, not by a speculative analysis, but by acting freely.

To elaborate on these distinctions, and find guidance in them, is the work of this conclusion.

1)   The Enlightenment is not the source of the Puritan project; the Puritan project rejects the Enlightenment.

To separate these two is a fundamental task for any historian of America. It's not an easy task. This is due to some simultaneity of the two and to a sometimes conscious, sometimes unconscious conflation of the two from the very start of our history by leading Americans.

When we say "all men are created equal" and when we dedicate ourselves to promoting "the general welfare" and securing "the blessings of liberty to ourselves and our posterity," we are endorsing the Enlightenment. When we honor our nation in song by calling it "the land of the free and the home of the brave," the Enlightenment resonates in these moving lines. Again, when we pledge our allegiance to "one nation, under God, with liberty and justice for all," we are pledging to live in the halo of the Enlightenment.

If it's difficult to pinpoint the essence of this movement of the human spirit, it's partly because the Enlightenment was different things to those who were its champions. To Hume it was, surprisingly, a matter of liberating mankind from the tyranny of reason. To Hume's lifelong friend, Adam Smith, it was a matter of bringing rationality and clarity to the conduct of economic affairs. To Thomas Paine, it was the very Age of Reason made flesh. Further, while Voltaire, in company with Hume, saw the Enlightenment as freeing humans from the dictates of religion, Kant saw it as a matter of setting limits to reason so as to make room for faith.

Even though the Enlightenment was in general a kind of morning-after resolution in favor of sobriety following a night-long binge of religious intoxication and mayhem, it's not by accident that so many of its leading lights stopped short of atheism. When in his last years Thomas Paine was rejected by the same American people whose banner-carrier he'd been, it was on a charge of atheism. But this was a misreading. Paine's unrelenting theme from *Common Sense* to *The Age of Reason* was human rights. In pleading his case for them, Paine drew on the long tradition — at least as old as Aristotle — that rooted human rights in natural law. To Paine, as to the majority in that tradition, it seemed an implausibility to have natural law without a lawgiver. Therefore, Paine, the son of a Quaker father, stopped short of atheism and was a deist.

But Paine's explicit deism (God stands back and leaves it to us to run the world properly) was enough to do the trick — that is, it provided Puritan America sufficient cause to turn its back on him. Puritanism insists we are on a mission of purgation under the generalship of Divine Providence. Puritans seemingly are sure God wants us His instruments to take the world by the neck and shake it till its teeth rattle. Enlightenment deism shudders at the thought of such a mission.

In his advocacy of rights, Paine was of necessity a critic of privilege. Central to Puritanism however is a claim to privilege. The problem Voltaire, Hume, and so many other leaders of the Enlightenment, including Paine, had with religion is that it seemed of its nature, by a kind of inbuilt reflex, to turn from worshipping God to instituting claims of privilege on behalf of the worshippers. Belonging to God's party, one was superior to everyone else. Worse yet, in the case of the Puritans, the act of worship tended to be identified with a mission to subjugate the ungodly — if necessary, purge them from the earth. (One can see why puritanical Christians have so much trouble with jihadist

Muslims; the programs of the two are near mirror images, and like a man's two hands, neither can reshape itself to occupy smoothly the space of the other. "Success" in either camp stirs outrage in the other.) The elitist mission of the Puritans was then incompatible with the Enlightenment's affirmation of the equality and dignity of all humans.

To be honest, it's hard to dwell in the Enlightenment. We've seen already how the illuminating reflections of Adam Smith were perverted into mere defenses of greed by those preparing a space for Ayn Rand and the Friedmanesque business schools and lawyerly operations of America today. To catch something earlier on of this same mechanism by which Enlightenment principles are let slide into dilution and contradiction, we can note in the life of Thomas Paine that before he was rejected by American society, he was rejected by the French whose revolution he had come to France to celebrate. As in human history everywhere, the issue was privilege. While Paine went to France to participate in a triumph of human rights, the leaders there who came actually came to power there preferred to celebrate their extraordinary ascendancy over others; and their revolution degenerated into chaos and terror, with Paine imprisoned and spared only by happenstance from execution.

We find a dialectic at work by which things become their opposites. This leads to disappointment and confusion. If amid this murky flow of human affairs, one wishes to locate the core principle of the Enlightenment, I'd hazard one can hardly do better than Kant's aforementioned second formulation of the Categorical Imperative: "So treat humanity, whether in yourself or another, as never to regard it as a mere means." Simple as the wording is, one has only to attempt to abide by this imperative to find how totally it sets one in opposition to the current flow of American affairs. To echo what Chesterton says of Christianity, one can say of the Enlightenment: "We have not tried it and found it wanting; rather we've found it difficult and left it untried."

Taking Kant's Categorical Imperative as the litmus test of Enlightenment thinking, one defines the Enlightenment as an unyielding champion of human dignity. On the other hand, to understand the Puritan project one must realize Puritans had no allegiance whatever to this imperative. In the Puritan view, the majority of humankind are damned, ours not to reason why. What we must do to certify ourselves as among the non-damned is put ourselves in opposition to the great unwashed majority with every fiber of our being. The more thoroughgoing our effort to cleanse the earth of them, the more secure in God's blessing can we feel.

In place of the tolerant garden of the Enlightenment, what we encounter here is the inhumane root of American exceptionalism. It's interesting that today, when we congratulate ourselves on racial progress in America, we're usually speaking of a kind of accommodation of white society to the descendants of people we brought here from Africa. This accommodation—and it's of course both more than that, and still remains tragically incomplete—is really not so surprising. Blacks were always valued. Why else the labor of kidnapping them and transporting them across the Atlantic? (Eventually, even Thomas Jefferson came to realize that the most valuable harvest of Monticello was each fresh harvest of black children.) The blacks planted the cotton and picked it. They built the houses of the whites. They cooked their meals and raised their children. They taught music. What was there not to like?

To recapitulate lessons from an earlier chapter, we are almost never speaking of an accommodation to Indians when we speak of racial progress. This is because we whites never had any intention to accommodate. Ralph Ellison's truly "invisible man" was the Indian. The Indian was beyond the pale. The Indians were an anomaly of nature (signs indeed of nature's "fall"). Once the Indians showed they would not be tamed by us, they became certifiable agents of Satan—to be cast into outer darkness.

(If you can't take this in, read the documents—the diaries, accounts, letters, and speeches of the whites, and read too those reports which have been handed down to us of the astonished, outraged reactions of indigenous Americans. This whole bundle of material is given limited space in our curricula. If one asks a college class whether Frederick Douglass was a great American, the more alert and articulate among the students will say there's no doubt he was. If then one follows by asking if Chief Joseph was a great American, the same students will go mute. Some may try after a pause to recover, and say "Well, he really isn't a part of the story of America." And of course, in a sense, that answer is perfect. Genuine documents and preserved data about Indian/ white relations do nothing to sweeten The American Story. They're demoralizing, and, like the torture activities of the CIA, they're best kept from the young and impressionable.)

Amid the many squabbles and rivalries present in Massachusetts Bay Colony from the start, one point there was that was universally agreed: Indians had no rights. Those who couldn't subscribe to this self-evident truth were exiled from the colony. Practice followed readily on the heels of preachment, and the bonds of fellowship within Massachusetts Bay Colony were soon quickened and sealed with Indian blood. As recounted earlier, this occurred within the first six years when at Mystic Fort the whites carried out a just-at-dawn massacre of Indian men, women, and children. We seem to have conducted no reassessment in the aftermath of this event; rather the event was allowed to become a paradigm, a community-affirming ritual act, which we repeated again and again through two and a half centuries, till there was no more Indian opposition we need worry about.

There are people alive today whose grandparents lived through the culmination of this enterprise. Further, as I mentioned, when I was a kid, the Westerns I imbibed at the corner theater ended typically when the federal cavalry would arrive at the last possible moment and shoot every Indian in sight—while we, the juvenile audience, cheered furiously. It happened in a way similar to the way Americans, still juvenile, assembled recently in Times Square to chant "U.S.A.!" at news that Osama bin Laden had just been assassinated in his bedroom in front of his wife.[1]

Perry Miller, our foremost scholar of the mentality of Puritans, says tentatively in his *Errand in the Wilderness* that the Puritans seem to have provided a thread which persists throughout the rest of American history; but Miller—ever provocative—avoids specificity here, leaving it to the reader to take things further. One of Miller's students, Bernard Bailyn, says in his study of the

---

1. I guess one has to grant—for it seems almost a requisite for being considered a genuine American—that this recent evening was a great moment in American life. Perhaps it would have been even better if bin Laden had been subjected to Abu Ghraib type torture before death instead of being rendered a bloody dishrag by streams of machine gun bullets from all directions. As it was, the people in Times Square got a lot out of it. And President Obama did too.

ideological origins of our American Revolution that even before the crystallization of our thinking in the second half of the 1770s, there was a consensus throughout the colonies, passed down to the present, regarding the nature of American life, and that Puritanism was a part of this.

They need not have been so tentative and cautious. There was, by reason of the Puritan settlement process—with its decision not to seek any lasting accommodation to Indians—a strong bond forged from the start between "civilians" and "military." In the early days, in fact, the two groups were often one. René Girard hypothesizes it's frequently part of the pathology of human societies that they have been formed "against"—and that actual bloodletting is frequently what seals the bond that holds them together. This has been the case with the United States. While we think of the United States as conceived in a bloody revolution against England, this bloodletting is prominent from the first Puritan settlements. At all subsequent moments in "the Winning of the West" the settlers, hand in glove with the military, have reconfirmed their sense of themselves in Indian blood. When the West was won and we ran out of domestic candidates for our rituals of solidarity, we sought new candidates abroad. We've never been at a loss for how to commemorate our shared citizenship and re-consecrate our original bonds.

It was only in the nineteenth century, with writers like Thoreau, Frederick Douglass, Helen Hunt Jackson, and Mark Twain, and in time since, with writers and orators like Will James, Randolph Bourne, Eugene Debs, William Appleman Williams, Martin Luther King, Jr., Howard Zinn, Noam Chomsky, Chris Hedges, Naomi Klein (of Canada), John Perkins, and Norman Solomon, does it seem a concerted effort has been made to study the constantly refreshed bond in American life between our civilians and our military.[2]

---

2. Barton Bernstein of Stanford has attempted to extend Eisenhower's notion of threat from a military-industrial complex by directing attention to ever tighter bonds between the military and our allegedly civilian institutions of higher learning. The alumni magazine of the allegedly civilian institution of higher learning called Stanford has not let this critique pass without printing a commentary on Bernstein that charges him with being an agent of violence.

These authors sometimes try to soften their depictions of us Americans on the home front by indicating the manipulations to which we've been subjected by industrialists and military leaders and bad media and bad schooling. The point I suggest here is that such manipulations would not have been working so predictably all these years without some predisposition of the public to go along.

Puritanism in America begins with a mission to tame the wilderness and plant a New Eden. Taming the wilderness meant eliminating or immobilizing its savagery—its savages. Stretch though it may seem, that same zeal, with father-to-son biological continuity, is alive and active in the Monroe Doctrine, in our acceptance of a Manifest Destiny, in the Winning of the West, in the annexation of the Philippines, in the announcement of an Open Door (a door open to us) in China, in Wilson's grand crusade to make the world safe for democracy (and American commerce), in our effort through manipulation of the United Nations to establish a Pax Americana throughout the world since the end of the Second World War, in our efforts to contain the Soviet Union in the Cold War, and in our present open-ended and apparently un-endable War on Terrorism.

There will be more on this when we try to reflect on the distinction and relations between American society and the American state.

What we've been elaborating here is the non-identity, and in fact deep opposition, between Enlightenment ideals and this Puritan project that has such a hold on our dedication. It was John Winthrop who first attempted a conflation of the two. Speaking of the Massachusetts Bay Colony as "a city on a hill," Winthrop suggests that Puritans will light up the world by their example. We echo this ambition when we speak of America as "the last best hope of humankind," or when we refer to the president of the United States—as media newscasters still casually sometimes do—as "the leader of the free world."

For all the sweetness of our rhetoric, we noted the Puritans soon swooped down from the sacred hill to wreak mayhem on everything that moved on two legs. The example thereby given was something less than the tolerant and beautiful thing one might have hoped. It proved more a matter of "making an example of" than a matter of "setting an example for." Convenience and dishonesty were facilitated by Winthrop's use of Enlightenment rhetoric.

Let's review, and incorporate in our conclusion some of the data from earlier in the book.

The pattern for action we proclaim is routinely humanitarian, but the practice is routinely Puritan. As noted, Polk (sometimes listed a Presbyterian, sometimes a Methodist—but a good Puritan either way) provides a clear instance. As Polk enters the White House, Texas is already ours; but Polk wants to add California (and why not all the land that lies between California and Texas as well?). He sends John Slidell to Mexico City to negotiate a purchase of California for $25,000,000. No one will talk to Slidell for, in the turmoil of Mexican politics, after the U.S. had annexed Texas, it would be political suicide for a Mexican politician to be found negotiating some further loss of land. In the ordinary uses of diplomacy, that would end the matter—at least for the time being. That doesn't happen. Frustrated, Polk decides to present Mexico's refusal to negotiate as itself a *casus belli*—such a breach of international law that he's entitled to go to Congress and request a declaration of war on the ground that a right of the United States has been grievously violated. It's no longer a mere piece of land he's seeking; he seeks rather to uphold the very fabric of international law. An effort at a landgrab has been elevated to an act to maintain the sanctity of international law.

Eventually, Polk was rescued from needing to stoop to quite such silliness, but the incident is worthy of our attention because its structure reveals a sad pattern in our way of doing foreign policy. No sane person (and Americans are mostly sane) really believes a nation has an obligation under international law to enter into negotiations for a sale of its land whenever a neighboring nation wishes to buy it. Yet the benefits of expanding westward were so manifest to Polk that he figured he could get by with such an argument if it was the best he could invent. He may have been right since the ploy he did use to get his declaration of war wasn't much better. The essence of the matter was to present America as the victim—the innocent but brave defender of justice. The Enlightenment was on our side. Our rival was the violator of rights and law—the God-rejected savage, if you will.

Sometimes we think the Puritan project was an offspring of the Enlightenment because we regard the Puritans as well read and remarkably articulate in the exposition of their views. They were. Perry Miller demonstrates this with a dazzling exploration of Puritan intellectual life in his *Errand into the Wilderness*. But we should avoid making a muddle of things. In an effort at disentanglement, let's consider twentieth-century President Woodrow Wilson. Here, certainly, one might think, is a child of the Enlightenment—wide in his grasp of history, a university professor, eloquent, proficient in scholarly works, and eventually a president of Princeton University. Yet if we look to his performance as president of the United States, we find the Enlightenment is employed to fulfill its traditional role in our foreign policy: it's there to legitimize the Puritan project.

In *The American Political Tradition*, Richard Hofstadter introduces his chapter on Wilson:

> Woodrow Wilson's father was a Presbyterian minister, his mother a Presbyterian minister's daughter, and the Calvinist spirit burned in them with a bright and imperishable flame. Their son learned to look upon life as the progressive fulfillment of God's will and to see man as "a distinct moral agent" in a universe of moral imperatives.... Deadly in earnest, rigid, self-exacting, Wilson suffered acutely from his Presbyterian training.... Capable himself of intense feelings of guilt, he projected his demand for unmitigated righteousness into public affairs, draining his intellectual capacity for tolerance. In an early essay on Burke he commented feelingly that "we should not expect a man to be easy and affable when he finds himself in a death-grapple with the enemies of his country."[3]

"Draining his intellectual capacity for tolerance" is a telling phrase. For Wilson had intellectual capacity second perhaps among American presidents only to Lincoln. By that I mean he could view a situation from five or ten angles when others in the room could see it only from one or maybe two. That he wished to act within the sphere of the Enlightenment seems evident from

---

3. Richard Hofstadter, *The American Political Tradition and the Men who Made It* (New York: Vintage, 1974), 309–10.

the recurring originality with which his speeches echoed it. At the outbreak of the First World War, he spoke of being "impartial in spirit as well as in action." He spoke of a "peace without victory," expressing his hope the war could end with neither side feeling vanquished and aggrieved. Later, when he felt the need to promote the war, he spoke of "a war to end all war," and "a war to make the world safe for democracy." After the war, he went to Versailles and lectured the victorious Allies at length on the need to allow all countries the right of "self-determination."

It fell apart. It was a tragedy in the Aristotelian sense where the downfall is the consequence of a flaw in the heroic protagonist. For Wilson could never free himself from the grip of the Puritan project. While he envisioned a postwar world in which natural law prevailed, one where justice and the rights and freedom of all were respected, he could never rid himself of the notion that the natural order was one in which white Anglo-Saxon Protestants—especially such as were bred in the United States—guided, tamed, and controlled everybody else.

His neutrality during the war was never genuine. With justified cynicism, we may say he believed in neutrality right up to the point where it might endanger the prosperity America could reap during the war from sales to Britain and France; beyond that point, he did not observe it. Or, taking a larger measure of the man, let us say he believed in neutrality right up to the point where it might endanger a British/French victory; at that point, he no longer believed in it—and never had. Believing an Allied victory would be conducive to leadership of the world by the United States after the war, he could not, in the days before our entry, genuinely commit to any neutrality that would leave an Allied victory in jeopardy.

Eventually he sounded as ridiculous as Polk. In 1915, he claimed, as Hofstadter tells us, a kind of unalienable right of Americans to travel on belligerent British merchant ships in a war zone. Such travel of course rendered probable a loss of American lives amid the hostilities. When that happened, Wilson would thereby be in a position to reproach the Germans with illegally killing "neutral" American citizens. He seemed to imply to the Germans that so long as a "neutral" American was on a ship, the Germans had to regard it as free from attack even though it might carry a cargo of food and munitions in support of the Allied cause. To suggest such a claim in the name of international law was to make a mockery of international law, and the Germans of course understood this. When the battle in Europe reached such a crisis that Germany felt it could no longer afford any deference to Wilson's hoax, it began sinking all ships supporting the Allied cause, and America discarded the pretense of neutrality and became a direct and honest participant. The honesty was new, for as Hofstadter makes clear, the United States was a participant from the start.

In the matter of Wilson's advocacy of self-determination for nations everywhere, there was again an undermining duplicity. On the eve of the First World War, Wilson had said, "I am going to teach the South American republics to elect good men." When a certifiably bad man muscled his way to the presidency of Mexico, and when this man added to his other disqualifications a lack of respect for the United States, Wilson saw him as setting a bad example, and sent troops to invade Mexico at Veracruz. Our troops remained until, in the ferment of the Mexican revolution, a new Mexican president came to the fore. While Wilson may have felt he had done the Mexican people a favor, it should surprise no one that there was widespread Mexican resentment of the American intrusion. Again, some four years later, in the aftermath of the First World War, Wilson sent a military force to Russia to protect the Russians from making mistakes similar to those to which Mexicans were prone. It's difficult to get a coherent account of just what Wilson thought he was doing. It's been charged against him that the main effect of our intervention in Russia was to prolong a chaotic state of affairs there at the cost of many Russian lives. George Kennan (a champion of a proactive policy toward Russia at the end of the Second World War) attempts a sympathetic account of how Wilson arrived at his policy, but ends by saying Wilson acted in complete ignorance of facts on the ground.

What these bookend events at the start and the end of the First World War suggest is that Wilson was prone to quixotic bungling in the exercise of diplomacy. While he believed in the right of people everywhere to self-determination, he was tolerant of the results only so long as what the foreigners strove for met his approval. Where their aspirations fell short, it was the office of the U.S. president to correct them. The president should do so with lethal military force if necessary.

During the war itself, Wilson (who'd often denounced the war as inhumane and as a war being fought for unworthy purposes) was routinely inhumane in persecuting and prosecuting dissenters who continued to say things Wilson no longer thought convenient. Pursuit and persecution of dissenters continued until Wilson's administration ended in 1921—more than two years after the war itself ended.

William Appleman Williams cites a onetime admirer of Wilson, Raymond Robins, as follows:

> Wilson was a great man but he had one basic fault. He was willing to do anything for people except get off their backs and let them live their own lives. He would never let go until they forced him to and then it was too late. He never seemed to understand there's a big difference between trying to save people and trying to help them. With luck you can help 'em—but they always save themselves.[4]

That Wilson envisioned himself and the United States as savior of others calls to mind how Massachusetts Bay Colony dealt with Quakers. Winthrop's successor as Governor, John Endecott, was willing to accommodate to Quakers if they'd give up their heretical notion of an Inner Light and would convert to Christianity—by which Endecott meant Calvinism as interpreted by Puritans. Short of that, he was willing to allow them to depart from the Puritan community. When both these generous alternatives were rejected, Endecott did what any godly person would do in such circumstances: he had them hanged.

Similar to the manner in which much that Wilson did in foreign policy violated the spirit of the Enlightenment, so, more explicitly, much that he did on the home front violated our Bill of Rights (our great effort to install Enlightenment principles at the core of our Constitution). This needs saying, not to heap coals on his head. Life itself did that. In the course of a couple years, Wilson lost the respect first of the leadership of the Senate, then that of the surrendering Germans, then that of the victorious

---

4. William Appleman Williams, *The Tragedy of American Diplomacy* (New York: Dell, 1962), 82–83.

Allies, and finally the respect of the generation of Americans who had twice elected him president. We need to note that the Wilson administration was not an outstanding moment of idealism but a stark example of how the Puritan project, alive and at the center of things in the twentieth century, trumped the spirit of the Enlightenment at just the moment it was most emphatically invoking it.

The maneuver has become such a staple of our foreign policy it seems almost trite to speak of it. In a generation some forty years after Wilson, our deep objection to the Castro revolution in Cuba was that it was not carried forward under American auspices and was not directed by American leaders. It violated our Monroe Doctrine and the hegemony we thought we had achieved over Cuba. We packaged our opposition however as an enlightened effort to resist a godless communism of Soviets who were intervening illegally in the western hemisphere and were out to destroy freedom everywhere. We insisted our opposition was simply a necessary response by the nation charged with leading the free world.

To bring this matter up to the time of writing: recently, having warned the Palestinians of Gaza not to elect the Hamas Party as its leadership, we now leave them with two options: having defied us, they can vacate Gaza and go God knows where; or they can stay in Gaza and die. The deaths are under way, and they proceed with our funding and with our approval and guidance. John Winthrop and John Endecott were never more clear than we. While baptized in the waters of the Enlightenment, the rivers in which we do our daily swimming are those of the Puritan project.

2) American society then is not the state; yet while our state often pursues projects very harmful to our society (thereby manifesting the two are not identical), the state wouldn't be able to do this with such regular and predictable ease were there not some predisposition in our society to go along.

The second-to-last paragraph of Randolph Bourne's remarkable indictment "War Is the Health of the State" is as follows (slightly shortened, and with the addition of a bracketed word):

Nothing is more obvious...than that every one of us comes into society as into something in whose creation we had not the slightest hand....By the time we find ourselves here we are caught in a network of customs and attitudes, the major directions of our desires and interests have been stamped on our minds, and by the time we have emerged from tutelage and reached the years of discretion when we might conceivably throw [direct] our influence to the reshaping of social institutions, most of us have been so molded into the society and class we live in that we are scarcely aware of any distinction between ourselves as judging, desiring individuals and our social environment. We have been kneaded so successfully that we approve of what our society approves, desire what our society desires, and add to the group our own passionate inertia against change, against the effort of reason, and the adventure of beauty.[5]

It would be difficult to over praise this paragraph. Each word-choice registers. Bourne combines insight with careful articulation. Trouble is, the gist of his paragraph here complicates the direction in which he's been arguing. He's labored eloquently to make a distinction between a generally wholesome and innocent populace (one believing presumably in the platitudes of the Enlightenment) and a duplicitous and manipulative state. Good society, bad state. Now he finds he must acknowledge a kind of original-sin arrangement built into the very structure of human existence. We are what our social forebears have chosen us to be. In a sense, it doesn't matter whether we are "society" or whether we are "state." What W.A. Williams calls "the dead inertia of the past" weighs equally on all. We are all equally innocent and all equally guilty.

Bourne's essay stops about here—ended either by the "Spanish flu" which ends his life, or perhaps stopped simply by the quandary into which his thought had carried him.

---

5. Randolph Bourne, *The State* (1918, available at http://fair-use.org/randolph-bourne/the-state/).

While Bourne formats the problem in universal terms, it's really in its exceptional and highly dramatic form in American history that Bourne is struggling with it. What he has come up against is the Puritan project. The long hand of Winthrop and company has been discovered in our heart of hearts, setting the values and paradigms by which we judge and live—and by which we decide whom to let live. And Bourne's acknowledgement carries with it the ring of truth. Surely the past is irreformable. There is absolutely nothing we can do to turn it into a different past.

Yet defending the innocence of us Americans becomes problematic as one reflects on the ease with which we have lent ourselves to cruel and violent enterprise. Bourne's poignant phrase "our own passionate inertia" points to the complicated reality here. We are victims of a cruel tradition—and this is a point Bourne very much wants to make. But we are willing victims—we have ingested the things that wound our souls. What does emerge clear in this sociological reflection is that it undermines one of the favorite tropes of would-be reformers; it cuts the ground out from under those who say: "let's return to the good ole days."

At the center of Barry Goldwater's conservatism was his conviction we must return to some Eden-like and forthright innocence of ours. The same conviction inspires the Tea Party movement today. My hunch is that this conviction is currently held with deliberate and conscious dedication by the much-denounced Koch brothers. We must strengthen the strong. That is what we did in the past and should do now. Handicapped parking spaces are a mistake. Human progress depends on enhancing the strong without regard to the price paid by the weak. Nietzsche has said exploitation is the law of life; he invites the strong to engage in it without remorse. He does this in *Beyond Good and Evil*. Ayn Rand echoes Nietzsche. What makes us Americans peculiarly open to this teaching is that we believe "strength" is the sign that God has befriended us and predestined us to grace. We white Americans come into the world not into the hands of an angry God, but into the hands of some very aggressive Puritans who immediately begin molding us into replicas of themselves.

For this reason, a genuine opposition to the class which includes the Koch brothers is almost impossible to mount among us; beyond our outbursts of rhetorical denunciation, there's a longstanding emotional flirtation with what they hold dear. Even that is too weak. There's a longstanding dedication. A people whose elected representatives recently voted one hundred percent for violence against the ill-fed, ill-washed, near defenseless people of Gaza can have no real argument with the Koch brothers.

What about the "good ole days"? When were they? Were they at the beginning when we were slaughtering Indians and hanging Quakers? Were they in the long years thereafter when, Northerner together with Southerner, we were accepting Africans kidnapped from their farming communities in Africa, and insisting we were the rightful owners of their labor? Think of the use of black women as "bed wenches" and of the disregard for their family relations by Christian whites who commodified them, treating them and theirs as disposable income. Think what such commercialization meant as members of black families were sold severally to the highest bidder or were separated to be handed over to the most insistent debt collector. (Do some black women have "attitude" today? How could they not?) Perhaps the golden days were when Thomas Jefferson would leave off overseeing the whipping of a slave boy at his nail factory so he could retire to his study and write eloquently on the equality of man. Perhaps the golden days were those of Andrew Jackson, slave-master and heroic hater of Indians. Here was a man, admired greatly in his own day, and admired still—a man on horseback who, in the midst of setting up pet banks or managing the spoils system, could turn at the blink of an eye and promote sending thousands of Cherokee on a trail of tears from their ancestral lands. Then there were the days of his protégé, James Polk. He too was respected and prosperous by reason of the slaves he acquired; he didn't exhaust himself with the undoing of Indians but rather with the taking of land from Mexicans. To this day there are historians who complain he's never gotten the full measure of credit he deserves.

Not to make too long a list, there was Teddy Roosevelt, as genuine a believer that might makes right as one could ask for. As noted, he cites among the chief benefactors of humankind those who purged the West of savages to make way for civilization. He was a legitimate offspring of the ancestors he praised. He helped purge Cuba of savage Spaniards in order to replace these arrogant Spaniards with ourselves. Later as president, he cheered on his good friend Leonard Wood as Wood purged the Philippines of savage Filipinos. He was and remains what most Americans regard as an exemplary president.

Putting sarcasm to one side, the truth of the matter is there were no good old days. When one hears the claim there were, one should ready oneself for fresh calls to violence.

From the age of nine, I've been fascinated by seeing in newsreels the faces and gestures of young men in landing barges, many of whom were less than thirty minutes from death on a foreign shore. While I've been moved beyond speech at the courage and grace of these Americans who fought the Second World War, nonetheless I fear the feelings of those who celebrate and remember with me. I fear lest in their nostalgia, they will keep those days going on forever. In many ways we remain in the midst of such days, guaranteeing our children and grandchildren will know them too, and know them first hand.

But as Bourne acknowledges, taking up a critical stance toward our past is very inconvenient. Where, if not to the past, is one to look for inspiration and direction?

Bourne speaks at the end of the paragraph cited above of "the effort of reason, and the adventure of beauty." It is, I think, not in celebration of our wars, but by rational reflection on the paramount accommodation in America's history that we can find something of the beauty and sense of direction we need—if we have the deeper courage to go there.

Our history does have something to say about accommodations. The fundamental accommodation of American history is the one between blacks and whites. I don't say it is achieved. Rather it's a work in progress. We whites often think of it I fear as a gradual process wherein whites have brought blacks to accommodate to the exigencies of living in white society. In actual fact, the accommodation is much more interesting than that, for—as is the general nature of accommodations—the process has been mutual and reciprocal. If whites have been the teacher, they have also been the student; if blacks have been the student, they have also been the teacher.

This accommodation is so imperfect, by reason of many kinds of fear and countless eruptions of hatred and bloodshed, that we may hesitate. Indeed, the reader may be incredulous. If however we want a future better than our past, it's especially here we can hope to learn something. When I speak of this accommodation of whites and blacks, more precisely what I have in mind is the still halting, deeply conflicted and imperfect accommodation of whites to blacks. In the face of all that's still lacking to whites in their capacity for this accommodation, it impresses me as the foremost success in American history. (More important even than the electric light bulb of Edison; more important than the Model T of Ford.)

After the Civil War, American blacks had no real choice but to stay pretty much where they were, and to achieve there what they could in the uncharted waters of emancipation. It turned out that the accommodation the mainstream was willing to make to them—in the North as well as in the South—was very limited. With the stoicism by which they'd survived more than two centuries of bondage, black Americans tested their new opportunities as best they could.

Amid Jefferson's stupefying list of black limitations set forth in his *Notes on Virginia* (read the list; the man was no sage), Jefferson conceded that blacks seemed good at music. They were. And they combined this gift with a Christian hope and with patience towards others' shortcomings that was altogether beyond Jefferson's reach. (This patience could of course bother Marx, and did bother Richard Wright and Malcolm X, and many others.)

When blacks were first introduced to the Bible, they knew where Egypt was. It was the plantation on which they lived. They recognized who the Egyptians were. The Egyptians were these light-skinned people of stunted affectivity who held them in bondage. As for Jesus, they understood—as their white handlers did not—that the sympathies of Jesus were with the orphan and the widow, the hungry, the unjustly treated, the despised. While for the whites, a sign of their election to grace was their success as oppressors, the blacks understood intuitively what a failed reading of the Bible that was. (The whites' special reading of the Bible was the bedrock of The American Story, and I suspect no black has ever been taken in by it.)

Blacks exercised their talent for music particularly along two lines. One was music that registered with equal force their sense of distress and their hope for deliverance. These "spirituals" initiated the gospel tradition which became the foundation for so much of the world's music from then till now. The other was music dealing with their deep dependence on personal relations, particularly the dependence of black men on the caring love and respect received from black women in a time of near utter humiliation.[6]

We call such music "soul." (It's well named, for this music emerges in response to an attempt to annihilate the souls of blacks.)

The themes of the gospel music and the soul music have never been in opposition to each other. The longing for salvation is common to both, and the passion voiced in each blends into the other. Whites have long been surprised by the easy conjunction here of religious sensibility and human sensuality—and find the result exotic and arresting. One can surmise that the African communities from which American blacks were taken were innocent of Calvin's withering touch on human sensibility.

Nowhere is the tutelage exercised by blacks more evident than in this matter of music. (This is matter greatly encumbered today by ill-directed efforts at political correctness; many in our universities get it wrong; musicians on the other hand understand the matter intuitively.) As just suggested, even in the days of slavery, the inhabitants of the Big House would hear the musical laments and musical celebrations (often in the same song) of those whose freedom they had done what they could to cancel. The inhabitants of the Big House were "captivated"—as well they should have been—and would invite the blacks "up" for the edification of themselves and their guests.

Antebellum accounts clearly attest that whites were impressed by this music. What can get lost in the mists of political correctness is how this white interest came to effect change in white

---

6. James Baldwin sets the mood for such music tellingly in *Go Tell It on the Mountain* (New York: Dell, 1980):

> They had been very happy together, in the beginning, and until the end he had been very good to her, had not ceased to love her, and tried always to make her know it. No more than she had been able to accuse her father had she been able to accuse him. His weakness she understood, and his terror, and even his bloody end. What life had made him bear, her lover, this wild, unhappy boy, many another stronger and more virtuous man might not have borne so well. (193)

aesthetic capacity. The beginnings of American minstrelsy can be given a too-complicated treatment as a result.

Minstrelsy probably began with blacks publically satirizing themselves in music for the amusement of themselves and of whites. If one wishes to pour out outrage at such a terrible self-violation of human dignity, well, be my guest. It seems to me a failure of human imagination to do so. From birth, American blacks enjoy privileged insight into human hypocrisy; conditions of their birth gift them with this. In the centuries of slavery, though, they could hardly make public sport of whites. Whites were, they knew, mysteriously challenged when it came to humor. So the original "Jim Crow" (perhaps the first minstrel) and others did what they could to clown and make mirth, but with circumspection. Satire on blacks could be performed publicly before both races; satire on whites had better be reserved for discreet performance in the slave quarters.

What's really quite wonderful about this—less sinister I'd say than subsequent critics, black and white, realize—is that, sooner than one might expect, whites who were looking on at black minstrelsy were saying: "Hey, let me try that!" Not much reflection has been expended on what that meant. The easy, politically correct, judgment is that whites were piling on. "If blacks are getting positive approval, and being rewarded by whites for demeaning blacks, I want a piece of the action. I can mock blacks better than they can." What this neat judgment leaves out is attention to the underlying humane context and intent of the music and the humor. For that, we do well to look back to the motivations for plantation music mentioned above.

When whites put on blackface, what they were often working toward was a more intimate entry into black music. If you want to say, "Well, then, they were attempting to kidnap black music just as they had kidnapped blacks," again, be my guest. But music doesn't work that way. The original white "covers" of black music had a singular honesty; whites put on blackface to do these covers, saying in effect, "If you want to know the sources of this music, I'm showing them to you."

What was being conducted, more perhaps than consciously realized, was an experiment in empathy. The white performer wanted to get into the shoes and skin of the black. Or, if you find that metaphor cloying and repugnant, you can reverse it:

the black Americans' music had gotten "under the skin" of the whites.[7]

Even in antebellum days, a process of tutelage and nurturing had been under way. The parched souls of aesthetically challenged Puritans were being washed in the redeeming waters of black sensibility. (Do you think that's over the top? To take a prominent instance from a later moment in the process, think of the millions of white Americans who responded to the ominous message of the First World War by entering the Jazz Age. The Jazz Age had roots other than the discredited worship of Progress that had been the white man's faith. This black music became balm and comfort food for the wounded hopes of whites.)

As I speak of a gradual accommodation of whites and blacks in America's history up to now, notice I'm not repeating a bromide about white Americans teaching blacks how to fit into white society. It should be clear by now I'm saying something quite different. True, there's always a reciprocal dimension to accommodations (and I do think along with Booker T. Washington—as updated by the Warren Court—that it's important for the skills necessary for economic success in America to be shared across the races). But a fundamental countermovement was in play: slowly, in the face of great resistance, and with many awkward starts and cruel rejections, blacks have been educating white Americans toward a more sensitive and humane understanding of others and—more basically and haltingly—to a more realistic sense of the shortcomings of the whites' own religiously impoverished souls. (To the extent that Martin Luther King Day serves any authentic purpose currently, it is to celebrate this.)

Blacks began bringing whites around through their music—a music now very nearly the idiom for music everywhere. (They've also done it through athletic skills—performances of grace under

---

7. In its later phases, in the first half of the twentieth century, the role of young Jewish musicians can't be exaggerated as a catalyst in accelerating the crossover of this music. Out of their own legacy of hardship and persecution, these brash young men, whose families were fresh from the ghettoes of Eastern Europe, "got" black music in advance of mainstream white America. Jolson said he'd never felt at home on stage till he put on blackface.

pressure. Think Jackie Robinson. Think Muhammad Ali. Think Bill Russell and Magic Johnson, Michael Jordan, Kobe Bryant, LeBron James, and Steph Curry.) And, as just suggested, they've done it too through a far more accurate and down-to-earth understanding of Christianity than their old-time plantation handlers (the Jefferson crowd) intended.

The sermons at typical black churches evidently owe less to Calvin and more to Jesus than has been the norm at white churches in America. So when Martin Luther King tried to bring the religious experience of blacks in America to bear upon American foreign policy, white America wouldn't let him. He was ridiculed in our mainstream press and by our president as being "intrusive" and "out of his league"—dismissed in President Johnson's revealing phrase as "just a nigger preacher after all." Then he was assassinated. Today, unfortunately, his eloquent teaching that injustice anywhere is a threat to justice everywhere is largely ignored on the day dedicated to his memory; in the eyes of King, in contrast to the good Puritan, the obligation to respect the rights and freedom of foreign peoples was quite real—and violence toward others in order to impose our will was violation and sin. (Were King alive today, one can be confident he would greet our veterans, returned from Iraq, with compassion and love; no doubt he would credit them with sincerity. But one familiar with the speeches of his final twelve months cannot imagine him congratulating them by saying: "Thank you for your service to our country." For this reason, those speeches are now seldom featured on the day dedicated to his memory.)

Our strong resistance to a black understanding of Christianity shows there's still a way to go; our Puritan heritage stands in the way. Black literature provides a kind of bridge. Through the works of David Walker and Frederick Douglass, Langston Hughes and Richard Wright, Ralph Ellison and James Baldwin, Maya Angelou and Alice Walker and Toni Morrison, to name a few, there has been an opportunity for whites to take in the texture of black lives and black aspirations more accurately than in earlier days. Not irrelevantly, in the two hundred and more years since the beginnings of black minstrelsy, black stand-up comics have in the last four or five decades been able to take on white audiences and get them laughing to the point of tears at the contradictions and hypocrisy of our white-dominated society. Dick Gregory, Richard Pryor, Eddie Murphy, and Chris Rock are prominent examples. More recently, reviving a style from the earliest days, there's the raunchy, minstrel-like honesty and down-to earth humor of Steve Harvey—judging from the laughter of audiences, as liberating to whites as to blacks.

This is mentioned, not to congratulate blacks but to locate where there remains hope for some change of direction in our American mainstream. True, some blacks, particularly in politics and law, have sold out—just like so many others—to the worst aspects of American ambition and American opportunism; and the system has rewarded them. But there's reason to believe the majority of blacks know too much and feel too strongly for that. If whites are becoming aware of the inconsistencies of our traditional story, and are looking around for a new and more realistic commentary on who we are, blacks have been and are now becoming increasingly a source and catalyst for white self-understanding. As I say, it's unlikely any black has ever taken seriously The American Story.

It's not then to some golden moment of our past we should look for remedies. The most positive thing in our history has been the gradual, halting—sometimes furiously resisted—steps of accommodation that sons and daughters of Puritan forefathers have made toward comprehending the struggles and riches of black culture in the face of white oppression and white resistance. An understanding of these struggles sweetens our temper, shames our arrogance, and redirects our shared society to more wholesome goals. It's from this, if anywhere, we can hope still to become responsible citizens of global society and conservers of the planet. (There's even hope we whites may someday forgive ancestral Native Americans for all the bad things we've done to them, and that we may begin to be tutored by their unslaughtered descendants who continue to breathe among us. The wisdom we tried to bury under the corpses of our Indian predecessors can, if we have the humility to accept it, yet help us toward redemption. In the meantime, we can look to Indians as a warning. In the nineteenth century, as time was then running out for them by reason of our actions, so time today, by reason of closely related current actions, is running out for the rest of us.)

3) So, while it's true we're all products of our past, that doesn't mean our past is our destiny—doesn't mean we're doomed by it.

Some of the most refreshing voices among American historians and commentators, past and current are those of Perry Miller, Richard Hofstadter, William Appleman Williams, Howard Zinn, Noam Chomsky, Barton Bernstein, and Chris Hedges. It's not that these scholars all agree; but they all tend to take ideology seriously. They think the ideas in our minds are of great importance, and that we cannot have much understanding of our past unless we attend to them. This makes these authors interesting to read—the more so because their approach is not familiar.

It's not that the rest of Americans have no ideology; it's just that most of us tend not to pay attention to the ideology out of which we act. Hofstadter wrote an entire book on anti-intellectualism in America.

It may be that Hume is the culprit here. (Or it's more probable he just articulated well what was to become the American mindset.) Reason, says Hume, does not call the shots in our ethical behavior; rather our emotions do. We act in accord with our inclinations and affectivity.

There is, to be sure, at least a half-truth in what Hume says. When I am wondering whether or not I should go to the beach today, it's probably not by a logical deduction but by an inclination, an appetitive disposition, that I'll resolve the matter. What Hume and we Americans seem insufficiently attentive to is that the general scheme of my affections—the organic whole of my affectivity—is no doubt deeply saturated with my ideology (something that does involve a network of—at least informal—reasonings and convictions). While Hume would have it that reason typically enters after the decision is made, and that then—when it does arrive—comes in the form of a rationalization, this can seem on reflection a bit glib. A more attentive phenomenology might reveal reasoning has been there from the start, predetermining what parts of my affectivity I will bring to bear upon the options under consideration. To state the matter in more general terms, Hume seems to disregard that one of the things to which one's affectivity is most inclined is one's ideology. That for

Americans, it's typically an unexamined ideology does not make it any the less dynamic. Here Freud is more useful than Hume.

In fact, a great deal of harm seems to have been occasioned by our American inattention to ideology. First of all, we don't notice our own; instead we will say that our preferences are simply for the natural order of things. (Some of us are able to say, for instance, it's quite natural to go to Africa and behead a lion named Cecil there.) Secondly, we're not alert to ideology in others. It doesn't occur to us, for instance, that Native Americans had (have!) ideologies of their own. We seem to have been so simple as to think their minds were simply examples of Locke's blank and chalk less slate — an empty tablet awaiting the slash of our writing instruments. Ditto for the minds of laborers drawn from Africa. Ditto for Mexicans, for Filipinos, for Vietnamese, Central Americans, and all classes of Muslims.

It's for this reason we've been so ready to go along with Wilson's "I will teach the people of South America to elect good presidents." It fits a pattern. In Chile, when the people elected Allende, Kissinger and our CIA knew better, and worked effectively to empower those opponents of Allende who drove him to commit suicide. In Iran, when Iranians elected Mossadegh, TR's grandson Kermit Roosevelt, Jr., of our CIA, pitched in to correct the outcome of their vote. When Ronald Reagan saw that the Nicaraguans had made a mistake in electing Daniel Ortega, he sponsored the Contras. The Contras, working closely with our CIA (and with people funding our clandestine operation by smuggling drugs into America's ghettoes), were — most of us felt — merely attempting to restore things to normal. Earlier, when Cubans made the mistake of choosing Castro, JFK worked hard for Castro's assassination. Earlier yet, Eisenhower knew that if the Vietnamese were left free to conduct the elections we had promised in the Geneva Accords, the Vietnamese would mistakenly have chosen Ho Chi Minh. In the interest of democracy Eisenhower called off the elections. More recently, less than a decade ago, we gave a clear and unmistakable warning to the Palestinians of Gaza not to vote Hamas into office as their leadership. Once they'd ignored us and done so anyway, in July, 2014, our entire Congress rose as one person and encouraged the Israeli government to punish the misguided civilians of Gaza. The obliging Israelis did so, killing roughly four hundred Gazan children to make the important point that violence never pays. Recently, when Egyptians voted a less-than-moderate

Muslim party into office, we worked successfully with Egyptian dissidents to bring about a coup. More recently still, we acted similarly in the Ukraine, assisting a coup in the Ukraine to reverse the election there and reduce Russian influence. We are now doing all we can to keep Putin from intruding into the stability we so artfully worked to establish. A decade ago, we destroyed the governmental structure of Iraq lest Saddam Hussein develop weapons of mass destruction, and currently we're naturally disappointed that the government we helped install in Saddam's place hasn't done better with the rich opportunity we provided—namely the opportunity to rebuild Iraq from the ground up. For all of this, we have never apologized; for after all, we've only been doing what comes naturally to us who bear responsibility for keeping the world free.

(OK, that's almost the last time I'll do that.)

We have always wanted to think, as one can observe, that in whatever we do, we're simply acting in accord with common sense. Yet the premises out of which we've operated have been bizarre, peculiar, and inhumane. Throughout all that, we've never quite abandoned the principles of the Enlightenment; we've reserved them to demand—often with threats and with violent force raining down from the sky—that our rivals and enemies abide by them. In particular, we want to teach them that opposition to us should always be non-violent. In order to teach from a position of power, we're working night and day—at tremendous cost to the American taxpayer—to refine still further our unrivaled nuclear arsenal.

Why is there today such general malaise (that word again!) among those who aspire to a reform of our actions "before it is too late"? It is not that it's so hard to decide what we want. The general shape of the desired result of reform is not too obscure. FDR did a good job in formulating it in his vision of the Four Freedoms: (1) freedom of speech, everywhere; (2) freedom of religion, everywhere; (3) freedom from hunger and want (due to lack of healthy habitat, lack of shelter, lack of adequate clothing), everywhere; (4) freedom from war and the threat of war, everywhere.

The source of our malaise is we do not see how to get from A (our present situation) to B (the desired result of reform). Our malaise is well founded. For to get from A to B, we must first become aware of the way our lifestyle, and the ideology that justifies it, hold us back from the result we want. For this reason I started this book with a general discussion of our disinvestment—moral as well as monetary—regarding education. Other chapters on "convenient skepticisms" and "false hopes" may have seemed extraneous; but really they too touch the heart of the matter. For here lie (in both senses) the strategic defenses for the mindset we hold. We hold these defenses with white knuckles, and we will not easily let them go.

Alternatives are not unimaginable. One can catch glimpses of opportunities for change in our past. Perhaps in the success of our Revolutionary War, we could have recognized that the noble premise we presented as motive for our revolt—all men are created equal—was ground not only for our assertions against England but ground too for Indian and black assertions against us successful ex-colonial whites. We did not do this because it was not convenient. We let our noble profession get ground to dust beneath our feet.

In the years immediately following the furor of the War of 1812, during the administration of J.Q. Adams, we could have followed Adams' lead toward internal improvements and provision for decent lives of all Americans, while learning to live within the boundaries of that time and by discontinuing our unjust treatment of black Americans. We chose Jackson instead.

Toward the end of the century, came the turbulent 1890s—never given the attention they deserve. Henry Adams reflects on this time in his autobiography, but demonstrates only how feckless he and the other intellectuals of the time had become. The time was the afterglow of the North's victory. It was the age of the Robber Barons—a time presaging the oligarchy we citizens united now endure. It was the Gilded Age. During this time we would celebrate the final cleansing of the Great Plains from savagery. It was a time in which we welcomed "Redemption" in the South, with Jim Crow laws restoring black Americans to their proper place—an action enjoying the tacit approval of the North. Having done what we could to subdue the people of color within our boundaries, we were now ready for Cubans and Filipinos. And after that, we were ready to extend our protection to the Chinese. Surprisingly, even as we congratulated ourselves amid so many successes, a time had come of frightening economic depression. The flaw in the economy was that the farmer and the industrial laborer often had insufficient funds to buy even ordinary goods amid the immense surpluses spewing from their farms and factories.

In other words, it was a time in which we were making all the wrong decisions.

Why rehash this? The intent is to emphasize how extensively we average Americans have been implicated in a disastrous commitment to the Puritan project. Largely, the commitment was unexamined and unchallenged.

Here the ideological detectives (Perry Miller, Richard Hofstadter, and company) are on the right track. Money does not quite run the show, as Marx might claim it does. (Neither, for that matter, it would seem, does Freudian libido.) In the final analysis, ideology has the upper hand. When in the Civil War, hundreds of young white soldiers of the South hurled their bodies into what was a virtual crematorium at Cemetery Ridge, it was not for money or economic advantage; neither, surely, was it for sex. It was pure ideology. Most of them neither owned slaves nor probably expected to. Rather, Virginia had been invaded! Georgia, for God's sake, was threatened! Their culture and custom had been despised. It was too much to take. And the North was just as blinded by ideology as was the South. The commitment to profit-taking at any cost was unyielding.

We charge Muslims with eccentricity and barbarism because they would sooner kill fellow human beings —and themselves into the bargain—than see their culture despised and changed. We should know better than to so charge them. We are very much cut from the same cloth. People will kill and be killed sooner than change their minds. In fact, this resistance to mind-change seems especially strong among us children of Puritans.

And so the final question. Can we, in the face of a manifest need to do so, change our minds? Can we abandon an unexamined and bankrupt ideology?

A concern for our children is perhaps our strongest motive to do so. If we insist, as we have been insisting, that anyone thinking and acting differently from the way we do is a threat to our national security, and if we continue trying to structure the politics and economics of the planet to accommodate a Puritan sense of economic rationality, and if we try to enforce this with the might of our military technology, we will end by declaring just about everyone in the world a terrorist. People everywhere will begin acting in accord with the label we have assigned them. Our grandchildren's lives will be bleak beyond present imagination.

I've argued that, while a terrible racism continues to corrode our hearts, the best place to look for lessons toward relief is, ironically, to the history of homegrown white racism against blacks. Our attention to this history over the last half-century has already contributed to our liberation in a variety of meaningful ways. The prejudices of parents and grandparents are happily becoming inexplicable to our young. Currently, when our police profile blacks, our very police—longtime emblems of security to white America—are becoming inexplicable to young Americans of all races.

Note that thousands of young blacks and young whites are marrying across the color line, and millions will follow. Even now multitudes of older white and black Americans stand with unstrained smiles to applaud and encourage the brides and grooms. Perhaps more importantly, parents who have absented themselves from attending such weddings are finding their grandchildren irresistible. The children of these unions are cherished and will be cherished by all their relatives—all sides reconciled by the deepest urges of human nature.

In addition to a blending of races, out of the successes of the civil-rights struggle have spun liberations of women, of Latinos, of the handicapped, and of gays and lesbians. (One can almost hear the shudder of American conservatives: "See! We warned you.")

One must hope that from these successes there will come a mellowing and gradual leavening of our Puritan sensibility. One hopes too that, for the sake of our children, the sensibility that develops will lead to a fresh connection with habitat while habitat is still there. The choice for that must come in the first half of this century, and can happen only if a residual wholesomeness in the people is able to refuse the blandishments—recognize the insanity—of a majority of those now leading our corporations.

History need not be a doom. It can liberate us. It can liberate us if we address it honestly. We have to admit that The American Story is an elaborate myth now in the process of crumbling. The cake of our Puritan custom is falling apart. While the Puritan myth has long been effective in providing some cohesion, it was always in fact a myth embedded in bigotry. The "America" of that myth, as it loses its creditability, is becoming altogether inadequate to hold things together—either for us, or as the pivot of the world. Whether we will abandon it in time to become an America that deserves our dedication is up to us.

Bibliography

Agar, Herbert. *The People's Choice: From Washington to Harding*. Safety Harbor, Fla.: Simon Publications, 2001.

Baker, Russ. *Family of Secrets*. New York: Bloomsbury Press, 2009.

Beard, Charles. *An Economic Interpretation of the Constitution of the United States*. New York: Macmillan, 1935.

Berlin, Adele, and Marc Zvi Brettler, eds. *The Jewish Study Bible*. New York: Oxford University Press, 1999.

Bernstein, Barton J., ed. *Towards a New Past: Dissenting Essays in American History*. New York: Random House, 1967.

Bernstein, Barton J. and Matusow, Allen J., eds. *Twentieth-Century America: Recent Interpretations*. New York: Harcourt Brace Jovanovich, 1972.

Berry, Thomas. *The Dream of the Earth*. San Francisco: Sierra Club Books, 1990.

Chomsky, Noam. *Failed States: The Abuse of Power and the Assault on Democracy*. New York: Henry Holt, 2006.

Collier, John. *Indians of the Americas*. New York: W.W. Norton, 1947.

Douglass, James W. *JFK and the Unspeakable: Why He Died and Why It Matters*. Maryknoll, N.Y.: Orbis Books, 2008.

Edwards, Jonathan. *Basic Writings*. New York: Signet Classic, 1966.

Friedman, Milton. "The Social Responsibility of Business is to Increase its Profits." *New York Times Magazine*, September 13, 1970. 32-33, 122-124.

Hedges, Chris. *War Is a Force That Gives Us Meaning*. New York: Public Affairs, 2002.

Hertsgaard, Mark. *The Eagle's Shadow*. New York: Farrar, Straus & Giroux, 2003.

Hofstadter, Richard. *Anti-Intellectualism in American Life*. New York: Vintage Books, 1962.

———. *The American Political Tradition*. New York: Vintage Books, 1974.

Jacoby, Susan. *The Age of American Unreason*. New York: Vintage Books, 2009.

Johnson, Chalmers. *Blowback: The Costs and Consequences of American Empire*. New York: Henry Holt, 2004.

Kennan George F. *American Diplomacy 1900–1950*. Chicago: University of Chicago Press, 1951.

———. *Russia and the West*. New York: Mentor Books, 1961

Klein, Naomi. *This Changes Everything: Capitalism vs. the Climate*. New York: Simon & Schuster, 2014.

Mahan, Alfred Thayer. *The Influence of Sea Power Upon History*. Boston: Little, Brown, 1890.

Marcuse, Herbert. *Eros and Civilization: A Philosophical Inquiry into Freud*. New York: Vintage, 1962.

Merry, Robert W. *A Country of Vast Designs*. New York: Simon & Schuster, 2009.

Miller, Perry. *Errand into the Wilderness*. Cambridge, Mass.: Harvard University Press, 1981.

Miller, Perry, ed. *The American Puritans: Their Prose and Poetry*. Garden City, N.Y.: Anchor Books, 1956.

Nash, Gary B., Julie Roy Jeffrey, et al., eds. *The American People: Creating a Nation and a Society*. 2nd ed. New York: Harper & Row, 1990.

Perkins, John. *Confessions of an Economic Hit Man*. San Francisco: Barrett-Koehler, 2004.

———. *The Secret History of the American Empire*. New York: Dutton, 2007.

Robinson, Charles M., III. *A Good Year to Die*. New York: Random House, 1995.

Roosevelt, Theodore. *The Winning of the West*. New York: G.P. Putnam's Sons, 1889.

Segal, Charles M., and Stineback, David C., eds. *Puritans, Indians & Manifest Destiny*. New York: G.P. Putnam's Sons, 1977.

Smith, Adam. *The Wealth of Nations*. New York: Penguin, 1981.

Solomon, Norman. *War Made Easy: How Presidents and Pundits Keep Spinning Us into Death.* Hoboken, N.J.: John Wiley & Sons, 2005.

Thoreau, Henry David. *Walden and Other Writings.* New York: Modern Library, 1950.

Toland, John. *The Rising Sun.* 2 vols. New York: Random House, 1970.

Turner, Frederick Jackson. "The Significance of the Frontier in American History." Speach from 1893; reprint of New York: Henry Holt, 1921 edition, Project Gutenberg, 2007. http://www.gutenberg.org/ebooks/22994.

Turner, Frederick W., III. "Red Man, White Man, Man on the Moon." *Evergreen Review*, July 1970.

Twain, Mark, and Charles Dudley Warner. *The Gilded Age: A Tale of Today.* Hartford: American, 1873.

Twain, Mark. *The Autobiography of Mark Twain, Vol. 1.* Berkeley: University of California Press, 2010.

Weber, Max. *The Protestant Ethic and the Spirit of Capitalism.* New York: Charles Scribner's Sons, 1958.

Williams, William Appleman. *The Tragedy of American Diplomacy.* New York: Dell, 1962.

Zimmermann, Warren. *First Great Triumph.* New York: Farrar, Straus & Giroux, 2002.

Zinn, Howard. *A People's History of the United States.* New York: HarperPerennial Modern Classics, 2005.

About the Author

Tom O'Neill has held many jobs. To recount some:

After he left the Jesuit Order—where he had the leisure to learn something of Aristotle's thinking (a wonderful experience)—he became for a number of years a social worker in child welfare in Compton, California; after that he served as a more than ordinarily inept teacher of English to islanders in the western Pacific—among whom he greatly enjoyed living for five years; later still, for a quarter of a century before his recent retirement, he was a sometimes adequate instructor in philosophy and religion at Las Positas College in Livermore, California. He is now retired and lives in Livermore. Until her recent death, he was the fortunate husband of the beautiful and remarkably practical Jung-Kang O'Neill, the ever-diligent mother of their two children: Christopher and Natasha (who continue to make his life interesting).

Index